T0310408

Valuing Pass-Through Entities

The Wiley Finance series contains books written specifically for finance and investment professionals as well as sophisticated individual investors and their financial advisors. Book topics range from portfolio management to e-commerce, risk management, financial engineering, valuation and financial instrument analysis, as well as much more. For a list of available titles, visit our Web site at www.WileyFinance.com.

Founded in 1807, John Wiley & Sons is the oldest independent publishing company in the United States. With offices in North America, Europe, Australia and Asia, Wiley is globally committed to developing and marketing print and electronic products and services for our customers' professional and personal knowledge and understanding.

Valuing Pass-Through Entities

ERIC J. BARR

WILEY

Wiley publishes in a variety of print and electronic formats and by print-on-demand. Some material included with standard print versions of this book may not be included in e-books or in print-on-demand. If this book refers to media such as a CD or DVD that is not included in the version you purchased, you may download this material at http://booksupport.wiley.com. For more information about Wiley products, visit www.wiley.com.

Library of Congress Cataloging-in-Publication Data:

Barr, Eric J., author.
   Valuing pass-through entities / Eric J. Barr.
      pages cm
   Includes index.
   ISBN 978-1-118-84866-1 (cloth); ISBN 978-1-118-84861-6 (epub);
ISBN 978-1-118-84868-5 (ePDF); ISBN 978-1-118-93669-6 (obook)
   1. Business enterprises—Taxation–Law and legislation—United States. 2. Business enterprises—Valuation—United States. 3. Tax assessment—Law and legislation—United States. 4. Valuation—Law and legislation—United States. 5. Income tax—Law and legislation—United States. I. Title.
   KF6450.B37 2014
   343.7306'8—dc23

                                                            2014022326

Printed in the United States of America

10 9 8 7 6 5 4 3 2 1

This book is dedicated to my wife, Linda; my children, Aimee, David, and Lori; and my granddaughter, Brooke, who fill me with inspiration, magic, and love.

Contents

Foreword

Pass-through entities have been an enigma to many valuation professionals over the years. Experts from Nancy Fannon to Chris Treharne to Dave Dufendach have all written extensively on pass-through entities, and specifically, S corporations. In this book, Eric Barr takes the handling of pass-through entities to new heights. Starting with the first chapter and continuing on to the last, Eric takes the reader through the byzantine nuances of valuing pass-through entities.

Valuation can be a daunting undertaking, akin to a paint-by-number picture without the numbers. In the introductory chapter, Eric lays the foundation by covering the basic building blocks of valuation. But unlike other valuation treatises, *Valuing Pass-Through Entities* provides a succinct, yet comprehensive overview of valuation fundamentals before tackling the often-thorny issue of valuing pass-through entities. And even more refreshing is Eric's weaving in the historical perspective that has given rise to these unique business structures, and how that historical perspective has changed over time. Like many endeavors, the original purpose for which pass-through entities were created has long since been forgotten. But understanding the genesis of pass-through entities provides a rich fabric from which the valuation professional can create a more understandable, and accurate, pass-through entity valuation. Eric's book provides the tools that allow for such a rich understanding.

And don't let me forget the deep technical construct that Eric builds throughout his book. Drawing upon his 40 years of experience, Eric provides a practical, well-reasoned journey through the pass-through entity landscape. From insights on the federal tax structure to changes in individual income tax rates, Eric explores rational business behavior and how such behavior is influenced by the overall tax system. Not being content with mere observations, Eric then provides a framework and structure that allow the valuation professional to address what he terms the *PTE conundrum*.

The practical side of Eric's book can be found in the many checklists and illustrations that accompany the narrative portions of each chapter. The examples are easy to follow, intuitive, and rational. And because there are so many permutations in the PTE conundrum, there are a lot of examples. Think about fair market value, fair value, investment value, and strategic value when combined with a merger or acquisition, estate or gift tax valuation, or in a divorce setting, and the number of permutations gets enormous. Although there isn't an example for every conceivable permutation, there are plenty of examples that will make you think through the process in a much more organized way.

Eric is the first valuation expert to attempt to solve the PTE conundrum, and he probably won't be the last. However, Eric's contribution to the body of knowledge goes a long way toward bringing the disparate approaches, and often contrary views, together in an easy to read and understandable book. So grab a cup of coffee, a valuation report, and Eric's book for a good read about the PTE conundrum.

—Neil J. Beaton
Managing Director
Alvarez & Marsal Valuation Services
Seattle, Washington

Preface

I have addressed many complex accounting, valuation, and forensic issues during my approximately 40-year career. In my work, with only one notable exception, I have generally found a consensus in technical literature, the industry, or expert opinions on the proper way to handle an issue. That notable exception is how or even whether one should tax-affect the earnings of a partnership, S corporation, limited liability company, or sole proprietorship (collectively, pass-through entities, or PTEs) when valuing such business ownership interests. I call this the *PTE conundrum*.

There have been many qualified, experienced professionals who have analyzed the PTE conundrum. It is a topic that has been the subject of articles and books. It has been contested in numerous litigations, in different courts, with varying facts and circumstances. In my opinion, there has been no lack of attention to this issue—only a lack of consensus and clarity.

I decided to take on this issue and started reading many court decisions, articles, and so on. Then I experimented with different Excel models, trying to develop a simple and understandable model that could properly address the different relevant possibilities that a potential buyer/seller would face when buying/selling an ownership interest in a PTE as compared with buying/selling an ownership interest in a C corporation. In time, my model evolved into something that I thought was practical, thorough, and worthy of consideration by the valuation community and users of our work, such as lawyers, judges, and purchasers of PTEs.

Tommy Lasorda, the former manager of the Los Angeles Dodgers, has said that there are players who make things happen, there are players who watch things happen, and there are players who wonder what happened. In certain respects, valuation analysts are the same as the players described by Mr. Lasorda. Since I had developed deep convictions on how to address the PTE conundrum, I decided I could no longer sit on the sidelines and watch things happen. I needed to get on the field and make things happen. It's safe on the sidelines, but it's much more fun being on the field of play.

My challenge was how to effectively communicate my findings, which were too long for a series of articles. The solution was this book. What follows is a discussion of the reasons for operating a business in the form of a PTE, how the appraisal community has tried to address the PTE conundrum, my proposed solution, and a detailed sensitivity analysis of each of the factors potentially impacting the valuation of PTEs under different facts and circumstances. I have always found it effective to communicate a message through a story, so I've also illustrated my solution to the PTE conundrum in a case study through the eyes of the parties to a hypothetical transaction. Since most interesting stories are told with some degree of emotion or humor, I tried to include both. Bob and all of the characters have a compulsive "get it right" attitude, a healthy skepticism, and patience—attributes that are useful when trying to value or purchase/sell a business.

The analyses contained in the following pages are based on 2013 federal income tax laws. Although we can say with certainty that such laws will change over time and that the calculations contained herein are subject to modification, the theories underlying the calculations will still hold true.

Please enjoy my contribution to the PTE conundrum discussion.

Acknowledgments

This book includes the thoughtful input of exceptionally talented professionals who generously contributed their time and expertise. My sincere and deep appreciation to Ashok Abbott, John E. Barrett Jr., Neil J. Beaton, Jay A. Soled, and Steven A. Loeb for their important contributions to the business valuation and income tax chapters. Also, a special thank-you to Sheila V. Sybrant, editor extraordinaire. To this list I add Sheck Cho, Lia Ottaviano, and all of their colleagues at John Wiley & Sons, who were easy to work with and polished my work into the text you have before you.

Writing a book was quite an undertaking and a remarkable learning experience. At times exhilarating, at times eye-opening, it was never boring or a grind. Of course it took longer than expected, therefore requiring the understanding, encouragement, and support of my partners, which I enthusiastically received from my firm's cofounders, O. David Fischer and Spencer V. Wissinger. Monica Kaden, a very experienced and respected colleague, was always there as a sounding board and provided focus and clarity. I thank each of you.

Over the course of my career, I have been fortunate to work with colleagues who contributed to my development as a professional advisor and critical thinker. So it is with deep appreciation that I acknowledge and thank Ronald G. Weiner, Ted M. Felix, Joseph P. Cipolla Jr., and Barry S. Sziklay.

As a baby boomer born to Depression-era parents, I was the first in my immediate family to attend college and learn a profession. My parents, Harold and June Barr, always stressed the importance of education, integrity, and hard work. I am the person I am today because of my parents, and it is with great pleasure and love that I publicly recognize and thank both of you.

My greatest source of inspiration and support is my wife, Linda. As a fourth-grade teacher, her frequent admonition to "show, don't tell" still reverberates. Make it simple, package your message in a story, and make it the type of text that you would want to read—all key messages—were the touchstones of my communication style. Her ever-present encouragement, love, and faith in me enabled me to see this project through to its completion. Thank you.

About the Author

Eric J. Barr is a founder and comanaging member of Fischer Barr & Wissinger LLC in Parsippany, New Jersey. He is a certified public accountant, accredited in business valuation and certified in financial forensics (all designations of the American Institute of Certified Public Accountants); a certified valuation analyst (a designation of the National Association of Certified Valuation Analysts [NACVA]); and a certified fraud examiner (a designation of the Association of Certified Fraud Examiners [ACFE]).

Mr. Barr has more than 40 years of public accounting experience specializing in litigation support, consulting, and traditional accounting and auditing services. He provides consulting and expert witness services in connection with the valuation of control and minority business interests, matrimonial dissolutions, shareholder/member disputes, estate/gift planning, mergers/acquisitions/disposals, purchase price allocations, and employee stock issuances. He has performed investigations to determine the amount of lost profits, fraud, marital lifestyle, and equitable distribution.

Mr. Barr is called upon to speak at seminars, conferences, and webinars of various professional groups. He has been published in the *Wall Street Journal* (online edition), the *CPA Journal*, the *Value Examiner*, and *Business Valuation Update*. He is a member of the editorial board of the *Value Examiner*.

He received his BS in accounting at the State University of New York at Buffalo.

CHAPTER 1

Introduction

In our daily lives we have come to expect—even demand—comfort, convenience, and choice. When we desire entertainment, we click on the remote and at our fingertips are hours of television viewing. When we want to speak with someone, we take out our portable telephone and dial the number, and we are instantly in conversation with someone who may be far away. We can change the climate in our home from hot to cold and back to hot simply by moving a dial. We can access encyclopedias with a few computer keystrokes. There is fast food, ethnic food, gluten-free food, carbohydrate-free food, fat-free food, and so on. Never before has so much been available so quickly to so many people.

Curiously, it seems like very few people—myself included—care how all of these things happen. I don't know what enables my car to do what it does. I don't know why my television, telephone, refrigerator, or any other household appliance works. Ask me why certain diets are better for me— I don't know and I don't care. It only matters to me that these things work when I want them to.

You may ask why any of this matters in a book about valuing pass-through entities. The reason is that if you are like the consumer who is described in the previous two paragraphs, looking for a quick and simple method to everything, including valuing any pass-through entity under any circumstance, then this book is not for you. This book does not offer a simple how-to valuation manual because there are no simple answers to complex valuation questions. This book is for business appraisers and users of business appraisals who need to look behind the curtain and understand the choices and issues associated with valuing a pass-through entity. It describes the process of developing a supportable, proper pass-through entity valuation conclusion.

DEFINITION OF VALUE

Value has been described by many people in many ways. Karl Marx said that "[n]othing can have value without being an object of utility."[1] Publius Syrus said that "[e]verything is worth what its purchaser will pay for it."[2] Contradicting Publius Syrus was John Ruskin, who said, "A thing is worth precisely what it can do for you; not what you choose to pay for it."[3] And leave it to Mark Twain to cleverly illustrate value: "Each person is born to one possession which outvalues all his others—his last breath."[4] For purposes of this book in connection with business appraisals, *value* is defined as the risk-adjusted present value of the future economic returns associated with the ownership of a business interest.

BEAUTY AND VALUE

Value, like beauty, is in the eye of the beholder. What may have extraordinary beauty to someone may not be beautiful to another. The same holds true regarding the value of a business ownership interest. A business ownership interest may have great value to one person but not another. Therefore, one's perspective greatly impacts value.

When valuing a business interest, the appraiser must gain an understanding of the control attributes of the business ownership interest being appraised and the purpose of the appraisal. Let's discuss both of these factors.

Control versus Noncontrolling Interests

The business interest being appraised may permit the holder to exercise the prerogatives of control. When valuing a controlling interest in an entity, the controlling interest generally has greater value than the minority interest, all other things being equal. The issue of control relates to various factors, the most important of which is the ability of the controlling owner to make decisions and select strategies without regard to minority owners. Due to the absence of control in a minority interest, the appraiser of a minority equity interest may need to consider a reduction beyond the mere pro rata value of the minority owner's interest in the entity. Thus, when valuing a business

---

[1]BrainyQuote, http://www.brainyquote.com/quotes/quotes/k/karlmarx157970.html.
[2]The Quotations Page, http://www.quotationspage.com/quote/34596.html.
[3]John Ruskin, "Athena in the Heart," in *The Works of John Ruskin: The Queen of the Air*, 123, 147 (1874).
[4]TwainQuotes, http://www.twainquotes.com/Life.html.

ownership interest, it is important to be mindful of the degree of control associated with the subject interest.

Standards of Value

The next consideration is the purpose of the business appraisal. There are many different reasons that a business appraisal is required:

1. Transactions (including, but not limited to, leveraged buyouts, employee stock ownership plans, employee compensation plans, and initial public offerings)
2. Litigation (matrimonial dissolution, bankruptcy, contractual disputes, owner disputes, and employment and intellectual property disputes)
3. Compliance-oriented engagements (financial reporting and tax matters (i.e., corporate reorganizations, S corporation conversions, estate and gift tax compliance, purchase price allocations, and charitable contributions))
4. Planning-oriented engagements (estate and gift tax planning, mergers and acquisitions, and personal financial planning)[5]

The purpose of the valuation will determine the perspective from which the valuation is being performed:

1. A known holder or seller (often referred to as the fair value standard of value in a dissenting shareholder rights or matrimonial dissolution context)[6]
2. A known or hypothetical buyer (also known as the investment value standard of value)
3. Fair market value, which has been defined as

> [t]he price at which the property would change hands between a willing buyer and a willing seller when the former is not under any compulsion to buy and the latter is not under any compulsion to sell, both parties having reasonable knowledge of relevant facts. Court decisions frequently state in addition that the hypothetical buyer and seller are assumed to be able, as well as willing, to trade and to be

---

[5]Consulting Services Executive Committee, American Institute of Certified Public Accountants, "Valuation of a Business Ownership Interest, Security, or Intangible Asset," 5 (June 2007).

[6]Under U.S. generally accepted accounting principles, *fair value* has a different meaning not utilized in this text.

well informed about the property and concerning the market for such property.[7]

It is critical to understand the standard of value because a different perspective may yield a different investment return. For example, the holder of a controlling equity ownership interest may enjoy certain synergistic benefits with other businesses that an unaffiliated investor may not have. Conversely, the investor may be able to access sources of financing, provide depth of management, have a lower cost of capital, implement efficiencies, and so forth, that provide an investor a greater return than the present owner can achieve. In addition, one standard of value may be impacted by federal and state laws (i.e., fair market value), whereas a different standard of value may not. Accordingly, different perspectives and standards of value yield different risk-adjusted returns—and ultimately different values. There is no single approach that is applicable to all appraisals.

PREMISE OF VALUE

There are two fundamental premises upon which a company may be valued: as a going concern or as if in liquidation.[8] The value of a company is most often determined to be the higher of these two values. This concept is consistent with the real estate appraisal concept of "highest and best use," which requires an appraiser

> to consider the . . . optimal use of the assets being appraised under current market conditions. If a business [is expected to] command a higher price as a going concern[,] then it should be valued as such. Conversely, if a business [is expected to] command a higher price if it is liquidated, then it should be valued as if in liquidation.[9]

---

[7]Rev. Rul. 59–60, 1959-1 C.B. 237, § 2.01(as defined in § 20.2031-1(b) of the Estate Tax Regulations (§ 81.10 of the Estate Tax Regulations 105) and § 25.2512-1 of the Gift Tax Regulations (§ 86.19 of Gift Tax Regulations 108).
[8]In liquidation, a company can be valued (1) as an "assemblage of assets but not in current use in the production of income"; (2) "on a piecemeal basis . . . as part of an orderly disposition"; and (3) "on a piecemeal basis . . . as part of a forced liquidation." Charles A. Wilhoite, *Defining and Estimating "Value" in the LLC Setting*, 10–12 (July 20, 2013), available at http://www.willamette.com/pubs/presentations2/wilhoite_aba_conf_2013.pdf (quoting *Valuing a Business*, 33 [4th ed., 2000]).
[9]William P. Dukes, "Business Valuation Basics for Attorneys," *Journal of Business Valuation and Economic Loss Analysis* 1(1) (2006).

For purposes of this text, we have assumed a going-concern premise of value for the concepts and examples provided herein.

APPROACHES TO VALUE

Our next step is to consider the different approaches to valuation. There are three generally accepted approaches to value:

■ The *income approach* determines the value of

"a business, business ownership interest, security, or intangible asset using one or more methods that convert anticipated benefits into a present value single amount." The application of the income approach establishes value by methods that discount or capitalize earnings and/or cash flow, by a discount or capitalization rate that reflects market rate of return expectations, market conditions, and the relative risk of the investment.[10]

■ The *market approach* calculates the value of

"a business, business ownership interest, security, or intangible asset by using one or more methods that compare the subject to similar business, business ownership interests, securities, or intangible assets that have been sold." Generally, this can be accomplished by a comparison to publicly traded guideline companies or by an analysis of actual transactions of similar businesses sold. It may also include an analysis of prior transactions in the company's stock, if any.[11]

■ The *asset (cost) approach* requires estimates of the individual market values of the subject company's assets and liabilities, if applicable, to

---

[10]James R. Hitchner and Michael J. Mard, *Financial Valuation Workbook*, 27 (3rd ed., 2011) (quoting "International Glossary of Business Valuation Terms," in *American Institute of Certified Public Accountants, Statement on Standards for Valuation Services*, no. 1, at 45, app. B, http://www.aicpa.org/InterestAreas/ForensicAndValuation/ Membership/DownloadableDocuments/Intl%20Glossary%20of%20BV%20Terms .pdf).

[11]*Id.* (quoting "International Glossary of Business Valuation Terms," in *American Institute of Certified Public Accountants, Statement on Standards for Valuation Services*, no. 1, at 46, app. B, http://www.aicpa.org/InterestAreas/ForensicAndValuation/ Membership/DownloadableDocuments/Intl%20Glossary%20of%20BV%20Terms .pdf).

derive an adjusted net asset value (i.e., equity value). The asset approach is often referred to as a *balance sheet approach*.

There are two methods that are often considered when employing the income approach: the capitalization of earnings method and the discounted future returns method (or permutations of these methods). There are also two methods that are often considered when employing the market approach: the guideline transaction method and the guideline public company method.

When considering the potential for different permutations of control, standards of value, valuation approaches, and valuation methods, there are 30 different potentially viable valuation calculations that must be considered, as shown in Table 1.1.

TABLE 1.1 Potential Valuation Calculations

	Controlling Interest	Noncontrolling Interest
Income Approach		
Value to Seller		
Capitalization of Earnings Method	1	2
Discounted Future Returns Method	3	4
Value to Buyer		
Capitalization of Earnings Method	5	6
Discounted Future Returns Method	7	8
Fair Market Value		
Capitalization of Earnings Method	9	10
Discounted Future Returns Method	11	12
Market Approach		
Value to Seller		
Guideline Transaction Method	13	14
Guideline Public Company Method	15	16
Value to Buyer		
Guideline Transaction Method	17	18
Guideline Public Company Method	19	20
Fair Market Value		
Guideline Transaction Method	21	22
Guideline Public Company Method	23	24
Asset (Cost) Approach		
Value to Seller	25	26
Value to Buyer	27	28
Fair Market Value	29	30

Internal Revenue Code (IRC) Revenue Ruling 59–60 recognizes that there is not one and only one way to value a business ownership interest, stating thus:

> A determination of fair market value, being a question of fact, will depend upon the circumstances in each case. No formula can be devised that will be generally applicable to the multitude of different valuation issues arising in estate and gift tax cases.[12] Often, an appraiser will find wide differences of opinion as to the fair market value of a particular stock. In resolving such differences, he should maintain a reasonable attitude in recognition of the fact that valuation is not an exact science. A sound valuation will be based upon all the relevant facts, but the elements of common sense, informed judgment and reasonableness must enter into the process of weighing those facts and determining their aggregate significance.[13]

Just as we want instant gratification when we turn on the television, clients and users of business appraisals want instant gratification when they ask their valuation questions. However, as evidenced by all of the valuation calculation possibilities noted earlier, the work needed to complete each analysis, and the guidance set forth in Revenue Ruling 59–60, there is no quick, reliable way to shortcut the process; in other words, there is no one-size-fits-all solution.

THE PTE CONUNDRUM

Even when two valuation consultants agree as to the degree of control, the standard of value, the approach, and the method to apply, they may still conclude that the subject ownership interest has a significantly different value. Valuation conclusions often differ because the inputs used to apply a particular methodology may be very different. Valuation analysts may have different expectations as to the future earnings potential, costs, or riskiness of a business. There are many other issues that complicate the valuation analysis. One issue is that there are different types of business entities, that is, C corporations, S corporations, partnerships, limited liability

---

[12]Although Revenue Ruling 59–60, § 3.01, specifically addresses the use of the fair market standard of value in connection with estate and gift tax valuations, the guidance set forth therein with respect to the approach to valuation also applies to other standards of value in situations other than estate and gift tax valuation.
[13]Rev. Rul. 59–60, 1959-1 C.B. 237, § 3.01.

companies (LLCs), and sole proprietorships. Depending on the form of the entity, different tax laws govern the recognition of income and losses at the entity and owners' level.[14] The after-tax cash flows to an owner can be materially different depending on the entity form. Accordingly, entity form may impact value.

When the after-tax net income of a C corporation is distributed to its owners, there is a second level of income taxes (a tax on dividend income) paid at the owner level. On the other hand, with rare exceptions, S corporations, partnerships, LLCs, and sole proprietorships do not pay income taxes at the entity level; such entities "pass through" their earnings and losses to their owners. Accordingly, S corporations, partnerships, LLCs, and sole proprietorships are collectively referred to herein as *pass-through entities (PTEs)*. The earnings of PTEs are therefore subjected to income tax only one time, at the owner level. Owners of interests in S corporations, partnerships, and LLCs are known as *shareholders* (or *stockholders*), *partners*, and *members*, respectively. The entity status as either a C corporation or a PTE can fundamentally impact after-tax future cash flows of a business ownership interest, and hence the value of that ownership interest. Table 1.2 illustrates this concept.

Applying the simplified assumptions contained in this example, the after-tax income for an owner of a PTE (60%) is 25 percent greater than the after-tax income for an owner of a C corporation (48%).

PTEs are often valued under the income approach and the market approach, utilizing data derived from public company transactions. Such

TABLE 1.2   Example of C Corp vs. PTE Income Available After All Income Taxes

	C Corp	PTE
Pretax income	100.0%	100.0%
Corporate tax income	40.0%	0.0%
Available earnings	60.0%	100.0%
Dividend tax rate [1]	12.0%	0.0%
Individual income tax rate	0.0%	40.0%
	12.0%	40.0%
Available after all income taxes	48.0%	60.0%

[1] The dividend tax is calculated in this example as follows:
Dividend tax rate (20%) multiplied by available earnings (60%) equals 12%.

---

[14] C corporations are subject to the Internal Revenue Code of 1986, as amended (IRC), subchapter C; partnerships are subject to IRC subchapter K; and S corporations are subject to subchapter S of chapter 1 of the IRC.

data would be presumed to be relevant as it reflects many thousands, even millions, of potentially relevant transactions between buyers and sellers. However, if a C corporation yields different after-tax investor returns than PTEs, how can a valuation analyst justify applying valuation multiples developed from tax-paying entities in connection with the valuation of a PTE? The answer is to somehow quantify the tax benefit, if any, associated with an entity's status as a PTE. The issue of how to quantify that tax benefit has vexed valuation analysts for years. I call this issue the *PTE conundrum*.

The PTE conundrum is a hotly debated topic among valuation analysts, with points of view evolving and changing over time. Certain valuation analysts ignore all entity-level income taxes, deeming such income taxes hypothetical, improper, and inappropriate. Some valuation analysts impose C corporation income taxes at maximum marginal rates on the earnings of a business for valuation purposes. Alternatively, an effective combined corporation federal and state tax rate of 40 percent is utilized by many valuation analysts. U.S. courts have issued varying and seemingly conflicting decisions on this issue, based on different facts and circumstances.

How to quantify the tax benefit of PTE status is a challenge when valuing companies for mergers and acquisitions, estate and gift tax purposes, marital dissolution, shareholder disputes, and other purposes. It is an issue when applying different standards of value, such as fair market value, fair value, and investment value.

The following chapters provide a potential solution to the PTE conundrum. The text includes a discussion of (1) applicable tax law, (2) different valuation approaches (the income, market, and cost approaches), and (3) standards of value (value to the holder/seller, value to the buyer, and fair market value). Significant cases and the manner in which different business appraisers have attempted to value the PTE tax benefit are presented and critiqued. Solutions, examples, and a sample case that illustrates the thought process and logic of parties to a hypothetical transaction are also contained in the following text.

CHAPTER 2

The History of Federal Statutory Tax Rates in Maximum Income Brackets and the Evolution of Different Forms of Business Entities

Abraham Lincoln caused the pass-through entity (PTE) conundrum. That's right, blame Honest Abe, who on October 3, 1862, signed the Act of 1862, the first law authorizing a U.S. income tax on individuals. The new law also provided for additional sales and excise taxes and introduced the inheritance tax. Never one to shrink away from a major issue, President Lincoln needed a new revenue source in order to help finance the Civil War, even though he believed "to secure each laborer the whole product of his labor, or as nearly as possible, is a most worthy object of any good government."[1] Prior to 1862, the government financed its operations from the collection of sales taxes and tariffs.

The Act of 1862 was the forerunner of the current Internal Revenue Code (IRC or Code). It required a person with earnings of $600–$10,000 per year to pay an income tax of 3 percent; a higher rate was applied to earnings in excess of $10,000. President Lincoln had the foresight to enact a progressive tax.[2]

---

[1] Abraham Lincoln, "Fragments on the Tariff (Aug. 1846–Dec. 1847)," *Abraham Lincoln: Speeches and Writings, 1832–1858* (Library of America, 1989).
[2] *U.S. Federal Individual Income Tax Rates History, 1862–2013* (Nominal and Inflation-Adjusted Brackets), www.taxfoundation.org.

In addition,

> [t]he Act of 1862 established the office of Commissioner of Internal
> Revenue. The Commissioner was given the power to assess, levy, and
> collect taxes, and the right to enforce the tax laws through seizure of
> property and income through prosecution. The [Commissioner's]
> powers and authority remain very much the same today.[3]

In 1872, after the Civil War, the income tax was eliminated even though
it proved to be a substantial revenue generator. It was revived in 1894 as an
attachment to the Wilson-Gorman Tariff Act, which called for a federal
income tax of 2 percent on incomes exceeding $4,000. This attempt at
taxation was challenged in U.S. federal courts.

> In *Pollock v. Farmers' Loan & Trust Co.*, 158 U.S. 601 (1895), the
> U.S. Supreme Court declared certain taxes on income . . . to be
> unconstitutionally unapportioned direct taxes. The [Supreme] Court
> reasoned that a tax on *income from property* should be treated as
> a tax on "property by reason of its ownership" and so should be
> required to be apportioned. The reasoning was that taxes on the
> rents from land, the dividends from stocks, and so forth, burdened
> the property generating the income in the same way that a tax on
> "property by reason of its ownership" burdened that property.[4]

On February 3, 1913, the Supreme Court's decision in *Pollock v.
Farmers' Loan & Trust Co.* was overruled with the passage of the Sixteenth
Amendment to the Constitution. The Sixteenth Amendment made the income
tax a permanent source of revenue for the federal government and "gave
Congress legal authority to tax . . . both individuals and corporations":[5]
"The Congress shall have power to lay and collect taxes on incomes, from
whatever source derived, without apportionment among the several States,
and without regard to any census or enumeration."[6]

---

[3]*History of the Income Tax in the United States*, Infoplease.com, www.infoplease
.com/ipa/A0005921.
[4]*Sixteenth Amendment to the United States Constitution*, Wikipedia, http://en.wikipe-
dia.org/wiki/Sixteenth_Amendment_to_the_United_States_Constitution (emphasis in
original). Article 1, Section 2, Clause 3 of the Constitution (1894) states thus: "Representatives and direct Taxes shall be apportioned among the several States which may
be included within this Union, according to their respective Numbers."
[5]*History of the Income Tax in the United States*, supra note 2.
[6]U.S. Constitution, amendment XVI.

In fiscal 1918, annual U.S. tax collections exceeded $1 billion for the first time, increasing to $5.4 billion by 1920. With the introduction of withholding taxes on wages in 1943, there were 60 million taxpayers. By 1945, tax collections increased to $43 billion, and have been increasing ever since.[7]

According to the *Internal Revenue Service Data Book, 2012*, covering the period from October 1, 2011, through September 30, 2012, during 2012 there were 237 million income tax returns filed, yielding net federal collections in excess of $2 trillion.[8] See the following tables, which present the numbers and types of income tax returns filed (Table 2.1) and the sources of revenues from each (Table 2.2).

ORIGINS OF THE UNITED STATES INTERNAL REVENUE CODE

Although there were codifications of U.S. statutes in 1874 and 1878, the IRC was initially codified in 1926 and then recodified in 1939, 1954, and 1986.

TABLE 2.1   Derived from Table 2 of 2012 *IRS Data Book*: Number of Returns Filed, by Type of Return—Fiscal Year Ended September 30, 2012 (in thousands)

Type of Return	
United States, total	$ 237,345
Income taxes, total	
C or other corporation	2,263
S corporation, Form 1120-S	4,580
Partnership, Form 1065	3,626
Individual	
Forms 1040, 1040-A, 1040-EZ	145,400
Forms 1040-C, 1040-NR, 1040NR-EZ, 1040-PR, 1040-SS	844
Individual estimated tax, Form 1040-ES	22,158
Estate and trust, Form 1041	3,061
Estate and trust, estimated tax, Form 1041-ES	400
Employment taxes	29,590
Estate tax	27
Gift, tax, Form 709	249
Excise taxes	1,197
Tax-exempt organizations	1,367
Supplemental documents	22,583

[7]*History of the Income Tax in the United States*, supra note 2.
[8]Department of the Treasury, Internal Revenue Service, *Internal Revenue Service Data Book, 2012*, at iii (2012).

TABLE 2.2 Derived from Table 1 of 2012 *IRS Data Book*: Collections and Refunds by Type of Tax—Fiscal Year Ended September 30, 2012 (in $ millions)

Type of Tax	Net Collections	Percentage of 2012 Totals
United States, total	$ 2,150,891	100.0%
Business income taxes, including Corporation and Tax-exempt organization unrelated business income tax	$ 237,491	11.0
Individual and estate and trust income tax		
Individual income taxes	1,048,735	48.8
Estate and trust income tax	15,041	0.7
Employment taxes		
Federal Insurance Contributions Act (FICA) and Self-Employment Insurance Contributions Act (SECA)	768,849	35.7
Unemployment insurance	7,053	0.3
Railroad retirement	4,765	0.2
Estate and gift taxes		
Estate	11,934	0.6
Gift	2,011	0.1
Excise taxes	55,011	2.6

Changing economic necessities, social imperatives, politics, the evolution of business practices, and other factors contributed to the recodifications and tax law changes subsequent to 1913. Here follows a brief discussion of certain provisions of each codification, its impact on the manner in which business was conducted, tax issues associated with each discrete period, and the evolution of tax law.

YEARS 1913 THROUGH 1938

After the passage of the Sixteenth Amendment, Congress established the schedule of 1913 federal income tax rates on individuals (the listed tax rates and brackets apply to all individuals, regardless of their status as single, married, married filing separately, or head of household): (see Table 2.3)[9]

---

[9]*U.S. Federal Individual Income Tax Rates History, 1862–2013* (Nominal and Inflation-Adjusted Brackets), www.taxfoundation.org.

TABLE 2.3   1913 Individual Income Tax Rates (Nominal and Inflation Adjusted, 2012)

1913 Marginal Tax Rate	Nominal Tax Brackets		Inflation Adjusted (2012) Using Average Annual CPU	
	Over	But Not Over	Over	But Not Over
1.0%	—	20,000	—	463,826
2.0%	20,000	50,000	463,826	1,159,566
3.0%	50,000	75,000	1,159,566	1,739,348
4.0%	75,000	100,000	1,739,348	2,319,131
5.0%	100,000	250,000	2,319,131	5,797,828
6.0%	250,000	500,000	5,797,828	11,595,657
7.0%	500,000	—	11,595,657	—

The seven different tax brackets in 1913 with a maximum rate of 7 percent reflected in Table 2.3 increased to 14 tax brackets in 1916 with a maximum rate of 15 percent. In 1917, there were 21 tax brackets with a maximum rate of 67 percent. By 1918, there were 56 tax brackets with a maximum rate of 77 percent![10] Table 2.4 summarizes the marginal federal income tax rates in maximum income brackets (nominal and inflation adjusted) for individuals during the period 1913–1938:[11]

Like President Lincoln, during the period from 1917 through 1921, President Woodrow Wilson passed revenue-generating income tax legislation as a source of funding the nation at war.

After World War I ended, Calvin Coolidge was elected president. President Coolidge stated in his inaugural address that "collecting more taxes than is absolutely necessary is only legalized larceny."[12] Under President Coolidge, maximum statutory individual income tax rates decreased to 25 percent.[13]

After the Roaring Twenties came the Great Depression, and federal income tax rates rose once again.

During the period from 1913 through 1938, partnerships and sole proprietorships were not the only form of conducting business. Business was also conducted through C corporations. Unlike partnerships, C

---

[10] *Id.*

[11] *Id.*

[12] www.brainyquote.com/quotes/authors/c/calvin_coolidge.html.

[13] *U.S. Federal Individual Income Tax Rates History, 1862–2013* (Nominal and Inflation-Adjusted Brackets), www.taxfoundation.org.

TABLE 2.4   Federal Individual Income Tax Rate History—Nominal Dollars—Income
Years: 1913–1938

	Married Filing Jointly			Single		
	Taxable Income Greater Than			Taxable Income Greater Than		
Year	Maximum Statutory Bracket	Nominal $	2012 Inflation Adjusted $	Maximum Statutory Bracket	Nominal $	2012 Inflation Adjusted $
1913	7.0%	500,000	11,595,657	7.0%	500,000	11,595,657
1914	7.0%	500,000	11,479,700	7.0%	500,000	11,479,700
1915	7.0%	500,000	11,366,040	7.0%	500,000	11,366,040
1916	15.0%	2,000,000	42,127,339	15.0%	2,000,000	42,127,339
1917	67.0%	2,000,000	35,874,063	67.0%	2,000,000	35,874,063
1918	77.0%	1,000,000	15,204,901	77.0%	1,000,000	15,204,901
1919	73.0%	1,000,000	13,271,329	73.0%	1,000,000	13,271,329
1920	73.0%	1,000,000	11,479,700	73.0%	1,000,000	11,479,700
1921	73.0%	1,000,000	12,826,480	73.0%	1,000,000	12,826,480
1922	58.0%	200,000	2,733,262	58.0%	200,000	2,733,262
1923	58.0%	200,000	2,685,310	58.0%	200,000	2,685,310
1924	46.0%	500,000	6,713,275	46.0%	500,000	6,713,275
1925	25.0%	100,000	1,311,966	25.0%	100,000	1,311,966
1926	25.0%	100,000	1,297,141	25.0%	100,000	1,297,141
1927	25.0%	100,000	1,319,506	25.0%	100,000	1,319,506
1928	25.0%	100,000	1,342,655	25.0%	100,000	1,342,655
1929	25.0%	100,000	1,342,655	25.0%	100,000	1,342,655
1930	25.0%	100,000	1,374,814	25.0%	100,000	1,374,814
1931	25.0%	100,000	1,510,487	25.0%	100,000	1,510,487
1932	63.0%	1,000,000	16,758,686	63.0%	1,000,000	16,758,686
1933	63.0%	1,000,000	17,661,077	63.0%	1,000,000	17,661,077
1934	63.0%	1,000,000	17,133,881	63.0%	1,000,000	17,133,881
1935	63.0%	1,000,000	16,758,686	63.0%	1,000,000	16,758,686
1936	79.0%	5,000,000	82,587,770	79.0%	5,000,000	82,587,770
1937	79.0%	5,000,000	79,720,139	79.0%	5,000,000	79,720,139
1938	79.0%	5,000,000	81,416,312	79.0%	5,000,000	81,416,312

corporations provided limited liability protection and were taxed at the entity
level at the federal income tax rates shown in Table 2.5.[14]

Chart 2.1 compares individual and C corporation statutory tax rates
from 1913 through 1938 based on the data contained in the preceding
tables. As is clearly illustrated in this chart, federal individual statutory
income tax rates in the maximum income bracket were substantially greater

---

[14]www.irs.gov/pub/irs-soi/02corate.pdf.

TABLE 2.5 Federal C Corporation Income Tax Rates—Years 1909–1938

Year	Rate Brackets or Exemptions	Rate [A] (Percent)
1909–1912	$ 5,000 exemption	1.0%
1913–1915	No exemption after March 1, 1913	1.0%
1916	None	2.0%
1917	None	6.0%
1918	$ 2,000 exemption	12.0%
1919–1921	$ 2,000 exemption	10.0%
1922–1924	$ 2,000 exemption	12.5%
1925	$ 2,000 exemption	13.0%
1926–1927	$ 2,000 exemption	13.5%
1928	$ 3,000 exemption	12.0%
1929	$ 3,000 exemption	11.0%
1930–1931	$ 3,000 exemption	12.0%
1932–1935	None	13.8%
1936–1937	First $ 2,000	8.0%
	Over $ 40,000	15.0%
1938	First $ 25,000	12.5% to 16.0%
	Over $ 25,000 [B]	19.0%

Notes:

[A] In addition to the rates shown, certain types of excess profits' levies were in effect in 1917–1921 and 1933–1945.

[B] Less adjustments: 14.025% of dividends received and 2.5% of dividends paid.

than federal corporation statutory income tax rates in the maximum income bracket.

During the period from 1913 through 1935, C corporation dividends were tax exempt for individual federal income tax reporting purposes. Hence, there was no "double tax" on C corporation profits prior to 1936. This benefit ended in 1936 when C corporation dividend income became fully taxable for individual federal income reporting tax purposes. The enactment of the Income Tax Assessment Act of 1936 that created a second level of taxation on C corporation income had a profound, negative effect on the economics of owning a C corporation.

Prior to 1936, limited liability protection and the disparity between high individual income tax rates, more favorable C corporation tax rates, and the absence of individual taxes on dividend income encouraged the formation of C corporations for the accumulation of wealth by very profitable businesses. Business owners were provided strong financial incentives to conduct their business in the form of a C corporation and then to retain such C corporation earnings in the business.

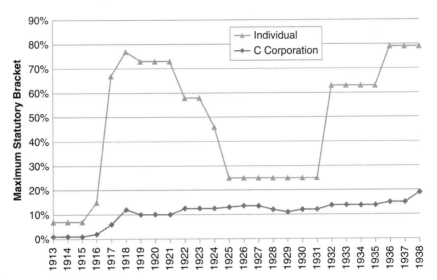

CHART 2.1 Individual (Married Filing Joint) versus C Corporation Statutory Tax Rates in Maximum Taxable Income Brackets, 1913–1938

During the period from 1913 through 1935, the transference of securities and other income-producing property to C corporations by wealthy individuals had become a common tax-avoidance strategy. Wealthy individuals reduced their overall federal income taxes by accumulating their assets in C corporations. Congress reacted to this commonplace taxpayer strategy by passing the Tariff Act of 1913, the Revenue Act of 1921, and the Revenue Act of 1934.

These acts created and refined the accumulated earnings tax, which provided disincentives for C corporations to retain and not distribute their earnings.

The original version of the tax first appeared in the Tariff Act of 1913, § II (a)(2), 38 Stat. 166 (1913). The tax was first enacted in its present form (taxing the corporate taxpayer) in the Revenue Act of 1921, § 220, 42 Stat. 247 (1921).[15]

This tax was also incorporated as part of subsequent regulations in the Internal Revenue Code.

---

[15]Norman G. Stone, "The Accumulated Earnings Tax: Displacement of the Avoidance Test and a Suggested Business Purpose Test," *British Columbia Law Review* 10(4), 919, n. 1 (July 1, 1969).

The accumulated earnings tax is "a tax imposed . . . [up]on companies with retained earnings deemed to be unreasonable and in excess of what is considered ordinary."[16] There is a presumption that such unreasonable accumulation of earnings in a C corporation is for the purpose of avoiding income taxes. This tax is a penalty tax that is added to C corporation income taxes.

Congress also tried to limit the use of C corporations as investment vehicles. In the Revenue Act of 1934, a *personal holding company* (PHC) was defined as a corporation that satisfied the following two criteria:

1. More than 50 percent of the value of its stock must be owned by five or fewer individuals (after attribution rules) "at any time during the last half of the taxable year."[17]
2. "At least 60 percent of its adjusted ordinary gross income . . . for the taxable year [must be] personal holding company income."[18] Adjusted ordinary gross income is derived by making several adjustments to gross income, including subtractions for capital gains and certain expenses associated with rental income.[19] PHC income consists primarily of dividends, interest, most royalties, annuities, and certain rental and compensation income.[20]

The Revenue Act of 1934 imposed a supplemental tax on PHCs. The PHC tax is imposed at the maximum individual dividend tax rate on PHC income; Congress's intention was to eliminate the tax savings that could be achieved under a rate structure in which individual income tax rates substantially exceeded corporate tax rates. This PHC tax is in addition to C corporation income taxes. In spite of repeated efforts to repeal the PHC tax, it remains in effect today.

YEARS 1939 THROUGH 1953

Internal Revenue Code of 1939: The tax statutes were re-codified by an Act of Congress on February 10, 1939, as the "Internal Revenue Code" (later known as the "Internal Revenue Code of 1939"). The 1939 Code was published as volume 53, Part I, of the United States

---

[16]*Accumulated Earnings Tax*, Investopedia, www.investopedia.com.
[17]I.R.C. § 542(a)(2).
[18]§ 542(a)(1).
[19]*Id.* § 543(b).
[20]*Id.* § 543(a).

Statutes at Large and as title 26 of the United States Code. Subsequent permanent tax laws enacted by the United States Congress updated and amended the 1939 Code.[21]

The period of 1939 through 1953 included the latter part of the Great Depression and World War II. The U.S. government's need for tax revenues increased during this period. As a result, maximum federal income tax rates were increased, rate brackets were reduced, and the income of more individuals was subjected to the maximum brackets. Table 2.6 summarizes the maximum marginal federal income tax rates and brackets for this time period.[22]

During this 15-year period, the maximum statutory federal income tax bracket increased from 79 (1939) to 92 percent (1953). Moreover, the

TABLE 2.6   Federal Individual Income Tax Rate History—Nominal Dollars—Income Years: 1939–1953

| | Married Filing Jointly | | | Single | | |
| | Taxable Income Greater Than | | | Taxable Income Greater Than | | |
Year	Maximum Statutory Bracket	Nominal $	2012 Inflation Adjusted $	Maximum Statutory Bracket	Nominal $	2012 Inflation Adjusted $
1939	79.0%	5,000,000	82,587,770	79.0%	5,000,000	82,587,770
1940	79.0%	5,000,000	81,997,857	79.0%	5,000,000	81,997,857
1941	81.0%	5,000,000	78,093,197	81.0%	5,000,000	78,093,197
1942	88.0%	200,000	2,817,104	88.0%	200,000	2,817,104
1943	88.0%	200,000	2,654,266	88.0%	200,000	2,654,266
1944	94.0%	200,000	2,609,023	94.0%	200,000	2,609,023
1945	94.0%	200,000	2,551,044	94.0%	200,000	2,551,044
1946	91.0%	200,000	2,354,810	91.0%	200,000	2,354,810
1947	91.0%	200,000	2,059,139	91.0%	200,000	2,059,139
1948	91.0%	200,000	1,905,344	91.0%	200,000	1,905,344
1949	91.0%	400,000	3,858,723	91.0%	200,000	1,929,361
1950	91.0%	400,000	3,810,689	91.0%	200,000	1,905,344
1951	91.0%	400,000	3,532,215	91.0%	200,000	1,766,108
1952	92.0%	400,000	3,465,570	92.0%	200,000	1,732,785
1953	92.0%	400,000	3,439,610	92.0%	200,000	1,719,805

[21]Internal Revenue Code, supra note 10.
[22]U.S. *Federal Individual Income Tax Rates History, 1862–2013* (Nominal and Inflation-Adjusted Brackets), www.taxfoundation.org.

nominal and 2012 inflation-adjusted amounts for the maximum statutory bracket plummeted. For married filing jointly taxpayers, the nominal taxable income for this bracket decreased from $5,000,000 (1939) to $400,000 (1953); for single taxpayers, the nominal taxable income for this bracket decreased from $5,000,000 (1939) to $200,000 (1953). Accordingly, more taxpayers were subjected to the highest of tax rates. During this period of high income taxes, Mark Twain's comments regarding income taxes were unfortunately accurate. He asked (and answered), "What is the difference between a taxidermist and a tax collector? The taxidermist takes only your skin."[23]

During this period, C corporations also experienced an increase in tax rates. Table 2.7 indicates the maximum statutory C corporation tax rates for the highest nominal income brackets from 1939 through 1953.[24]

During this period, similar to the period prior to 1939, federal individual statutory income tax rates in the highest income bracket continued to be much greater than federal corporation statutory income tax rates in the highest income bracket. See Chart 2.2, which was derived from Tables 2.6 and 2.7.

TABLE 2.7 Federal Corporation Income Tax Rate History—Nominal Dollars— Income Years: 1939–1953

Year	Top Corp Tax Rate	Top Tax Bracket (nominal $)
1939	19%	25,000
1940	24%	38,566
1941	31%	38,462
1942	40%	50,000
1943	40%	50,000
1944	40%	50,000
1945	40%	50,000
1946	38%	50,000
1947	38%	50,000
1948	38%	50,000
1949	38%	50,000
1950	42%	25,000
1951	51%	25,000
1952	52%	25,000
1953	52%	25,000

[23]*Mark Twain's Notebook* (Albert Bigelow Paine edition, 1935).
[24]www.irs.gov/pub/irs-soi/02corate.pdf.

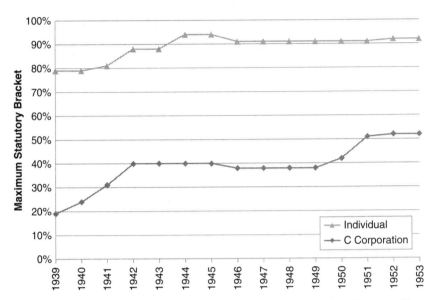

CHART 2.2   Individual (Married Filing Jointly) versus C Corporation Statutory Tax Rates in Maximum Taxable Income Brackets, 1939–1953

During this period, C corporation dividends were tax exempt from 1913 through 1935 and from 1940 through 1953; during 1936 through 1939, dividends were taxable at ordinary federal income tax rates.

YEARS 1954 THROUGH 1985

Internal Revenue Code of 1954: On August 16, 1954, in connection with a general overhaul of the Internal Revenue Service, the IRC was greatly reorganized by the 83rd United States Congress and expanded (by Chapter 736, Pub. L. 83–591). Ward M. Hussey was the principal drafter of the Internal Revenue Code of 1954. The code was published in volume 68A of the United States Statutes at Large. To prevent confusion with the 1939 Code, the new version was thereafter referred to as the "Internal Revenue Code of 1954" and the prior version as the "Internal Revenue Code of 1939." The lettering and numbering of subtitles, sections, etc., was completely changed. For example, section 22 of the 1939 Code (defining gross income) was roughly analogous to section 61 of the 1954 Code. The 1954 Code replaced the 1939 Code as title 26 of the United States Code.[25]

Topping out at 91 percent, the maximum statutory federal income tax rates immediately following the enactment of the 1954 Internal Revenue Code were historically very high, especially since it was not during the period of a world war or depression. Federal individual income tax rates for 1954 in the maximum income bracket decreased substantially during the 31-year period ending in 1985. The first major reduction was in 1964 under President Johnson, when the maximum rate fell from 91 to 77 percent, and further fell to 70 percent in 1965. Federal income tax rates in the maximum income bracket remained unchanged until President Reagan took office. In 1982, Congress lowered the federal income tax rate in the maximum individual bracket, this time to 50 percent. See Table 2.8.[26]

Even though individual income tax rates decreased substantially during this period, there were only slight decreases in the federal statutory income tax rate for businesses in the top C corporation income bracket (from 52% in 1954 to 46% in 1985). See Table 2.9.[27]

With enactment of the 1954 Code, C corporation dividends were once again taxable as ordinary income at the shareholder level (subject to certain annual exemptions). No longer did C corporations offer a tax shelter advantage to individuals in the maximum statutory income tax bracket. For the reasons illustrated in the following chapter, once dividends again became taxable in 1954, the second level of taxation of C corporation income greatly reduced the economic advantage of having a business operate as a C corporation relative to a PTE.

Chart 2.3 was derived from Tables 2.7 and 2.8.

S CORPORATIONS

Prior to 1958, there were only three choices for entrepreneurs starting a business: C corporations, partnerships, and sole proprietorships. All three choices had advantages and disadvantages. For shareholders of C corporations, the combination of high C corporation income taxes and a second level of taxation at the individual level on dividend income was extraordinarily burdensome. Partnerships and sole proprietorships were preferable to

---

[25]Internal Revenue Code, supra note 10.
[26]*U.S. Federal Individual Income Tax Rates History, 1862–2013* (Nominal and Inflation-Adjusted Brackets), www.taxfoundation.org.
[27]www.irs.gov/pub/irs-soi/02corate.pdf.

TABLE 2.8 Federal Individual Income Tax Rate History—Nominal Dollars—
Income Years: 1954–1985

| | Married Filing Jointly | | | | Single | | |
| | | Taxable Income Greater Than | | | | Taxable Income Greater Than | |
Year	Maximum Statutory	Nominal $	2012 Inflation Adjusted $	Maximum Statutory	Nominal $	2012 Inflation Adjusted $
1954	91%	400,000	3,414,037	91%	200,000	1,707,019
1955	91%	400,000	3,426,776	91%	200,000	1,713,388
1956	91%	400,000	3,376,382	91%	200,000	1,688,191
1957	91%	400,000	3,268,242	91%	200,000	1,634,121
1958	91%	400,000	3,177,772	91%	200,000	1,588,886
1959	91%	400,000	3,155,931	91%	200,000	1,577,966
1960	91%	400,000	3,102,622	91%	200,000	1,551,311
1961	91%	400,000	3,071,492	91%	200,000	1,535,746
1962	91%	400,000	3,040,980	91%	200,000	1,520,490
1963	91%	400,000	3,001,229	91%	200,000	1,500,614
1964	77%	400,000	2,962,503	77%	200,000	1,481,252
1965	70%	200,000	1,457,740	70%	100,000	728,870
1966	70%	200,000	1,417,247	70%	100,000	708,623
1967	70%	200,000	1,374,814	70%	100,000	687,407
1968	70%	200,000	1,319,506	70%	100,000	659,753
1969	70%	200,000	1,251,193	70%	100,000	625,597
1970	70%	200,000	1,183,474	70%	100,000	591,737
1971	70%	200,000	1,133,798	70%	100,000	566,899
1972	70%	200,000	1,098,536	70%	100,000	549,268
1973	70%	200,000	1,034,207	70%	100,000	517,104
1974	70%	200,000	931,416	70%	100,000	465,708
1975	70%	200,000	853,509	70%	100,000	426,755
1976	70%	200,000	807,009	70%	100,000	403,504
1977	70%	203,200	769,860	70%	102,200	387,203
1978	70%	203,200	715,544	70%	102,200	359,885
1979	70%	215,400	681,192	70%	108,300	342,494
1980	70%	215,400	600,177	70%	108,300	301,760
1981	70%	215,400	544,054	70%	108,300	273,543
1982	50%	85,600	203,661	50%	41,500	98,737
1983	50%	109,400	252,185	50%	55,300	127,475
1984	50%	162,400	358,865	50%	81,800	180,758
1985	50%	169,020	360,650	50%	85,130	181,648

TABLE 2.9   Federal Corporation Income Tax Rate History—Nominal Dollars—
Income Years: 1954–1985

Year	Top Corp Tax Rate	Top Tax Bracket (nominal $)
1953–1963	52.0%	25,000
1964	50.0%	25,000
1965–1967	48.0%	25,000
1968–1969	52.8%	25,000
1970	49.2%	25,000
1971–1974	48.0%	25,000
1975–1978	48.0%	50,000
1979–1983	46.0%	100,000
1984–1985	46.0%	1,405,000

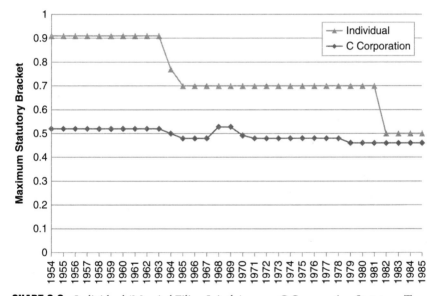

CHART 2.3   Individual (Married Filing Jointly) versus C Corporation Statutory Tax
Rates in Maximum Taxable Income Brackets, 1954–1985

C corporations because there was only one layer of income taxation on
partnership income (i.e., there was no entity-level income tax on partnership
earnings). However, owners of partnerships and sole proprietors were subject
to unlimited liability, unlike C corporation owners, who had limited liability
protection.

In response to the high tax versus unlimited liability dilemma facing entrepreneurs forming new businesses, President Eisenhower recommended the creation of the small business corporation (S corporation) to Congress. S corporations would be a PTE, similar to partnerships; the S corporation shareholders would have limited liability, similar to C corporation shareholders.

In 1958, Congress enacted legislation creating subchapter S of the IRC, subject to certain limitations:

1. S corporations could only have a limited number of shareholders.
2. S corporations could only have individuals and certain types of entities as shareholders.
3. S corporations could only have one class of stock.
4. S corporations could only be a domestic enterprise.[28]

Although certain details of these restrictions have changed over the years (i.e., increasing the number of allowable shareholders from 35 to 100; the liberalization of qualifying S corporation shareholders, that is, qualifying trusts, employee stock ownership plans, qualifying S corporations), these four types of restrictions remain in place.

As noted in "The History and Challenges of America's Dominant Business Structure,"

> [c]reation of the S corporation was a huge step forward in eliminating a devastating double tax and encouraging small and family business creation in the United States. Reducing an oppressive level of tax was an essential part of the legislation. As the Finance Committee noted at the time of passage, "permitting shareholders to report their proportionate share of the corporate income, in lieu of a corporate tax, will be a substantial aid to small business."[29]

Presently, there are more business entities filing U.S. federal income tax returns as S corporations than as C corporations, partnerships, or limited liability companies.[30]

---

[28]I.R.C. § 1361 (1954, as amended).
[29]*The History and Challenges of America's Dominant Business Structure*, S-Corp, www.s-corp.org/our-history.
[30]*IRS Data Book*, www.irs.gov.

TAX ON UNREASONABLE COMPENSATION

"[A] reasonable allowance for salaries or other compensation for personal services actually rendered" is permitted under IRC 162 as a tax-deductible business expense.[31] This clause "forms the basis for the law of reasonable compensation and effectively empowers the [IRS] to . . . police . . . compensation arrangements between an employer and an employee."[32]

The argument has been advanced that the reasonable compensation clause, originating in 1918, was intended to enlarge, rather than restrict, allowable compensation deductions. According to the enlargement theory, the excess profits tax of 1917 worked a hardship on closely held corporations, partnerships, and proprietorships that had not actually paid salaries to their shareholders, partners, or principals even though such individuals had performed services. The excess profits tax was computed on the basis of net income, which was determined under the Revenue Act of 1916. The net income of these taxpayers was overstated to the extent that they had failed to pay and deduct salaries. The Treasury Department responded in 1918 with a regulation permitting a taxpayer to deduct a reasonable amount designated as salary or compensation for personal service actually rendered in the conduct of such trade or business even though no such salary had actually been paid. Proponents of the enlargement theory argue that Congress incorporated the reasonable compensation clause in the Revenue Act of 1918 in order to furnish a statutory basis for the relief granted by the regulation interpreting the excess profits tax. Thus, they argue that Congress added the reasonable compensation clause to permit the deduction of a reasonable allowance for services actually rendered whether or not payment actually was made, and that there is no foundation in the statute for its use as a means of restricting the deduction of amounts that had actually been paid.[33] Notwithstanding this interpretation, it is clear that today the reasonable compensation clause stands as a limitation on the deductibility of compensation.

Shareholders of C corporations are incentivized to classify dividend distributions as compensation. The reason is that shareholder compensation is tax-deductible to the C corporation, whereas dividends are not. Classifying

---

[31]I.R.C. 162(a)(1).

[32]Sam G. Torolopoulos, *Position Paper Regarding: The Appropriateness of the Need for Management Compensation Studies Between Entities That Have Been Awarded EDC Benefits and U.S. Domiciled Corporation*, www.aticg.com/articles/IRC162PositionPaper .html.

[33]*Id.*

dividend distributions as tax-deductible compensation lowers a C corporation's taxable income.

The Internal Revenue Service (IRS) applies different factors to determine whether compensation is excessive. Unlike the accumulated earnings tax, which is a supplemental penalty tax, an IRS adjustment to reclassify compensation to dividends increases a C corporation's income tax burden. The excess compensation adjustment is not applicable to S corporations and other PTEs.

GENERAL UTILITIES DOCTRINE

The General Utilities Doctrine was eponymously named after a 1935 U.S. Supreme Court case entitled *General Utilities & Operating Co. v. Helvering*.[34] In this case, General Utilities distributed appreciated assets to its shareholders without recognizing a gain on the appreciation. If General Utilities had sold the appreciated assets and distributed its net proceeds, the company would have recognized a gain and paid corporation-level income taxes on the transaction.

The Court's decision was based on the general rule governing the nonrecognition of income tax on the distribution of appreciated assets that first appeared in the Revenue Act of 1918. The language in the Revenue Act of 1918 matched the language under the Revenue Acts of 1921, 1924, and 1926: "No gain or loss is realized by a corporation from the mere distribution of its assets in kind upon dissolution, however they may have appreciated or depreciated in value since their acquisition."[35]

This case was later interpreted to excuse the C corporation–level income tax on certain distributions of property by a corporation to its shareholders, whether the distribution took the form of a dividend, redemption, or liquidating distribution. It was incorporated into the Internal Revenue Code of 1954 as law.

This taxpayer-friendly law provided tax relief to owners of C corporations that distribute their assets and/or liquidate. Absent the General Utilities Doctrine, there would be one level of corporation income taxes on the sale or liquidation of assets; a second level of income taxes would be paid at the shareholder level on receipt of the distribution. The General Utilities Doctrine provisions in the 1954 IRC provided the shareholders of C corporations the same benefits—one level of taxation on a company's liquidation and distribution of assets—enjoyed by partnerships and S corporations.

---

[34]296 U.S. 200 (1935).
[35]Revenue Act of 1918, chapter 18, 40 Stat. 1057, 1081.

YEARS 1986 THROUGH 2013

Internal Revenue Code of 1954 . . . Relationship to Title 26 of the United States Code: The Tax Reform Act of 1986 changed the name of the 1954 Code to the "Internal Revenue Code of 1986" [and] is separately published as Title 26 of the United States Code.[36]

Commencing in 1987 following the enactment of the Internal Revenue Code of 1986, individual federal income tax rates in the maximum income bracket decreased from 50 percent (1986) to 38.5 percent (1987) and 28 percent (1988, 1989, and 1990). Thereafter, individual federal income tax rates in the maximum income bracket have ranged from 31 to 39.6 percent. Starting in 1993, the inflation-adjusted maximum income brackets have remained relatively constant. See Table 2.10.[37]

During this same period, the federal corporation income tax on maximum income brackets also decreased, from 46 percent (1986) to 35 percent (1993 to 2013). See Table 2.11.[38]

Chart 2.4 (derived from Tables 2.10 and 2.11) illustrates the continuing trend of convergence of maximum statutory federal individual income tax rates and C corporation tax rates during the period 1986–2013.

The federal tax rate on dividends received by individuals from C corporations also decreased during this period. From 1986 through 2002, dividend income was fully taxable, subject to certain exclusions. Commencing in 2003–2013, for the first time since 1953, the federal tax rate on dividend income received by individuals was lower than the tax rate on taxable income. For the period 2003–2012, the maximum federal dividend income tax rate was 15 percent; after 2012, the maximum federal dividend income tax rate is 20 percent (increased by a 3.8% surcharge under IRC section 1411). As discussed in detail later in this text, C corporation dividend tax rates that are lower than individual income tax rates have significant PTE valuation implications.

While the lowering of C corporation income tax and dividend tax rates benefited the owners of C corporations, the Internal Revenue Code of 1986 also contained provisions that did not benefit C corporations. The Internal Revenue Code of 1986 repealed the General Utilities Doctrine, providing yet another incentive for entrepreneurs to form their new enterprises as PTEs.

---

[36] Internal Revenue Code, supra note 10.

[37] *U.S. Federal Individual Income Tax Rates History, 1862–2013* (Nominal and Inflation-Adjusted Brackets), www.taxfoundation.org.

[38] www.irs.gov/pub/irs-soi/02corate.pdf.

TABLE 2.10   Federal Individual Income Tax Rate History—Nominal Dollars—Income Years: 1986–2013

	Married Filing Jointly			Single		
		Taxable Income Greater Than			Taxable Income Greater Than	
	Maximum Statutory Bracket	Nominal $	2012 Inflation Adjusted $	Maximum Statutory Bracket	Nominal $	2012 Inflation Adjusted $
1986	50.0%	175,250	367,120	50.0%	88,270	184,911
1987	38.5%	90,000	181,897	38.5%	54,000	109,138
1988	28.0%	29,750	57,738	28.0%	17,850	34,643
1989	28.0%	30,950	57,306	28.0%	18,550	34,347
1990	28.0%	32,450	57,003	28.0%	19,450	34,167
1991	31.0%	82,150	138,481	31.0%	49,300	83,106
1992	31.0%	86,500	141,553	31.0%	51,900	84,932
1993	39.6%	250,000	397,221	39.6%	250,000	397,221
1994	39.6%	250,000	387,304	39.6%	250,000	387,304
1995	39.6%	256,500	386,423	39.6%	256,500	386,423
1996	39.6%	263,750	385,949	39.6%	263,750	385,949
1997	39.6%	271,050	387,735	39.6%	271,050	387,735
1998	39.6%	278,450	392,211	39.6%	278,450	392,211
1999	39.6%	283,150	390,213	39.6%	283,150	390,213
2000	39.6%	288,350	384,457	39.6%	288,350	384,457
2001	39.1%	297,350	385,487	39.1%	297,350	385,487
2002	38.6%	307,050	391,867	38.6%	307,050	391,867
2003	35.0%	311,950	389,249	35.0%	311,950	389,249
2004	35.0%	319,100	387,842	35.0%	319,100	387,842
2005	35.0%	326,450	383,773	35.0%	326,450	383,773
2006	35.0%	336,550	383,283	35.0%	336,550	383,283
2007	35.0%	349,700	387,230	35.0%	349,700	387,230
2008	35.0%	357,700	381,443	35.0%	357,700	381,443
2009	35.0%	372,950	399,125	35.0%	372,950	399,125
2010	35.0%	373,650	393,421	35.0%	373,650	393,421
2011	35.0%	379,150	386,996	35.0%	379,150	386,996
2012	35.0%	388,350	388,350	35.0%	388,350	388,350
2013	39.6%	450,000	440,876	39.6%	400,000	391,890

LIMITED LIABILITY COMPANIES

Limited liability companies (LLCs) are relatively new, first emerging in Wyoming (1977).[39] LLCs are very similar to partnerships with one notable

---

[39]Susan Pace Hamill, "The Story of LLCs: Combining the Best Features of a Flawed Business Tax Structure," p. 295 at www.law.ua.edu/resources/misc.

TABLE 2.11 Federal Corporation Income Tax Rate History—Nominal Dollars—Income Years: 1986–2013

Year	Top Corp Tax Rate	Top Tax Bracket (nominal $)
1986	46%	1,405,000
1987	40%	1,405,000
1988–1992	34%	335,000
1993–2013	35%	18,333,333

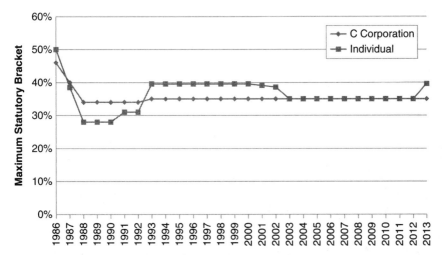

CHART 2.4 Individual (Married Filing Jointly) versus C Corporation Statutory Tax Rates in Maximum Taxable Income Brackets, 1986–2013

exception; the owners of LLCs have limited liability (similar to stockholders of corporations), whereas the partners of partnerships (with the exception of limited partners) have unlimited liability. This limited liability feature makes it a very attractive form of conducting business.

From 1977 through 1987, it remained unclear whether LLCs would be recognized as PTEs for federal tax reporting purposes. In 1988, the IRS issued Revenue Ruling 88–76, stating that a Wyoming LLC could be treated as a partnership. After the 1988 IRS ruling, the floodgates opened, and nearly every state enacted an LLC statute by 1996.[40] LLCs are now a widely recognized business form.

---

[40]*Id.*, pp. 296–297.

To be treated as a partnership, an LLC must have more than one owner (or member); single-member LLCs are treated as sole proprietorships for income tax reporting purposes. Unlike S corporations, there is no restriction on the number of owners. LLCs can have partnerships or S corporations as a member, but S corporations cannot have an LLC or a partnership as a shareholder. State law governs the formation process, the articles of organization, the duration of the LLC, and so forth.

SUMMARY

Chart 2.5, derived from Charts 2.1–2.4, illustrates the wide range in federal individual tax rates in the maximum income bracket during the period 1913–2013.

What a range! Immediately following its inception, federal individual statutory tax rates in the maximum income bracket soared during World War I, dipped during the Roaring Twenties, and then rose to new heights during the Great Depression and World War II, peaking at more than 90 percent. Such statutory rates would later plummet—by approximately 20 percent (to 70 percent) in the 1960s, and then again under President Reagan in the 1980s to a low of 28 percent. Since approximately 1990, federal statutory individual income tax rates in maximum income brackets have ranged between 30 and 40 percent. Very profitable businesses with taxable income in the maximum statutory

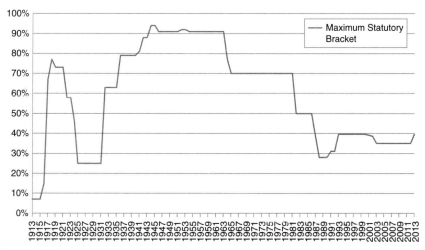

CHART 2.5   Married Filing Jointly Statutory Tax Rate in Maximum Income Bracket, 1913–2013

income bracket and operating as PTEs would be subject to these tax rates at the individual owner level.

Alternatively, businesses could operate as a C corporation and incur income taxes at the entity level. As shown in Chart 2.6, also derived from Charts 2.1–2.4, very profitable C corporations with taxable income in the maximum statutory corporation income bracket would subject their profits to the following C corporation tax rates in the maximum income tax bracket:

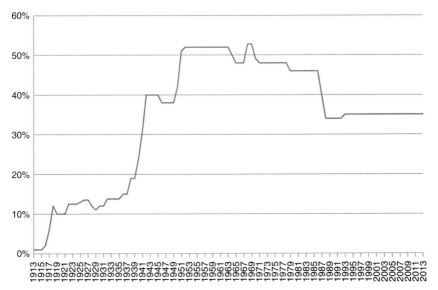

CHART 2.6   C Corporation Statutory Tax Rates in Maximum Taxable Income Brackets, 1913–2013

When the previous two charts are combined (see Chart 2.7), it is clearly seen that during the period prior to 1980, the federal individual income tax rates that were in the maximum income bracket were substantially higher than federal C corporation income tax rates in the maximum income bracket. Accordingly, through 1980, more highly profitable businesses were formed as C corporations than as PTEs. Laws were passed by Congress that sought to limit C corporation abuses (i.e., PHC, accumulated earnings tax, reasonable compensation, and General Utilities Doctrine repeal). Such tax laws, along with the narrowing of differences between the statutory income tax rates in the maximum income brackets of C corporations and individuals, resulted in a substantial increase in the number of businesses operating as PTEs after 1980.[41]

---

[41]See the annual *IRS Data Book*, available at www.irs.gov.

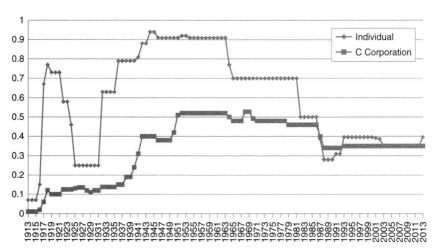

CHART 2.7 Individual (Married Filing Jointly) versus C Corporation Statutory Tax Rates in Maximum Taxable Income Brackets, 1913–2013

Congress also sought to limit C corporation benefits by passing laws making dividend distributions to individuals federally taxable (1936–1939 and after 1953). This created the second level of income taxation on C corporation profits discussed earlier and increased the economic cost of operating as a C corporation by reducing after-tax business profits available for the shareholder. See the comparison of individual federal income tax rates in the maximum income bracket in Table 2.12 and dividend tax rates from 1913 through 2013. The years highlighted in gray (i.e., 1913–1935, 1940–1953, and 2003–2013) have higher federal maximum statutory individual income tax rates than dividend tax rates.[42]

Table 2.13 compares maximum statutory dividend tax rates to individual income tax rates, and indicates the number of years where dividend rates were 0 percent; more than 0 percent but less than individual income tax rates; equal to individual income tax rates; and greater than individual income tax rates.

What the foregoing tables and charts clearly demonstrate is that even if a business has consistent levels of annual pretax operating profits, C corporation shareholders will receive substantially different after-tax cash flows depending on the tax year. For example, during certain years, the maximum statutory

---

[42]*U.S. Federal Individual Income Tax Rates History, 1862–2013* (Nominal and Inflation-Adjusted Brackets), www.taxfoundation.org, for maximum statutory individual income tax rates; for maximum dividend tax rates: Tax Foundation, Treasury Department and Commerce Clearing House.

TABLE 2.12 Comparison of Federal Maximum Statutory Tax Rates—Individual Income Tax Rates versus Dividend Tax Rates—Years 1913–2013

Year	Maximum Statutory Individual Income Tax Rates	Maximum Dividend Tax Rates
1913	7.0%	0.0%
1914	7.0%	0.0%
1915	7.0%	0.0%
1916	15.0%	0.0%
1917	67.0%	0.0%
1918	77.0%	0.0%
1919	73.0%	0.0%
1920	73.0%	0.0%
1921	73.0%	0.0%
1922	58.0%	0.0%
1923	58.0%	0.0%
1924	46.0%	0.0%
1925	25.0%	0.0%
1926	25.0%	0.0%
1927	25.0%	0.0%
1928	25.0%	0.0%
1929	25.0%	0.0%
1930	25.0%	0.0%
1931	25.0%	0.0%
1932	63.0%	0.0%
1933	63.0%	0.0%
1934	63.0%	0.0%
1935	63.0%	0.0%
1936	79.0%	79.0%
1937	79.0%	79.0%
1938	79.0%	79.0%
1939	79.0%	79.0%
1940	79.0%	0.0%
1941	81.0%	0.0%
1942	88.0%	0.0%
1943	88.0%	0.0%
1944	94.0%	0.0%
1945	94.0%	0.0%
1946	91.0%	0.0%
1947	91.0%	0.0%
1948	91.0%	0.0%
1949	91.0%	0.0%
1950	91.0%	0.0%

(*continued*)

TABLE 2.12 (*Continued*)

Year	Maximum Statutory Individual Income Tax Rates	Maximum Dividend Tax Rates	
1951	91.0%	0.0%	
1952	92.0%	0.0%	
1953	92.0%	0.0%	
1954	91.0%	91.0%	[2]
1955	91.0%	91.0%	[2]
1956	91.0%	91.0%	[2]
1957	91.0%	91.0%	[2]
1958	91.0%	91.0%	[2]
1959	91.0%	91.0%	[2]
1960	91.0%	91.0%	[2]
1961	91.0%	91.0%	[2]
1962	91.0%	91.0%	[2]
1963	91.0%	91.0%	[2]
1964	77.0%	77.0%	[1]
1965	70.0%	70.0%	[1]
1966	70.0%	70.0%	[1]
1967	70.0%	70.0%	[1]
1968	70.0%	70.0%	[1]
1969	70.0%	70.0%	[1]
1970	70.0%	70.0%	[1]
1971	70.0%	70.0%	[1]
1972	70.0%	70.0%	[1]
1973	70.0%	70.0%	[1]
1974	70.0%	70.0%	[1]
1975	70.0%	70.0%	[1]
1976	70.0%	70.0%	[1]
1977	70.0%	70.0%	[1]
1978	70.0%	70.0%	[1]
1979	70.0%	70.0%	[1]
1980	70.0%	70.0%	[1]
1981	70.0%	70.0%	[3]
1982	50.0%	50.0%	[3]
1983	50.0%	50.0%	[3]
1984	50.0%	50.0%	[3]
1985	50.0%	50.0%	[3]
1986	50.0%	50.0%	
1987	38.5%	38.5%	
1988	28.0%	28.0%	
1989	28.0%	28.0%	

TABLE 2.12 (*Continued*)

Year	Maximum Statutory Individual Income Tax Rates	Maximum Dividend Tax Rates
1990	28.0%	28.0%
1991	31.0%	31.0%
1992	31.0%	31.0%
1993	39.6%	39.6%
1994	39.6%	39.6%
1995	39.6%	39.6%
1996	39.6%	39.6%
1997	39.6%	39.6%
1998	39.6%	39.6%
1999	39.6%	39.6%
2000	39.6%	39.6%
2001	39.1%	39.1%
2002	38.6%	38.6%
2003	35.0%	15.0%
2004	35.0%	15.0%
2005	35.0%	15.0%
2006	35.0%	15.0%
2007	35.0%	15.0%
2008	35.0%	15.0%
2009	35.0%	15.0%
2010	35.0%	15.0%
2011	35.0%	15.0%
2012	35.0%	15.0%
2013	39.6%	20.0%

Notes:
[1] First $100 exempt.
[2] First $50 exempt.
[3] For 1981–1982, the first $200 of combined dividend and interest income ($400 for joint returns) is exempt. For 1981–1986, up to $750 ($1,500 for joint returns) of reinvested dividends of public utilities is exempt.

TABLE 2.13 History of Maximum Statutory Dividend Tax Rates

Number of Years When Maximum Statutory Dividend Tax Rates Were	
0%	37
More than 0%, less than individual tax rates	11
Equal to individual tax rates	53
Greater than individual tax rates	0

dividend tax rate could be in excess of 90 percent; in other years it could be 0 percent. The form of business and year of valuation can and often does have a substantial impact on business value.

The following is a summary of key matters noted in this chapter:

1. Federal individual income, dividend, and corporation income tax rates change; sometimes they change substantially, and sometimes they don't. Sometimes the rates change annually, and sometimes they don't.
2. During periods of world war, individual federal income tax rates in the maximum income bracket tend to be very high.
3. Federal individual and corporation income brackets change; sometimes they change substantially, and sometimes they don't. Sometimes the income brackets change annually, and sometimes they don't.
4. Rules governing calculation of taxable income change frequently.
5. The federal government has imposed penalty taxes when it identifies systemic abuses (or what the government perceives as abuse).
6. During the past 60 years, new forms of business ownership (i.e., S corporations and LLCs) were introduced; in the future, new forms may continue to be introduced.
7. Rules favoring one form of business ownership often change. For example, during the early part of the twentieth century, C corporations

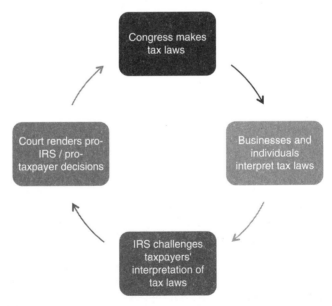

CHART 2.8 Evolution of Tax Law

with substantial taxable income provided income tax shelter for business owners. Many of the benefits that favored C corporations over PTEs during the first half of the twentieth century no longer exist.

8. In general, the evolution of tax law is based in part on the revenue needs of the U.S. government, the manner in which rules are interpreted, and the perception of abuses in the system.

Throughout the Code's history, a pattern emerges: Congress passes tax laws, taxpayers interpret the laws, the IRS challenges taxpayer interpretations, taxpayers and the IRS decipher the courts' decisions, and Congress passes new laws. This cycle of tax law evolution is graphically presented in Chart 2.8—and is unlikely to change in the future.

CHAPTER 3

Effective Federal Individual and Corporation Income Tax Rates

The preceding chapter analyzed statutory federal income tax rates in the maximum individual and corporation income brackets. Due to the progressivity of tax rates, the top 1 percent of taxpayers by income share reported approximately 17 percent of all adjusted gross income and paid approximately 37 percent of all income taxes in 2009. Thus, 63 percent of 2009 income taxes were paid by individuals not in the top 1 percent income bracket.[1] Accordingly, only a very small percentage of taxpayers are impacted by maximum income bracket tax rates. In this chapter we analyze the impact of tax rates on lower levels of income during the period 1913–2013.

How were lower-, middle-, and upper-income individuals affected by the rollercoaster ups and downs of income tax rates and changes in the IRC during the years 1913–2013? Do lower levels of income change the incentives for operating a business as a C corporation or a PTE? If so, when, why, and how were business values impacted by operating as a C corporation versus a PTE? What are the implications for business appraisers performing valuations in a changing tax environment?

To address these issues, this chapter provides the following discussion:

1. It analyzes three different hypothetical levels of annual, taxable income in 2012 Consumer Price Index (CPI) equivalent amounts of $10,000, $100,000, and $1,000,000. To simplify the analyses, state income taxes, itemized deductions, and exemptions are ignored, while statutory federal income tax rates are applied to each bracket of income.

---

[1]IRS, Statistics of Income, "Individual Income Tax Rates and Shares, 2009," www.irs .gov/pub/irs-soi/09inratesnap.pdf.

2. It calculates the effective federal individual income tax rates in each instance, for each year in the period 1913–2013, assuming a filing status of married filing jointly (prior to 1942, there were no married filing jointly filings). Federal individual income tax expense was calculated utilizing federal income tax tables found at Tax Foundation, www .taxfoundation.org. The effective federal individual income tax rate is equal to the total federal individual income tax expense divided by taxable income.

3. It calculates the effective federal C corporation income tax rate in each instance, for each year in the period 1913–2013. C corporation income tax expense was calculated utilizing federal income tax tables found at www.irs.go/pub/irs-soi/02corate.pdf. The effective federal C corporation income tax rate is equal to the total federal C corporation income tax expense divided by C corporation taxable income.

4. It calculates the effective federal tax rate on dividend income for each year in the period 1913–2013, utilizing federal income tax tables found at Tax Foundation, www.taxfoundation.org, Treasury Department, and Commerce Clearing House. The effective federal tax rate on dividend income is equal to the total federal dividend tax expense divided by C corporation taxable income.

5. It determines whether it was tax advantageous in each instance to operate as a C corporation or a PTE, absent other issues, for each year in the period 1913–2013.

6. It compares and analyzes the results under each example.

7. It identifies specific legislation that impacted the decision of taxpayers to operate as a C corporation or a PTE.

The analyses contained in this chapter provide greater clarity with respect to the impact of changing tax laws and rates on entity form, based on different levels of taxable income, during the period 1913–2013.

EFFECTIVE FEDERAL INCOME TAXES ON $10,000 OF 2012 CPI ADJUSTED TAXABLE INCOME, 1913–2013

In the preceding chapter, it was noted that during the 40-year period ending in 1953, federal individual income tax rates in the maximum income brackets were very high relative to C corporation rates in the maximum income bracket; this provided an incentive for very profitable businesses to operate as C corporations. How were businesses that earned lower levels of income impacted by C corporation and individual tax rates? Did they have the same incentives for operating as a C corporation? Let's find out.

Table 3.1 presents, for a business with $10,000 of 2012 CPI adjusted taxable income, the federal tax benefit (cost) of operating as a PTE versus a C corporation. The table presents a PTE's net after-tax income for a married filing jointly taxpayer (100%) less the effective federal individual income tax amount noted in the second numeric column. The amount that the owner would retain after tax by operating the business as a PTE is indicated by the column "NI." If the business operated as a C corporation, there were two levels of income taxes that would need to be considered: the C corporation income tax at the entity level and the tax on dividend distributions of C corporation income (dividend tax). These two levels of taxation are noted under the broad heading "Corp Tx" and "Div Tx." The difference between 100 percent and the sum of the effective C corporation and dividend taxes is the net after-tax amount retained by the C corporation owner, indicated in the column "NI."

For example, during 1920, a married couple with $10,000 of 2012 CPI adjusted taxable income ($871 in nominal dollars, before adjusting for inflation[2]) would retain 96 percent of their taxable income, after paying 4 percent of income taxes, by operating the business as a PTE. If that same married couple operated their business as a C corporation in 1920, they would incur no C corporation income tax expense because there was no C corporation income tax on the first $22,959 of taxable income ($2,000 in nominal dollars, before adjusting for inflation) and no dividend tax (there was no tax on dividend income until 1936). Hence, these taxpayers would have retained 100 percent of his business's taxable income if he operated as a C corporation. The difference in retained after-tax income between operating as a PTE (96% retained) and as a C corporation (100%) indicates that it would have been advantageous for this business to operate as a C corporation during 1920.

Individual Income Taxes

During the period 1913–1940, the individual federal income tax burden for taxpayers with $10,000 of CPI adjusted taxable income ranged from a low of 1 percent to a high of 6 percent, indicating limited tax rate volatility. Thereafter, the individual federal income tax burden increased substantially and, with the exception of the period 1977–1986, has remained in the range of 10 to 22 percent. As of 2013, the effective federal individual tax rate was at approximately the midpoint during this 101-year period—10 percent. Chart 3.1 is derived from Table 3.1, and illustrates the effective federal

---

[2]This figure is calculated as follows: $10,000 multiplied by the 1920 CPI of 20.00 divided by the 2012 CPI of 229.594.

TABLE 3.1 Federal Individual and C Corporation Income Tax History—Inflation Adjusted Using Average Annual CPI—Income Years: 1913–2013

| | $10,000 of 2012 CPI Adjusted Taxable Income | | | | | | | | |
| Year | Married Filing Jointly | | | | C Corporation | | | | |
	100.0%	FIT	NI	100%	Corp Tx	After Corp Tx	Div Tx	NI	MFJ v C Corp
1913	100.0%	1.0%	99.0%	100.0%	1.0%	99.0%	0.0%	99.0%	0.0%
1914	100.0%	1.0%	99.0%	100.0%	1.0%	99.0%	0.0%	99.0%	0.0%
1915	100.0%	1.0%	99.0%	100.0%	1.0%	99.0%	0.0%	99.0%	0.0%
1916	100.0%	2.0%	98.0%	100.0%	2.0%	98.0%	0.0%	98.0%	0.0%
1917	100.0%	2.0%	98.0%	100.0%	6.0%	94.0%	0.0%	94.0%	4.0%
1918	100.0%	6.0%	94.0%	100.0%	0.0%	100.0%	0.0%	100.0%	-6.0%
1919	100.0%	4.0%	96.0%	100.0%	0.0%	100.0%	0.0%	100.0%	-4.0%
1920	100.0%	4.0%	96.0%	100.0%	0.0%	100.0%	0.0%	100.0%	-4.0%
1921	100.0%	4.0%	96.0%	100.0%	0.0%	100.0%	0.0%	100.0%	-4.0%
1922	100.0%	4.0%	96.0%	100.0%	0.0%	100.0%	0.0%	100.0%	-4.0%
1923	100.0%	4.0%	96.0%	100.0%	0.0%	100.0%	0.0%	100.0%	-4.0%
1924	100.0%	2.0%	98.0%	100.0%	0.0%	100.0%	0.0%	100.0%	-2.0%
1925	100.0%	1.5%	98.5%	100.0%	0.0%	100.0%	0.0%	100.0%	-1.5%
1926	100.0%	1.5%	98.5%	100.0%	0.0%	100.0%	0.0%	100.0%	-1.5%
1927	100.0%	1.5%	98.5%	100.0%	0.0%	100.0%	0.0%	100.0%	-1.5%
1928	100.0%	1.5%	98.5%	100.0%	0.0%	100.0%	0.0%	100.0%	-1.5%
1929	100.0%	1.5%	98.5%	100.0%	0.0%	100.0%	0.0%	100.0%	-1.5%
1930	100.0%	1.5%	98.5%	100.0%	0.0%	100.0%	0.0%	100.0%	-1.5%
1931	100.0%	1.5%	98.5%	100.0%	0.0%	100.0%	0.0%	100.0%	-1.5%
1932	100.0%	4.0%	96.0%	100.0%	13.8%	86.2%	0.0%	86.2%	9.8%

TABLE 3.1 (*Continued*)

	Married Filing Jointly			$10,000 of 2012 CPI Adjusted Taxable Income C Corporation					
Year	100.0%	FIT	NI	100%	Corp Tx	After Corp Tx	Div Tx	NI	MFJ v C Corp
1933	100.0%	4.0%	96.0%	100.0%	13.8%	86.2%	0.0%	86.2%	9.8%
1934	100.0%	4.0%	96.0%	100.0%	13.8%	86.2%	0.0%	86.2%	9.8%
1935	100.0%	4.0%	96.0%	100.0%	13.8%	86.2%	0.0%	86.2%	9.8%
1936	100.0%	4.0%	96.0%	100.0%	12.5%	87.5%	3.5%	84.0%	12.0%
1937	100.0%	4.0%	96.0%	100.0%	12.5%	87.5%	3.5%	84.0%	12.0%
1938	100.0%	4.0%	96.0%	100.0%	12.5%	87.5%	3.5%	84.0%	12.0%
1939	100.0%	4.0%	96.0%	100.0%	12.5%	87.5%	3.5%	84.0%	12.0%
1940	100.0%	4.0%	96.0%	100.0%	15.4%	84.6%	0.0%	84.6%	11.4%
1941	100.0%	10.0%	90.0%	100.0%	21.0%	79.0%	0.0%	79.0%	11.0%
1942	100.0%	19.0%	81.0%	100.0%	25.0%	75.0%	0.0%	75.0%	6.0%
1943	100.0%	19.0%	81.0%	100.0%	25.0%	75.0%	0.0%	75.0%	6.0%
1944	100.0%	23.0%	77.0%	100.0%	25.0%	75.0%	0.0%	75.0%	2.0%
1945	100.0%	23.0%	77.0%	100.0%	25.0%	75.0%	0.0%	75.0%	2.0%
1946	100.0%	20.0%	80.0%	100.0%	21.0%	79.0%	0.0%	79.0%	1.0%
1947	100.0%	20.0%	80.0%	100.0%	21.0%	79.0%	0.0%	79.0%	1.0%
1948	100.0%	20.0%	80.0%	100.0%	21.0%	79.0%	0.0%	79.0%	1.0%
1949	100.0%	20.0%	80.0%	100.0%	21.0%	79.0%	0.0%	79.0%	1.0%
1950	100.0%	20.0%	80.0%	100.0%	23.0%	77.0%	0.0%	77.0%	3.0%
1951	100.0%	20.4%	79.6%	100.0%	28.8%	71.2%	0.0%	71.2%	8.4%
1952	100.0%	22.2%	77.8%	100.0%	30.0%	70.0%	0.0%	70.0%	7.8%
1953	100.0%	22.2%	77.8%	100.0%	30.0%	70.0%	0.0%	70.0%	7.8%

(*continued*)

TABLE 3.1 (Continued)

			$10,000 of 2012 CPI Adjusted Taxable Income						
	Married Filing Jointly			C Corporation					
Year	100.0%	FIT	NI	100%	Corp Tx	After Corp Tx	Div Tx	NI	MFJ v C Corp
1954	100.0%	20.0%	80.0%	100.0%	30.0%	70.0%	13.9%	56.1%	23.9%
1955	100.0%	20.0%	80.0%	100.0%	30.0%	70.0%	13.9%	56.1%	23.9%
1956	100.0%	20.0%	80.0%	100.0%	30.0%	70.0%	13.9%	56.1%	23.9%
1957	100.0%	20.0%	80.0%	100.0%	30.0%	70.0%	13.9%	56.1%	23.9%
1958	100.0%	20.0%	80.0%	100.0%	30.0%	70.0%	13.9%	56.1%	23.9%
1959	100.0%	20.0%	80.0%	100.0%	30.0%	70.0%	13.9%	56.1%	23.9%
1960	100.0%	20.0%	80.0%	100.0%	30.0%	70.0%	13.9%	56.1%	23.9%
1961	100.0%	20.0%	80.0%	100.0%	30.0%	70.0%	13.9%	56.1%	23.9%
1962	100.0%	20.0%	80.0%	100.0%	30.0%	70.0%	13.9%	56.1%	23.9%
1963	100.0%	20.0%	80.0%	100.0%	30.0%	70.0%	13.9%	56.1%	23.9%
1964	100.0%	16.1%	83.9%	100.0%	22.0%	78.0%	12.3%	65.7%	18.2%
1965	100.0%	14.3%	85.7%	100.0%	22.0%	78.0%	10.8%	67.2%	18.5%
1966	100.0%	14.3%	85.7%	100.0%	22.0%	78.0%	10.8%	67.2%	18.5%
1967	100.0%	14.3%	85.7%	100.0%	22.0%	78.0%	10.9%	67.1%	18.6%
1968	100.0%	14.3%	85.7%	100.0%	24.2%	75.8%	10.6%	65.2%	20.5%
1969	100.0%	14.4%	85.6%	100.0%	24.2%	75.8%	10.6%	65.2%	20.4%
1970	100.0%	14.4%	85.6%	100.0%	22.5%	77.5%	10.9%	66.6%	19.0%
1971	100.0%	14.4%	85.6%	100.0%	22.0%	78.0%	11.0%	67.0%	18.6%
1972	100.0%	14.5%	85.5%	100.0%	22.0%	78.0%	11.0%	67.0%	18.5%
1973	100.0%	14.5%	85.5%	100.0%	22.0%	78.0%	11.0%	67.0%	18.5%
1974	100.0%	14.6%	85.4%	100.0%	22.0%	78.0%	11.1%	66.9%	18.5%

TABLE 3.1 (*Continued*)

$10,000 of 2012 CPI Adjusted Taxable Income

Year	Married Filing Jointly				C Corporation				MFJ v C Corp
	100.0%	FIT	NI	100%	Corp Tx	After Corp Tx	Div Tx	NI	
1975	100.0%	14.7%	85.3%	100.0%	20.0%	80.0%	11.4%	68.6%	16.7%
1976	100.0%	14.8%	85.2%	100.0%	20.0%	80.0%	11.4%	68.6%	16.6%
1977	100.0%	0.0%	100.0%	100.0%	20.0%	80.0%	0.0%	80.0%	20.0%
1978	100.0%	0.0%	100.0%	100.0%	20.0%	80.0%	0.0%	80.0%	20.0%
1979	100.0%	0.0%	100.0%	100.0%	17.0%	83.0%	0.0%	83.0%	17.0%
1980	100.0%	0.7%	99.3%	100.0%	17.0%	83.0%	0.0%	83.0%	16.3%
1981	100.0%	2.0%	98.0%	100.0%	17.0%	83.0%	0.0%	83.0%	15.0%
1982	100.0%	2.3%	97.7%	100.0%	16.0%	84.0%	0.0%	84.0%	13.7%
1983	100.0%	2.4%	97.6%	100.0%	15.0%	85.0%	0.3%	84.7%	12.9%
1984	100.0%	2.7%	97.3%	100.0%	15.0%	85.0%	0.6%	84.4%	12.9%
1985	100.0%	2.7%	97.3%	100.0%	15.0%	85.0%	1.0%	84.0%	13.3%
1986	100.0%	2.5%	97.5%	100.0%	15.0%	85.0%	0.9%	84.1%	13.4%
1987	100.0%	12.6%	87.4%	100.0%	15.0%	85.0%	10.3%	74.7%	12.7%
1988	100.0%	15.0%	85.0%	100.0%	15.0%	85.0%	12.8%	72.2%	12.8%
1989	100.0%	15.0%	85.0%	100.0%	15.0%	85.0%	12.8%	72.2%	12.8%
1990	100.0%	15.0%	85.0%	100.0%	15.0%	85.0%	12.8%	72.2%	12.8%
1991	100.0%	15.0%	85.0%	100.0%	15.0%	85.0%	12.8%	72.2%	12.8%
1992	100.0%	15.0%	85.0%	100.0%	15.0%	85.0%	12.8%	72.2%	12.8%
1993	100.0%	15.0%	85.0%	100.0%	15.0%	85.0%	12.8%	72.2%	12.8%
1994	100.0%	15.0%	85.0%	100.0%	15.0%	85.0%	12.8%	72.2%	12.8%
1995	100.0%	15.0%	85.0%	100.0%	15.0%	85.0%	12.8%	72.2%	12.8%

(*continued*)

TABLE 3.1 (*Continued*)

$10,000 of 2012 CPI Adjusted Taxable Income

Year	Married Filing Jointly			C Corporation					
	100.0%	FIT	NI	100%	Corp Tx	After Corp Tx	Div Tx	NI	MFJ v C Corp
1996	100.0%	15.0%	85.0%	100.0%	15.0%	85.0%	12.8%	72.2%	12.8%
1997	100.0%	15.0%	85.0%	100.0%	15.0%	85.0%	12.8%	72.2%	12.8%
1998	100.0%	15.0%	85.0%	100.0%	15.0%	85.0%	12.8%	72.2%	12.8%
1999	100.0%	15.0%	85.0%	100.0%	15.0%	85.0%	12.8%	72.2%	12.8%
2000	100.0%	15.0%	85.0%	100.0%	15.0%	85.0%	12.8%	72.2%	12.8%
2001	100.0%	15.0%	85.0%	100.0%	15.0%	85.0%	12.8%	72.2%	12.8%
2002	100.0%	10.0%	90.0%	100.0%	15.0%	85.0%	8.5%	76.5%	13.5%
2003	100.0%	10.0%	90.0%	100.0%	15.0%	85.0%	0.0%	85.0%	5.0%
2004	100.0%	10.0%	90.0%	100.0%	15.0%	85.0%	0.0%	85.0%	5.0%
2005	100.0%	10.0%	90.0%	100.0%	15.0%	85.0%	0.0%	85.0%	5.0%
2006	100.0%	10.0%	90.0%	100.0%	15.0%	85.0%	0.0%	85.0%	5.0%
2007	100.0%	10.0%	90.0%	100.0%	15.0%	85.0%	0.0%	85.0%	5.0%
2008	100.0%	10.0%	90.0%	100.0%	15.0%	85.0%	0.0%	85.0%	5.0%
2009	100.0%	10.0%	90.0%	100.0%	15.0%	85.0%	0.0%	85.0%	5.0%
2010	100.0%	10.0%	90.0%	100.0%	15.0%	85.0%	0.0%	85.0%	5.0%
2011	100.0%	10.0%	90.0%	100.0%	15.0%	85.0%	0.0%	85.0%	5.0%
2012	100.0%	10.0%	90.0%	100.0%	15.0%	85.0%	0.0%	85.0%	5.0%
2013	100.0%	10.0%	90.0%	100.0%	15.0%	85.0%	0.0%	85.0%	5.0%

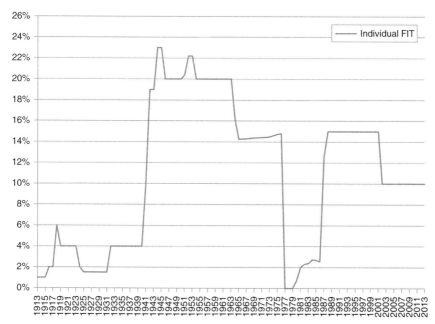

CHART 3.1 Effective Individual Income Tax Rates (MFJ) Assuming $10,000 of 2012 CPI Adjusted Taxable Income, 1913–2013

income tax burden of a married filing jointly taxpayer with $10,000 of CPI adjusted taxable income from 1913 to 2013.

C Corporation Income Taxes and Dividend Taxes

On the other hand, C corporations with $10,000 of taxable income during this period experienced much greater federal tax rate volatility. For example, during 1917, all C corporation income, regardless of income bracket, was subject to a federal income tax of 6 percent. This law changed in 1918, exempting the first $30,410 of 2012 CPI adjusted taxable income ($2,000 in nominal dollars) from income taxation; this first bracket of exempted taxable income would protect the C corporation in this example from income taxation through 1931 (see Table 2.5). Starting in 1932, all C corporation income was subject to income tax.

A new tax on C corporation dividend distributions commenced in 1936 and lasted until 1939. This tax on dividend income decreased after-tax income by an additional 3.5 percent during the period 1936–1939. This dividend tax was repealed effective 1940 but returned permanently in 1954 (see Table 2.12).

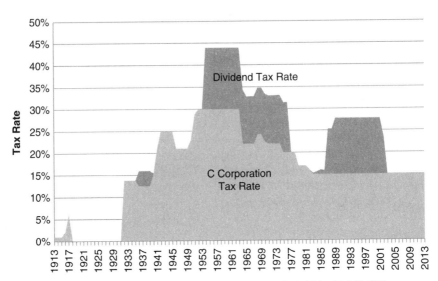

CHART 3.2 C Corporation and Dividend Tax Rates—$10,000 of 2012 CPI Adjusted Taxable Income, 1913–2013

Chart 3.2 summarizes the total corporation and dividend tax cost presented in Table 3.1 for an owner of a C corporation with $10,000 of 2012 CPI adjusted taxable income.

Comparison of PTE and C Corporation Income Taxes

The income-retained advantage of operating as a C corporation (negative amounts) and as a PTE (positive amounts) is graphically presented by year in Chart 3.3. See Table 3.1.

Based on the preceding charts and table, (1) during the years 1918–1931, it was tax advantageous for the owner of a business earning $10,000 of 2012 CPI adjusted taxable income to operate as a C corporation because there was no corporation income tax or dividend tax; and (2) during all other years, an owner of a PTE operating a business with $10,000 of taxable income would retain far more money than an owner of a C corporation with $10,000 of taxable income.

In summary, unlike businesses subject to tax rates in the maximum income brackets and except for the period 1918–1931, it has never been tax advantageous to operate a business with $10,000 of 2012 CPI adjusted taxable income as a C corporation.

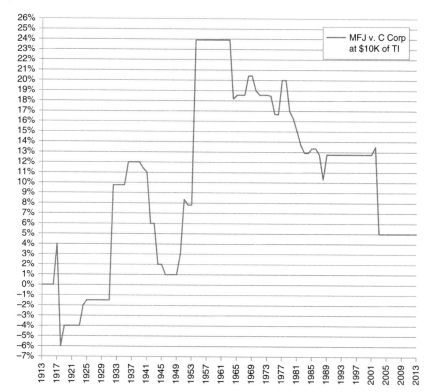

CHART 3.3 Benefit of MFJ versus C Corporation, 1913–2013, Assuming $10,000 of 2012 CPI Adjusted Taxable Income

EFFECTIVE FEDERAL INCOME TAXES ON $100,000 OF 2012 CPI ADJUSTED TAXABLE INCOME, 1913–2013

The next analysis examines a business with $100,000 of 2012 CPI adjusted taxable income and identifies in which years it was more advantageous to operate as a PTE and in which years it was more advantageous to operate as a C corporation.

Table 3.2 analyzes the income tax cost of operating a business as a PTE and as a C corporation, assuming $100,000 of 2012 CPI adjusted taxable income.

Individual Income Taxes

From data compiled in Table 3.2, Chart 3.4 illustrates the federal effective individual income tax expense of a PTE with $100,000 of 2012 CPI adjusted taxable income during the period 1913–2013.

TABLE 3.2 Federal Individual and C Corporation Income Tax History—Inflation Adjusted Using Average Annual CPI—Income Years: 1913–2013

| | Married Filing Jointly | | | C Corporation | | | | | |
| | $100,000 of 2012 CPI Adjusted Taxable Income | | | | | | | | |
Year	100.0%	FIT	NI	100%	Corp Tx	After Corp Tx	Div Tx	NI	MFJ v C Corp
1913	100.0%	1.0%	99.0%	100.0%	1.0%	99.0%	0.0%	99.0%	0.0%
1914	100.0%	1.0%	99.0%	100.0%	1.0%	99.0%	0.0%	99.0%	0.0%
1915	100.0%	1.0%	99.0%	100.0%	1.0%	99.0%	0.0%	99.0%	0.0%
1916	100.0%	2.0%	98.0%	100.0%	2.0%	98.0%	0.0%	98.0%	0.0%
1917	100.0%	3.4%	96.6%	100.0%	6.0%	94.0%	0.0%	94.0%	2.6%
1918	100.0%	8.7%	91.3%	100.0%	8.4%	91.6%	0.0%	91.6%	−0.3%
1919	100.0%	6.4%	93.6%	100.0%	7.3%	92.7%	0.0%	92.7%	0.9%
1920	100.0%	7.0%	93.0%	100.0%	7.7%	92.3%	0.0%	92.3%	0.7%
1921	100.0%	6.5%	93.5%	100.0%	7.4%	92.6%	0.0%	92.6%	0.9%
1922	100.0%	6.0%	94.0%	100.0%	9.1%	90.9%	0.0%	90.9%	3.1%
1923	100.0%	6.0%	94.0%	100.0%	9.1%	90.9%	0.0%	90.9%	3.1%
1924	100.0%	2.9%	97.1%	100.0%	9.1%	90.9%	0.0%	90.9%	6.2%
1925	100.0%	2.2%	97.8%	100.0%	9.6%	90.4%	0.0%	90.4%	7.4%
1926	100.0%	2.2%	97.8%	100.0%	10.0%	90.0%	0.0%	90.0%	7.8%
1927	100.0%	2.2%	97.8%	100.0%	9.9%	90.1%	0.0%	90.1%	7.7%
1928	100.0%	2.2%	97.8%	100.0%	7.2%	92.8%	0.0%	92.8%	5.0%
1929	100.0%	2.2%	97.8%	100.0%	6.6%	93.4%	0.0%	93.4%	4.4%
1930	100.0%	2.2%	97.8%	100.0%	7.1%	92.9%	0.0%	92.9%	4.9%
1931	100.0%	2.1%	97.9%	100.0%	6.6%	93.4%	0.0%	93.4%	4.5%
1932	100.0%	5.3%	94.7%	100.0%	13.8%	86.3%	0.0%	86.3%	8.4%

TABLE 3.2 (*Continued*)

	Married Filing Jointly			C Corporation					
				$100,000 of 2012 CPI Adjusted Taxable Income					
Year	100.0%	FIT	NI	100%	Corp Tx	After Corp Tx	Div Tx	NI	MFJ v C Corp
1933	100.0%	5.2%	94.8%	100.0%	13.8%	86.2%	0.0%	86.2%	8.6%
1934	100.0%	5.3%	94.7%	100.0%	13.8%	86.2%	0.0%	86.2%	8.5%
1935	100.0%	5.3%	94.7%	100.0%	13.8%	86.2%	0.0%	86.2%	8.5%
1936	100.0%	5.4%	94.6%	100.0%	13.5%	86.5%	4.3%	82.2%	12.4%
1937	100.0%	5.5%	94.5%	100.0%	13.5%	86.5%	4.4%	82.1%	12.4%
1938	100.0%	5.4%	94.6%	100.0%	12.8%	87.2%	4.4%	82.8%	11.8%
1939	100.0%	5.4%	94.6%	100.0%	12.8%	87.2%	4.3%	82.9%	11.7%
1940	100.0%	5.4%	94.6%	100.0%	15.7%	84.3%	0.0%	84.3%	10.3%
1941	100.0%	13.8%	86.2%	100.0%	21.4%	78.6%	0.0%	78.6%	7.6%
1942	100.0%	23.5%	76.5%	100.0%	25.6%	74.4%	0.0%	74.4%	2.1%
1943	100.0%	23.9%	76.1%	100.0%	25.7%	74.3%	0.0%	74.3%	1.8%
1944	100.0%	27.3%	72.7%	100.0%	25.7%	74.3%	0.0%	74.3%	-1.6%
1945	100.0%	27.4%	72.6%	100.0%	25.7%	74.3%	0.0%	74.3%	-1.7%
1946	100.0%	25.1%	74.9%	100.0%	21.8%	78.2%	0.0%	78.2%	-3.3%
1947	100.0%	26.2%	73.8%	100.0%	22.0%	78.0%	0.0%	78.0%	-4.2%
1948	100.0%	26.9%	73.1%	100.0%	22.0%	78.0%	0.0%	78.0%	-4.9%
1949	100.0%	22.1%	77.9%	100.0%	22.0%	78.0%	0.0%	78.0%	-0.1%
1950	100.0%	22.2%	77.8%	100.0%	23.0%	77.0%	0.0%	77.0%	0.8%
1951	100.0%	23.0%	77.0%	100.0%	28.8%	71.3%	0.0%	71.3%	5.7%
1952	100.0%	25.1%	74.9%	100.0%	30.0%	70.0%	0.0%	70.0%	4.9%
1953	100.0%	25.1%	74.9%	100.0%	30.0%	70.0%	0.0%	70.0%	4.9%

(*continued*)

TABLE 3.2 (Continued)

| | Married Filing Jointly | | | C Corporation | | | | | |
| | | | | $100,000 of 2012 CPI Adjusted Taxable Income | | | | | |
Year	100.0%	FIT	NI	100%	Corp Tx	After Corp Tx	Div Tx	NI	MFJ v C Corp
1954	100.0%	22.6%	77.4%	100.0%	30.0%	70.0%	14.8%	55.2%	22.2%
1955	100.0%	22.6%	77.4%	100.0%	30.0%	70.0%	14.8%	55.2%	22.2%
1956	100.0%	22.6%	77.4%	100.0%	30.0%	70.0%	14.8%	55.2%	22.2%
1957	100.0%	22.8%	77.2%	100.0%	30.0%	70.0%	14.9%	55.1%	22.1%
1958	100.0%	23.0%	77.0%	100.0%	30.0%	70.0%	15.0%	55.0%	22.0%
1959	100.0%	23.1%	76.9%	100.0%	30.0%	70.0%	15.0%	55.0%	21.9%
1960	100.0%	23.2%	76.8%	100.0%	30.0%	70.0%	15.1%	54.9%	21.9%
1961	100.0%	23.2%	76.8%	100.0%	30.0%	70.0%	15.1%	54.9%	21.9%
1962	100.0%	23.3%	76.7%	100.0%	30.0%	70.0%	15.1%	54.9%	21.8%
1963	100.0%	23.4%	76.6%	100.0%	30.0%	70.0%	15.2%	54.8%	21.8%
1964	100.0%	20.9%	79.1%	100.0%	22.0%	78.0%	15.3%	62.7%	16.4%
1965	100.0%	19.6%	80.4%	100.0%	22.0%	78.0%	14.4%	63.6%	16.8%
1966	100.0%	19.8%	80.2%	100.0%	22.0%	78.0%	14.4%	63.6%	16.6%
1967	100.0%	19.9%	80.1%	100.0%	22.0%	78.0%	14.5%	63.5%	16.6%
1968	100.0%	20.1%	79.9%	100.0%	24.2%	75.8%	14.1%	61.7%	18.2%
1969	100.0%	20.4%	79.6%	100.0%	24.2%	75.8%	14.3%	61.5%	18.1%
1970	100.0%	20.8%	79.2%	100.0%	22.5%	77.5%	15.0%	62.5%	16.7%
1971	100.0%	21.1%	78.9%	100.0%	22.0%	78.0%	15.3%	62.7%	16.2%
1972	100.0%	21.3%	78.7%	100.0%	22.0%	78.0%	15.4%	62.6%	16.1%
1973	100.0%	21.7%	78.3%	100.0%	22.0%	78.0%	15.6%	62.4%	15.9%
1974	100.0%	22.6%	77.4%	100.0%	22.0%	78.0%	16.1%	61.9%	15.5%

TABLE 3.2 (*Continued*)

$100,000 of 2012 CPI Adjusted Taxable Income

Year	Married Filing Jointly			C Corporation					MFJ v C Corp
	100.0%	FIT	NI	100%	Corp Tx	After Corp Tx	Div Tx	NI	
1975	100.0%	23.4%	76.6%	100.0%	20.0%	80.0%	17.2%	62.8%	13.8%
1976	100.0%	24.0%	76.0%	100.0%	20.0%	80.0%	17.4%	62.6%	13.4%
1977	100.0%	20.5%	79.5%	100.0%	20.1%	79.9%	14.3%	65.6%	13.9%
1978	100.0%	21.4%	78.6%	100.0%	20.2%	79.8%	14.9%	64.9%	13.7%
1979	100.0%	21.6%	78.4%	100.0%	17.6%	82.4%	15.7%	66.7%	11.7%
1980	100.0%	23.6%	76.4%	100.0%	17.9%	82.1%	16.9%	65.2%	11.2%
1981	100.0%	25.4%	74.6%	100.0%	18.1%	81.9%	17.9%	64.0%	10.6%
1982	100.0%	23.8%	76.2%	100.0%	17.2%	82.8%	17.0%	65.8%	10.4%
1983	100.0%	21.9%	78.1%	100.0%	16.3%	83.7%	16.0%	67.7%	10.4%
1984	100.0%	21.2%	78.8%	100.0%	16.3%	83.7%	15.7%	68.0%	10.8%
1985	100.0%	21.1%	78.9%	100.0%	16.4%	83.6%	15.7%	67.9%	11.0%
1986	100.0%	20.9%	79.1%	100.0%	16.4%	83.6%	15.5%	68.1%	11.0%
1987	100.0%	21.0%	79.0%	100.0%	15.7%	84.3%	16.0%	68.3%	10.7%
1988	100.0%	20.5%	79.5%	100.0%	15.3%	84.7%	16.2%	68.5%	11.0%
1989	100.0%	20.6%	79.4%	100.0%	15.7%	84.3%	16.1%	68.2%	11.2%
1990	100.0%	20.6%	79.4%	100.0%	16.2%	83.8%	16.0%	67.8%	11.6%
1991	100.0%	20.5%	79.5%	100.0%	16.6%	83.4%	15.9%	67.5%	12.0%
1992	100.0%	20.4%	79.6%	100.0%	16.8%	83.2%	15.7%	67.5%	12.1%
1993	100.0%	20.4%	79.6%	100.0%	17.1%	82.9%	15.6%	67.3%	12.3%
1994	100.0%	20.3%	79.7%	100.0%	17.3%	82.7%	15.5%	67.2%	12.5%
1995	100.0%	20.4%	79.6%	100.0%	17.5%	82.5%	15.5%	67.0%	12.6%

(*continued*)

TABLE 3.2 (Continued)

$100,000 of 2012 CPI Adjusted Taxable Income

Year	Married Filing Jointly			C Corporation					MFJ v C Corp
	100.0%	FIT	NI	100%	Corp Tx	After Corp Tx	Div Tx	NI	
1996	100.0%	20.4%	79.6%	100.0%	17.7%	82.3%	15.4%	66.9%	12.7%
1997	100.0%	20.3%	79.7%	100.0%	17.8%	82.2%	15.3%	66.9%	12.8%
1998	100.0%	20.2%	79.8%	100.0%	18.0%	82.0%	15.2%	66.8%	13.0%
1999	100.0%	20.3%	79.7%	100.0%	18.1%	81.9%	15.2%	66.7%	13.0%
2000	100.0%	20.4%	79.6%	100.0%	18.3%	81.7%	14.4%	67.3%	12.3%
2001	100.0%	20.2%	79.8%	100.0%	18.8%	81.2%	15.0%	66.2%	13.6%
2002	100.0%	19.1%	80.9%	100.0%	19.0%	81.0%	14.0%	67.0%	13.9%
2003	100.0%	17.0%	83.0%	100.0%	19.3%	80.7%	12.1%	68.6%	14.4%
2004	100.0%	17.1%	82.9%	100.0%	19.7%	80.3%	12.0%	68.3%	14.6%
2005	100.0%	17.2%	82.8%	100.0%	20.2%	79.8%	12.0%	67.8%	15.0%
2006	100.0%	17.2%	82.8%	100.0%	20.6%	79.4%	11.9%	67.5%	15.3%
2007	100.0%	17.1%	82.9%	100.0%	21.0%	79.0%	11.9%	67.1%	15.8%
2008	100.0%	17.2%	82.8%	100.0%	21.5%	78.5%	11.8%	66.7%	16.1%
2009	100.0%	16.8%	83.2%	100.0%	21.4%	78.6%	11.8%	66.7%	16.5%
2010	100.0%	17.0%	83.0%	100.0%	21.6%	78.4%	11.8%	66.6%	16.4%
2011	100.0%	17.1%	82.9%	100.0%	22.0%	78.0%	11.7%	66.3%	16.6%
2012	100.0%	17.1%	82.9%	100.0%	22.3%	77.8%	11.7%	66.1%	16.8%
2013	100.0%	17.0%	83.0%	100.0%	22.6%	77.4%	15.5%	61.9%	21.1%

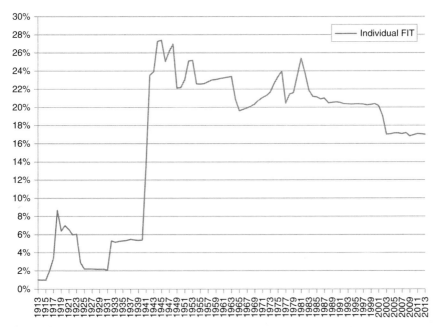

CHART 3.4   Effective Individual Income Tax Rates (MFJ) Assuming $100,000 of 2012 CPI Adjusted Taxable Income, 1913–2013

C Corporation Income Taxes and Dividend Taxes

Chart 3.5 illustrates how the tax burden of operating as a C corporation climbed steadily over the period 1913–1953, plateaued at approximately 45 percent during the mid-1950s, and has remained in the range of approximately 30 to 40 percent commencing in 1964.

Comparison of PTE and C Corporation Income Taxes

From data compiled in Table 3.2, Chart 3.6 illustrates the tax benefit (cost) of operating as a PTE relative to a C corporation during the period 1913–2013. During only 7 of the 101 years in this period was it tax advantageous for a business earning $100,000 of 2012 CPI adjusted taxable income to operate as a C corporation.

EFFECTIVE FEDERAL INCOME TAXES ON $1 MILLION OF 2012 CPI ADJUSTED TAXABLE INCOME, 1913–2013

The last of the three examples considers the effective federal income tax burden on $1 million of 2012 CPI adjusted taxable income.

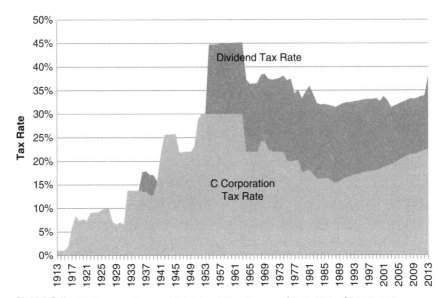

CHART 3.5   C Corporation and Dividend Tax Rates—$100,000 of 2012 CPI Adjusted Taxable Income, 1913–2013
Source: Table 3.2.

Intuitively, an individual with $1 million of taxable income should be in the maximum income tax bracket. After all, it has been more than 70 years since a married filing jointly taxpayer with nominal taxable income of $1 million was not in the maximum income bracket. In 1941, $1 million of nominal taxable income would place a married filing jointly taxpayer in the 79 percent marginal tax bracket; there were still two higher income brackets ($2 million to $5 million income bracket having a marginal tax rate of 80%, and more than $5 million of income with a marginal tax rate of 81%).[3] How different is the result if we analyze the data based on $1 million of 2012 CPI adjusted taxable income and not nominal taxable income? It is *very* different.

Pieter Geyl said, "Parallels in history, however indispensable and frequently instructive, are never wholly satisfactory, because each phenomenon is embedded in its own circumstances, never to be repeated, from which it cannot be completely detached."[4] This statement is clearly illustrated when we consider CPI adjusted amounts in lieu of nominal dollars. For example, we

---

[3]*U.S. Federal Individual Income Tax Rates History, 1862–2013* (Nominal and Inflation-Adjusted Brackets), www.taxfoundation.org.

[4]Pieter Geyl, "Toynbee's System of Civilizations," in Pieter Geyl, Arnold J. Toynbee, and Pitirim A. Sorokin, *The Pattern of the Past: Can We Determine It?* (Boston: Beacon Press, 1949).

CHART 3.6 Benefit of MFJ versus Corporation, 1913–2013, Assuming $100,000 of 2012 CPI Adjusted Taxable Income

find that when we convert the $1 million of 1941 nominal taxable income to 2012 CPI adjusted taxable income, the amount inflates to $15,618,639! On the other hand, $1 million of 2012 CPI adjusted taxable income is equivalent to 1941 nominal taxable income of $64,026. Therefore, $1 million of 2012 CPI adjusted taxable income places a married filing jointly taxpayer in the seventeenth of 32 income tax brackets, at a marginal tax rate of 63 percent, far below the statutory tax rates in the maximum income brackets.[5]

We should expect that the federal effective individual income tax rate of a married filing jointly taxpayer with $1 million of 2012 CPI adjusted taxable income would be higher than a married filing jointly taxpayer with $10,000 and $100,000 of 2012 CPI adjusted taxable income. This is indeed the case. However, the statutory tax rate of a married filing jointly taxpayer in the

---

[5]*U.S. Federal Individual Income Tax Rates History, 1862–2013* (Nominal and Inflation-Adjusted Brackets), www.taxfoundation.org.

maximum income bracket is far greater than the rates incurred in the $1 million example. Let's examine the year 1920, the highest effective tax rate during the period 1913–1938.

As shown in Table 3.3, during 1920, a married filing jointly taxpayer with $1 million of 2012 CPI adjusted taxable income incurred an effective federal income tax of 28.1 percent. The marginal federal tax rate for this taxpayer was 50 percent, and he would have been in the forty-fourth-highest income bracket. However, there were 56 federal income brackets during 1920, ranging from a low of 4 percent to a high of 73 percent.[6] Clearly, $1,000,000 of 2012 CPI adjusted taxable income did not burden a married filing jointly taxpayer with statutory federal tax rates in the maximum income bracket.

What is noteworthy about this analysis is that during each year in the period 1913–1953 (with the exception of 1936–1939 when the scope of income was broadened to include the receipt of dividend payments), there was a tax savings associated with functioning as a C corporation versus a PTE for businesses with $1 million of 2012 CPI adjusted taxable income.

Individual Income Taxes

During much of the twentieth century, there were several dozen annual federal income brackets that subjected each increment in taxable income to larger and larger progressive federal individual income tax rates. Although $1 million is a significant amount of money, even in 2012 CPI adjusted dollars, it did not result in federal effective individual tax rates of taxpayers in the maximum income bracket during the period 1913–2013. In fact, the federal effective individual tax rates in our example were far less than such maximum income bracket rates.

Chart 3.7, derived from Table 3.3, summarizes the effective federal income tax rates of a married filing jointly taxpayer with $1 million of 2012 CPE adjusted taxable income during the period 1913–2013.

C Corporation Income Taxes and Dividend Taxes

There were far fewer income tax brackets for C corporations than for individuals during the period 1913–2013. Accordingly, more of the taxable income in this example fell into the maximum income bracket, making the federal effective tax rates under the C corporation scenario more closely approximate the annual statutory income tax rates in the maximum income bracket. The lowering of the C corporation and the dividend tax rates during

---

[6] *U.S. Federal Individual Income Tax Rates History, 1862–2013* (Nominal and Inflation-Adjusted Brackets), www.taxfoundation.org.

TABLE 3.3 Federal Individual and C Corporation Income Tax History—Inflation Adjusted Using Average Annual CPI—Income Years: 1913–2013

$1,000,000 of 2012 CPI Adjusted Taxable Income

Year	Married Filing Jointly			C Corporation					MFJ v C Corp
	100.0%	FIT	NI	100%	Corp Tx	After Corp Tx	Div Tx	NI	
1913	100.0%	1.5%	98.5%	100.0%	1.0%	99.0%	0.0%	99.0%	-0.5%
1914	100.0%	1.5%	98.5%	100.0%	1.0%	99.0%	0.0%	99.0%	-0.5%
1915	100.0%	1.5%	98.5%	100.0%	1.0%	99.0%	0.0%	99.0%	-0.5%
1916	100.0%	2.7%	97.3%	100.0%	2.0%	98.0%	0.0%	98.0%	-0.7%
1917	100.0%	11.1%	88.9%	100.0%	6.0%	94.0%	0.0%	94.0%	-5.1%
1918	100.0%	26.6%	73.4%	100.0%	11.6%	88.4%	0.0%	88.4%	-15.0%
1919	100.0%	25.1%	74.9%	100.0%	9.7%	90.3%	0.0%	90.3%	-15.4%
1920	100.0%	28.1%	71.9%	100.0%	9.8%	90.2%	0.0%	90.2%	-18.3%
1921	100.0%	25.8%	74.2%	100.0%	9.7%	90.3%	0.0%	90.3%	-16.1%
1922	100.0%	23.5%	76.5%	100.0%	12.2%	87.8%	0.0%	87.8%	-11.3%
1923	100.0%	23.9%	76.1%	100.0%	12.2%	87.8%	0.0%	87.8%	-11.7%
1924	100.0%	17.7%	82.3%	100.0%	12.2%	87.8%	0.0%	87.8%	-5.5%
1925	100.0%	14.1%	85.9%	100.0%	12.7%	87.3%	0.0%	87.3%	-1.4%
1926	100.0%	14.2%	85.8%	100.0%	13.1%	86.9%	0.0%	86.9%	-1.1%
1927	100.0%	14.1%	85.9%	100.0%	13.1%	86.9%	0.0%	86.9%	-1.0%
1928	100.0%	13.9%	86.1%	100.0%	11.5%	88.5%	0.0%	88.5%	-2.4%
1929	100.0%	13.9%	86.1%	100.0%	10.6%	89.4%	0.0%	89.4%	-3.3%
1930	100.0%	13.7%	86.3%	100.0%	11.5%	88.5%	0.0%	88.5%	-2.2%
1931	100.0%	12.8%	87.2%	100.0%	11.5%	88.5%	0.0%	88.5%	-1.3%
1932	100.0%	20.1%	79.9%	100.0%	13.8%	86.2%	0.0%	86.2%	-6.3%

(continued)

TABLE 3.3 (Continued)

$1,000,000 of 2012 CPI Adjusted Taxable Income

Year	Married Filing Jointly				C Corporation				MFJ v C Corp
	100.0%	FIT	NI	100%	Corp Tx	After Corp Tx	Div Tx	NI	
1933	100.0%	19.3%	80.7%	100.0%	13.8%	86.2%	0.0%	86.2%	−5.5%
1934	100.0%	21.6%	78.4%	100.0%	13.8%	86.2%	0.0%	86.2%	−7.8%
1935	100.0%	22.0%	78.0%	100.0%	13.8%	86.2%	0.0%	86.2%	−8.2%
1936	100.0%	22.4%	77.6%	100.0%	16.5%	83.5%	16.4%	67.1%	10.5%
1937	100.0%	23.0%	77.0%	100.0%	16.6%	83.4%	16.8%	66.6%	10.4%
1938	100.0%	22.7%	77.3%	100.0%	17.0%	83.0%	16.3%	66.7%	10.6%
1939	100.0%	22.4%	77.6%	100.0%	17.0%	83.0%	16.2%	66.8%	10.8%
1940	100.0%	31.3%	68.7%	100.0%	24.0%	76.0%	0.0%	76.0%	−7.3%
1941	100.0%	46.9%	53.1%	100.0%	30.6%	69.4%	0.0%	69.4%	−16.3%
1942	100.0%	58.8%	41.2%	100.0%	40.0%	60.0%	0.0%	60.0%	−18.8%
1943	100.0%	59.9%	40.1%	100.0%	40.0%	60.0%	0.0%	60.0%	−19.9%
1944	100.0%	65.0%	35.0%	100.0%	40.0%	60.0%	0.0%	60.0%	−25.0%
1945	100.0%	65.4%	34.6%	100.0%	40.0%	60.0%	0.0%	60.0%	−25.4%
1946	100.0%	64.0%	36.0%	100.0%	38.0%	62.0%	0.0%	62.0%	−26.0%
1947	100.0%	66.7%	33.3%	100.0%	38.0%	62.0%	0.0%	62.0%	−28.7%
1948	100.0%	68.3%	31.7%	100.0%	38.0%	62.0%	0.0%	62.0%	−30.3%
1949	100.0%	54.4%	45.6%	100.0%	38.0%	62.0%	0.0%	62.0%	−16.4%
1950	100.0%	54.7%	45.3%	100.0%	37.5%	62.5%	0.0%	62.5%	−17.2%
1951	100.0%	56.8%	43.2%	100.0%	45.9%	54.1%	0.0%	54.1%	−10.9%
1952	100.0%	60.4%	39.6%	100.0%	47.2%	52.8%	0.0%	52.8%	−13.2%
1953	100.0%	60.5%	39.5%	100.0%	47.3%	52.7%	0.0%	52.7%	−13.2%

TABLE 3.3 (*Continued*)

$1,000,000 of 2012 CPI Adjusted Taxable Income

Year	Married Filing Jointly			C Corporation					MFJ v C Corp
	100.0%	FIT	NI	100%	Corp Tx	After Corp Tx	Div Tx	NI	
1954	100.0%	56.8%	43.2%	100.0%	47.3%	52.7%	23.5%	29.2%	14.0%
1955	100.0%	56.7%	43.3%	100.0%	47.3%	52.7%	23.5%	29.2%	14.1%
1956	100.0%	57.0%	43.0%	100.0%	47.4%	52.6%	23.6%	29.0%	14.0%
1957	100.0%	57.6%	42.4%	100.0%	47.5%	52.5%	23.8%	28.7%	13.7%
1958	100.0%	58.2%	41.8%	100.0%	47.6%	52.4%	24.0%	28.4%	13.4%
1959	100.0%	58.3%	41.7%	100.0%	47.7%	52.3%	24.0%	28.3%	13.4%
1960	100.0%	58.6%	41.4%	100.0%	47.7%	52.3%	24.1%	28.2%	13.2%
1961	100.0%	58.8%	41.2%	100.0%	47.8%	52.2%	24.2%	28.0%	13.2%
1962	100.0%	59.0%	41.0%	100.0%	47.8%	52.2%	24.3%	27.9%	13.1%
1963	100.0%	59.3%	40.7%	100.0%	47.9%	52.1%	24.4%	27.7%	13.0%
1964	100.0%	52.9%	47.1%	100.0%	44.8%	55.2%	23.7%	31.5%	15.6%
1965	100.0%	50.0%	50.0%	100.0%	43.3%	56.7%	23.4%	33.3%	16.7%
1966	100.0%	50.4%	49.6%	100.0%	43.4%	56.6%	23.6%	33.0%	16.6%
1967	100.0%	50.9%	49.1%	100.0%	43.5%	56.5%	23.8%	32.7%	16.4%
1968	100.0%	51.5%	48.5%	100.0%	48.1%	51.9%	21.5%	30.4%	18.1%
1969	100.0%	52.2%	47.8%	100.0%	48.3%	51.7%	21.8%	29.9%	17.9%
1970	100.0%	53.1%	46.9%	100.0%	45.3%	54.7%	24.1%	30.6%	16.3%
1971	100.0%	53.7%	46.3%	100.0%	44.3%	55.7%	25.0%	30.7%	15.6%
1972	100.0%	54.2%	45.8%	100.0%	44.4%	55.6%	25.2%	30.4%	15.4%
1973	100.0%	55.0%	45.0%	100.0%	44.6%	55.4%	25.6%	29.8%	15.3%
1974	100.0%	56.5%	43.5%	100.0%	45.0%	55.0%	26.3%	28.7%	14.8%

(*continued*)

TABLE 3.3 (Continued)

$1,000,000 of 2012 CPI Adjusted Taxable Income

Year	Married Filing Jointly				C Corporation				MFJ v C Corp
	100.0%	FIT	NI	100%	Corp Tx	After Corp Tx	Div Tx	NI	
1975	100.0%	57.6%	42.4%	100.0%	42.2%	57.8%	28.8%	29.0%	13.4%
1976	100.0%	58.3%	41.7%	100.0%	42.6%	57.4%	29.0%	28.4%	13.3%
1977	100.0%	58.2%	41.8%	100.0%	42.9%	57.1%	28.5%	28.6%	13.2%
1978	100.0%	59.0%	41.0%	100.0%	43.2%	56.8%	29.0%	27.8%	13.2%
1979	100.0%	59.5%	40.5%	100.0%	39.9%	60.1%	31.7%	28.4%	12.1%
1980	100.0%	60.7%	39.3%	100.0%	40.6%	59.4%	32.3%	27.1%	12.2%
1981	100.0%	61.6%	38.4%	100.0%	41.1%	58.9%	32.8%	26.1%	12.3%
1982	100.0%	47.0%	53.0%	100.0%	41.3%	58.7%	26.3%	32.4%	20.6%
1983	100.0%	46.3%	53.7%	100.0%	41.3%	58.7%	25.6%	33.1%	20.6%
1984	100.0%	45.9%	54.1%	100.0%	41.5%	58.5%	25.1%	33.4%	20.7%
1985	100.0%	45.9%	54.1%	100.0%	41.7%	58.3%	25.0%	33.3%	20.8%
1986	100.0%	45.8%	54.2%	100.0%	41.8%	58.2%	24.9%	33.3%	20.9%
1987	100.0%	36.5%	63.5%	100.0%	37.7%	62.3%	21.9%	40.4%	23.1%
1988	100.0%	27.2%	72.8%	100.0%	34.0%	66.0%	17.7%	48.3%	24.5%
1989	100.0%	27.3%	72.7%	100.0%	34.0%	66.0%	17.7%	48.3%	24.5%
1990	100.0%	27.3%	72.7%	100.0%	34.0%	66.0%	17.7%	48.3%	24.5%
1991	100.0%	29.8%	70.2%	100.0%	34.0%	66.0%	19.3%	46.7%	23.5%
1992	100.0%	29.8%	70.2%	100.0%	34.0%	66.0%	19.3%	46.7%	23.5%
1993	100.0%	35.9%	64.1%	100.0%	34.0%	66.0%	22.4%	43.6%	20.5%
1994	100.0%	35.9%	64.1%	100.0%	34.0%	66.0%	22.5%	43.5%	20.6%
1995	100.0%	35.9%	64.1%	100.0%	34.0%	66.0%	22.5%	43.5%	20.6%

TABLE 3.3 (*Continued*)

$1,000,000 of 2012 CPI Adjusted Taxable Income

Year	Married Filing Jointly			C Corporation					MFJ v C Corp
	100.0%	FIT	NI	100%	Corp Tx	After Corp Tx	Div Tx	NI	
1996	100.0%	35.9%	64.1%	100.0%	34.0%	66.0%	22.5%	43.5%	20.6%
1997	100.0%	35.9%	64.1%	100.0%	34.0%	66.0%	22.5%	43.5%	20.6%
1998	100.0%	35.9%	64.1%	100.0%	34.0%	66.0%	22.4%	43.6%	20.5%
1999	100.0%	35.9%	64.1%	100.0%	34.0%	66.0%	22.4%	43.6%	20.5%
2000	100.0%	36.0%	64.0%	100.0%	34.0%	66.0%	22.5%	43.5%	20.5%
2001	100.0%	35.5%	64.5%	100.0%	34.0%	66.0%	22.2%	43.8%	20.7%
2002	100.0%	34.9%	65.1%	100.0%	34.0%	66.0%	21.7%	44.3%	20.8%
2003	100.0%	31.9%	68.1%	100.0%	34.0%	66.0%	9.9%	56.1%	12.0%
2004	100.0%	31.9%	68.1%	100.0%	34.0%	66.0%	9.9%	56.1%	12.0%
2005	100.0%	32.0%	68.0%	100.0%	34.0%	66.0%	9.9%	56.1%	11.9%
2006	100.0%	32.0%	68.0%	100.0%	34.0%	66.0%	9.9%	56.1%	11.9%
2007	100.0%	31.9%	68.1%	100.0%	34.0%	66.0%	9.9%	56.1%	12.0%
2008	100.0%	32.0%	68.0%	100.0%	34.0%	66.0%	9.9%	56.1%	11.9%
2009	100.0%	31.8%	68.2%	100.0%	34.0%	66.0%	9.9%	56.1%	12.1%
2010	100.0%	31.9%	68.1%	100.0%	34.0%	66.0%	9.9%	56.1%	12.0%
2011	100.0%	31.9%	68.1%	100.0%	34.0%	66.0%	9.9%	56.1%	12.0%
2012	100.0%	31.9%	68.1%	100.0%	34.0%	66.0%	9.9%	56.1%	12.0%
2013	100.0%	34.5%	65.5%	100.0%	34.0%	66.0%	13.2%	52.8%	12.7%

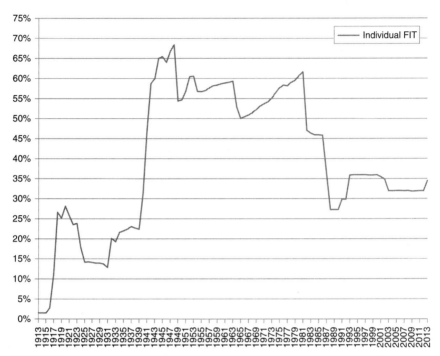

CHART 3.7   Effective Individual Income Tax Rates (MFJ) Assuming $1 Million of 2012 CPI Adjusted Taxable Income, 1913–2013

the latter portion of the period 1913–2013 lowered the tax burden of C corporation stockholders.

Chart 3.8 illustrates the effective federal income tax burden of (1) a C corporation and (2) the tax on dividend income of a married filing jointly taxpayer, assuming $1 million of 2012 CPE adjusted taxable income during the period 1913–2013, utilizing data compiled in Table 3.3.

Comparison of PTE and C Corporation Income Taxes

For married filing jointly taxpayers with $1 million of 2012 CPI adjusted taxable income, the period 1913–1953 was vastly different from the period 1954–2013. During this earlier period, operating one's business in the form of a C corporation enabled shareholders to retain far more income, after-tax, than a PTE. This abruptly changed when the scope of income broadened to include the receipt of dividend payments (dividend tax), which existed briefly from 1936 through 1939 and was subsequently made a permanent part of the IRC in 1954. Once the dividend tax was signed into law, operating one's

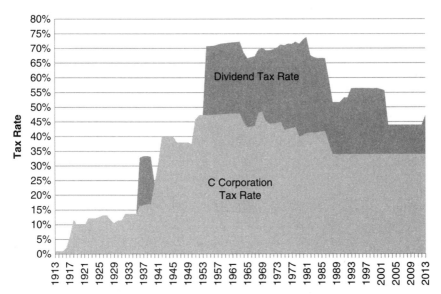

CHART 3.8 C Corporation and Dividend Tax Rates—$1 Million of 2012 CPI Adjusted Taxable Income, 1913–2013

business in the form of a PTE enabled owners to retain more income, after-tax, than a C corporation.

Using the data compiled in Table 3.3, Chart 3.9 illustrates the federal tax benefit of operating a business with $1 million of 2012 CPI adjusted taxable income as a C corporation versus a PTE during the period 1913–2013.

SUMMARY

The three examples presented in this chapter illustrate the impact of different facts on income tax consequences. When analyzing 2012 CPI adjusted taxable income of $10,000, $100,000, and $1 million for each year in the period 1913–2013, the following observations are noted:

1. The same amount of CPI adjusted taxable income generated substantially different effective federal individual income tax expenses depending on the year of calculation.
2. The same amount of CPI adjusted taxable income generated substantially different federal corporate income taxes and federal dividend tax expenses depending on the year of calculation.

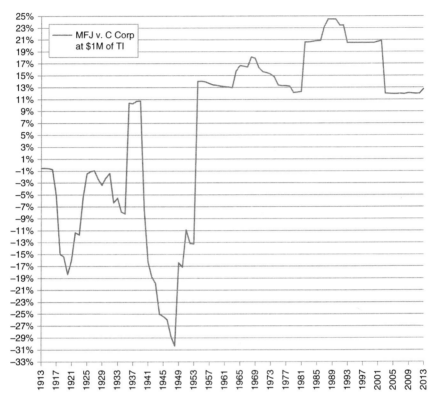

CHART 3.9 Benefit of MFJ versus C Corp, 1913–2013, Assuming $1 Million of 2012 CPI Adjusted Taxable Income

3. During any year, the decision to operate a business as a PTE or as a C corporation was significantly impacted by its level of taxable income.
4. The amount of the federal tax benefit of operating a business as a PTE or a C corporation was very different depending on both the year and the amount of taxable income.

From these findings, the following can be inferred:

1. Operating a business in the form of a PTE may provide a tax savings benefit in some years but not in other years.
2. Operating a business in the form of a C corporation may provide a tax savings benefit in some years but not in other years.
3. After-tax cash flows to the investor are substantially impacted by entity form.

4. After-tax cash flows to the investor change when income tax rates change.
5. If entity form and tax laws both impact after-tax cash flows to the investor, then both factors must be considered when valuing PTEs.

It therefore is incumbent on the valuation analyst to take into consideration the form of entity, magnitude of taxable income, and tax laws in effect as of the valuation date. Moreover, it is important to consider known or knowable changes in tax laws at the time of the valuation. If it is known that income tax rates will change, then it is appropriate to incorporate the changed rates into the valuation analysis. Failing to take into consideration changes in tax rates could lead to an analysis whereby incorrect after-tax cash flows are incorporated into the valuation conclusion. This could occur, for example, when applying tax rates in effect during 2000 to a 2010 valuation. This issue will be discussed in greater detail when discussing the applicability of certain court findings based on 2000 tax rates and tax laws to the period after 2002.

CHAPTER 4

Comparison of Different Entity Forms

P revious chapters examined the differences in after-tax returns of business ownership interests stemming from whether a business was formed as a C corporation or as a PTE. However, there are other considerations when choosing an appropriate form of business entity, such as the appropriate form of PTE to select, the impact of PTE form on the presentation of financial statements under generally accepted accounting principles (GAAP), borrowing issues, and so forth. In consideration of these other issues, this chapter accomplishes the following:

- Compares the benefits and limitations of PTEs and C corporations over the course of a business's life, commencing at the start-up phase, moving on to the operating phase, and ending with the wind-down/liquidation/ sale phase.
- Contrasts different types of PTEs.
- Describes differences between financial statements of C corporations and those of PTEs.
- Explains the issues considered by banks when lending to PTEs.
- Discusses the prevalence of different forms of PTEs as compared with C corporations.
- Analyzes the issues associated with converting from one form of business entity to another.

BUSINESS LIFE CYCLE

Choosing a business entity form is often influenced by the stage of the business's life cycle, the owner's plans, and the owner's ultimate exit strategy. Different facts and circumstances will cause one company to choose to operate as a C corporation, while another will be better able to achieve its goals operating as an S corporation, partnership, or LLC. A discussion of the relative advantages and disadvantages of the different business entity forms (under current tax law), from their evolutions as start-ups through their sale/ liquidation, follows.

Start-Up Phase

Many companies experience losses when they first open for business. Such losses could result from, among other things, the initial costs associated with purchasing property and equipment; development of customized software; recruiting, training, and retaining staff; and marketing and promotion. These costs are often incurred before significant revenues are generated. The resulting losses are funded either by the equity owners of the business via debt, capital contributions, or third-party debt.

A company operating as a PTE passes through to its owners business losses incurred during the start-up phase. The owners can then offset such losses against other income, subject to certain passive loss rules, basis limitations, and so on. An owner's ability to recognize such losses as they are incurred, for individual income tax reporting purposes, effectively reduces the pretax investment by the tax benefit of the business loss. This is often a substantial and timely source of reimbursement for PTE business owners. Such tax refunds can be recycled back into the PTE, providing an additional source of funding to businesses.

C corporations do not pass through losses to owners. Instead, such losses are accumulated, carried forward, and available to be offset against the future taxable income of the C corporation. No current tax benefit is therefore realized from a start-up net operating loss of a C corporation. When the tax benefit of the net operating loss is ultimately realized by the C corporation, it is realized in future nominal dollars as opposed to CPI adjusted present value dollars. Also, the tax rate at which such net operating loss carryforwards are realized may be lower than the tax rate of the PTE owner. Hence, the C corporation net operating loss carryforward tax benefit accumulated during the start-up phase may be less valuable than a net operating loss incurred by a PTE.

Nevertheless, the deferred tax benefit of a C corporation's net operating loss carryforward creates an asset, which is recognized for financial statement reporting purposes under GAAP in the United States. This deferred tax asset can add value to a company seeking angel investors, venture capital funding, or other sources of equity. No such deferred tax asset is recognized for PTEs under GAAP.

A start-up (or mature) company may experience an uninsured loss related to employee negligence, weather-related damage, product liability, and so forth. Entities that offer limited liability protection, such as C corporations, S corporations, and LLCs, shield their owners from third-party claims and uninsured losses. However, entities that lack limited liability protection, such as general partnerships and sole proprietorships, do not.

Operating Phase

As discussed in the preceding chapters, reduced overall personal and business-level income taxes provide a strong incentive for PTE formation (for all years after 1953).

PTEs also are able to eliminate the adverse effect of two types of IRS audit adjustments to which C corporations are exposed: (1) a tax on excess compensation (when owners' compensation expense is deemed unreasonable and is reclassified as a nondeductible corporate dividend) and (2) a tax on accumulated earnings (in those cases where the IRS deems that the company's accumulated earnings are in excess of its future operating needs, the IRS imputes a hypothetical dividend distribution on such excess accumulated earnings).

Sale of Business

There are three form-of-entity issues that potentially impact the value that could be realized from the sale of a business ownership interest:

1. Double taxation on sale of assets
2. The "BIG" tax
3. The tax benefit of the purchaser's goodwill

Double Taxation on Sale of Assets   As explained in Chapter 2, before 1986, corporate liquidations could occur on a tax-free basis, subjecting the C corporation shareholders to only one level of taxation. Starting in 1986, when a C corporation sells its assets, there are now potentially two levels of income taxes: (1) the income taxes paid by the selling C corporation on the taxable gain on the sale of assets and (2) a second level of taxation paid by the C corporation's shareholders when they receive the liquidating distribution. PTEs only incur one level of taxation by the owners on the sale of a business or its assets.[1] This PTE characteristic distinguishes it as being more favorable than C corporations for many owner-managed businesses.

---

[1]The exception is the "BIG" Tax, discussed herein.

"BIG" Tax   S corporations are subject to a tax on any appreciated assets held on the day a C corporation converts to S status. If a business always operated in the form of an S corporation, this tax would not apply. The tax results on the later sale of any such appreciated assets within a defined period of time under the IRC. This tax is often referred to as a tax on built-in gains (or "BIG" tax). It applies to liquidating and nonliquidating distributions made by S corporations starting in 1986.

The BIG tax became law as part of the 1986 Tax Reform Act. The BIG tax was intended to prevent circumvention of the two-tier tax on C corporations converting to S corporation status during the first 10 years of the S corporation's existence. This was the law from 1986 until 2008. The holding period during which the BIG tax would be incurred was reduced from 10 years after the conversion date to 7 taxable years for tax years beginning in 2009 and 2010, and 5 years for taxable years beginning in 2011–2013.

Appreciated assets subject to BIG tax recognition include, but are not limited to, accounts receivable (for cash basis taxpayers); property and equipment; inventory; investments; and intangible assets such as goodwill, trademarks, patents, copyrights, customer lists, and proprietary technology. Such appreciated assets may be deemed to exist even if they do not appear on a company's balance sheet. An S corporation subject to the BIG tax would pay a corporation-level tax on the sale of the assets at the highest corporation rate; then, after reduction for corporation taxes paid, the gain on sale would immediately pass through to the S corporation shareholder. As a C corporation (i.e., absent an S corporation conversion), such gain on sale would occur at whatever the C corporation's applicable tax rate would be (which could be less than the maximum rate); the shareholder would later pay tax on the liquidating or nonliquidating dividend only when it was received.

Tax Benefit of the Purchaser's Goodwill   The tax treatment of the purchase of an equity ownership interest in a C corporation, S corporation, LLC, or partnership may have very different tax consequences, which may ultimately impact the after-tax cost of a purchase.

> When a PTE or C corporation purchases the equity interests of another entity, the purchase price (buyer's outside tax basis) may exceed the owner/member/partner's equity of the acquired entity (company's inside tax basis). There is a materially different tax result if the subject interest is an equity interest in an LLC or partnership as compared with an S corporation or a C corporation. Where the subject interest is an equity ownership interest in an LLC or partnership, the acquirer could make an election under IRC Section 754. This election would enable the acquirer to record an adjustment to

the internal tax basis of the assets acquired based upon the purchase price. The purchaser would then be able to allocate the purchase price to each of the assets and liabilities acquired, including goodwill. This process is similar to the accounting for a purchase of assets under Generally Accepted Accounting Principles.

Where the interest being sold is the capital stock of an S corporation or a C corporation, no such election is available without adverse tax consequences. Accordingly, the taxable basis of the assets of the acquired company (inside basis) remains unchanged, and the buyer does not receive any immediate tax benefit from the goodwill acquired.[2]

Goodwill is amortizable on a straight-line basis over a 15-year period for federal income tax reporting purposes. The amount allocable to goodwill impacts the after-tax cost to an acquirer and, where the amount is substantial, could possibly affect the price that could be realized on a sale pursuant to the investment or fair market standards of value. See Chapter 7 for a more detailed explanation of the benefits associated with a purchaser's ability to amortize goodwill and the benefits associated with purchasing the equity of a partnership or LLC versus the purchase of the equity of an S corporation or C corporation.

BENEFITS AND LIMITATIONS OF PTEs

Although they are all PTEs, S corporations, LLCs, and partnerships are different from one another. The owners of a general partnership are subject to unlimited liability;[3] this is not so with C corporations, S corporations, LLCs, and limited partners of limited partnerships.[4] On the other hand, LLCs and partnerships can have special allocations of owners' income, which is not the case with S corporations.

C corporations can have different classes of capital stock (e.g., preferred stock and common stock) that provide preferences with respect to dividend distributions, receipt of proceeds on sale or liquidation, and other rights. These differing rights are not permitted for S corporations, with some specific

---

[2]Eric J. Barr, "Are Limited Liability Companies Worth More Than S Corporations?," *Business Valuation Update* 18(12) (Dec. 2012), 2.
[3]General partners of limited partnerships are subject to unlimited liability; limited partners of limited partnerships have limited liability.
[4]A limited partner cannot engage in the management of the limited partnership and continue to have limited liability.

exceptions. In addition, C corporations can offer different stock compensation arrangements that benefit certain shareholders but not others.

There are statutory limitations and restrictions on S corporations regarding the number of shareholders (currently, 100),[5] entity form of the shareholder, and citizenship of the shareholder. Certain local taxing jurisdictions do not recognize S corporation status. Moreover, shareholders can terminate the S corporation election unless restricted from doing so by a company's articles of incorporation, bylaws, or other agreements or by operation of law. These same limitations do not exist for C corporations and other PTEs.

Summary of PTE Benefits and Limitations

Table 4.1 summarizes the benefits and limitations of each entity form.

FINANCIAL STATEMENTS OF C CORPORATIONS AND PTEs

C corporations pay income taxes at the business-entity level. Financial statements contained in public C corporation Securities and Exchange Commission (SEC) registration statements and interim and annual filings present corporation income tax expense as a separate line item on the face of the *statement of operations* (also referred to as the *income statement*). This corporation income tax expense is often more than 20, 30, or even 40 percent of pretax income. Footnotes to the financial statements of publicly owned C corporations that are prepared in conformity with GAAP provide descriptive income tax information regarding, among other things, the following:

- Current and deferred income tax expenses.
- Income tax expense allocated between continuing and discontinued operations.
- Reconciliation of income tax expense using applicable statutory rates to the income tax expense presented on the financial statements.
- Income tax benefits recognized with respect to any net operating loss carryforwards.
- Income taxes payable and receivable.
- The components of current and noncurrent deferred income tax assets and deferred income tax liabilities.
- Valuation allowances for deferred tax assets that may not be realized.

---

[5]An S corporation exceeds the shareholder limit if it has more than the permissible number of shareholders at any particular time during the taxable year.

TABLE 4.1 Comparison of C Corporations and PTEs

	C Corp	S Corp	LLC & Ltd. Partnership	General Partnership
Benefits of PTEs				
1 Avoids federal income tax at entity level	No	Yes	Yes	Yes
2 Limits exposure to excess compensation adjustment	No	Yes	Yes	Yes
3 Limits exposure to accumulated earnings tax	No	Yes	Yes	Yes
4 Avoids double taxation on sale of business	No	Yes	Yes	Yes
5 Special allocations [A]	Yes	No	Yes	Yes
6 Limited liability to owners [B]	Yes	Yes	Yes	No
Limitations of PTEs				
1 Number of owners [C]	No	Yes	No	No
2 Type of owners [D]	No	Yes	No	No
3 Multiple classes of ownership [E]	Yes	No	Yes	Yes
4 Risk of termination of form of entity [F]	No	Yes	No	No
5 Recognition of entity status by all taxing jurisdictions	Yes	No	No	No
6 Eligible for employee qualified and nonqualified ownership plans	Yes	No	Yes	Yes
7 Active PTE earnings subject to self-employment taxes	N/A	No	Yes	Yes

Notes:

[A] Special allocations of taxable income and distributions are more common in LLCs and partnerships; C corporations can have multiples classes of capital stock, phantom stock, and bonus compensation arrangements.

[B] General partners of limited partnerships and general partnerships have unlimited liability. C corporation and S corporation shareholders, LLC members, and limited partners have limited liability.

[C] S corporations have a 100-shareholder limit.

[D] S corporation shareholders are limited to individuals, estates, certain trusts, banks, certain exempt organizations, and qualifying S corporations.

[E] S corporations may only have one class of stock outstanding. The only permitted distinction is voting versus nonvoting stock. Shares must confer identical ownership rights, including rights to dividend distributions and liquidation proceeds.

[F] S corporation election may be revoked by consent of stockholders holding more than 50 percent of outstanding shares of stock on the day the revocation is made. An S corporation election may also be revoked by operation of law (i.e., transfer to nonqualifying owner).

More detailed information regarding C corporation income taxes and GAAP requirements can be found in Financial Accounting Standards Board (FASB) ASC 740.

PTEs incur no federal income taxes or federal deferred income taxes at the entity level. Accordingly, federal current and deferred income tax assets, liabilities, and expenses are not presented on the financial statements of PTEs. When comparing the financial performance of a particular PTE to an entity (or entities) that are not PTEs, appropriate income tax normalization adjustments must be made. These normalization adjustments should be made in connection with the comparison of a PTE's performance to industry data for valuations, audits, and/or reviews, and trend analyses.

PTE STATUS AND BANK FINANCING

Based on my 40-plus years of public accounting experience, knowing and meeting with many bank lenders, and participation on numerous bank advisory boards, I have become keenly aware of the following:

1. Banks that focus on the "small-to-middle" market have found that a substantial number of their customers operate in the form of a PTE.
2. Lenders are sensitized to the fact that PTE business owners have personally paid the income tax on any entity-retained business profits.
3. Unlike C corporations, where there is a dividend tax on distributions of entity-level profits, the owner(s) of a PTE will generally incur no incremental income tax as a result of the distribution of business-retained profits. Accordingly, PTE business owners often view the money retained in the business as "theirs" and, absent any business reason for retaining funds in the business, will seek to withdraw it.
4. Banks try to limit the distribution of PTE-retained earnings by imposing restrictive covenants on PTE borrowers. Such restrictive covenants will often require compliance with liquidity, capitalization, debt service, and other ratios. Permitted distributions and owner compensation may also be limited by bank covenants.
5. Banks often require a PTE's owner(s) to personally guarantee the balance due under the note obligation. Sometimes, such personal guarantees can include the posting of outside collateral, letters of credit, and so on.
6. In some instances, banks require interim and annual financial reporting that includes combining the business and owner/guarantor's balance sheet and income statement. This is referred to as a global financial statement and is requested when a bank is looking to the owner/guarantor for repayment.

The good news is that many banks have learned how to address the nuances of lending to PTEs. The bad news is that PTE owners need to be aware that their bank may impose restrictions and debt covenants to which a comparably profitable C corporation would not be subjected.

PREVALENCE OF PTEs

The IRS tracks the number of entities filing on Federal Forms 1065 (Partnerships and LLCs), 1120S (S corporations), and 1120 (C corporations). Since the Tax Reform Act of 1986, many entities have been formed as, or converted to, PTEs. Evidence of this trend can be seen in Table 4.2, which is summarized from data contained in the annual *IRS Data Book*, available at www.irs.gov.

The number of PTEs filing income tax returns during the 10-year period ended December 31, 2012, increased from 5.7 million (2003) to 8.2 million (2012), while the number of C corporations filing income tax returns decreased from 2.6 million (2003) to 2.3 million (2012). According to data published by the IRS in June 2010,[6] this trend is expected to continue.

Table 4.3 presents data from Table 4.2 on a common-size basis, with each amount shown as a percent of that year's totals.

TABLE 4.2 *IRS Data Book*, Table 2—Summary of Number of Business Entity Income Tax Returns (in thousands)

Year	Total	Pass-Through Entities			C Corporation
		Total	Partnership	S Corporation	
2012	10,469	8,206	3,626	4,580	2,263
2011	10,432	8,119	3,574	4,545	2,313
2010	10,373	8,017	3,509	4,508	2,356
2009	10,537	8,061	3,565	4,496	2,476
2008	10,285	7,747	3,307	4,440	2,538
2007	9,704	7,196	3,097	4,099	2,508
2006	9,052	6,598	2,773	3,825	2,454
2005	8,793	6,299	2,665	3,634	2,494
2004	8,566	6,025	2,521	3,504	2,541
2003	8,271	5,711	2,381	3,330	2,560

[6]Document 6292, Office of Research, Analysis and Statistics, "Fiscal Year Return Projections for the United States: 2010–2017," revised June 2010.

TABLE 4.3   *IRS Data Book*, Derived from Table 2—Summary of Business Entity Income Tax Returns—Percent of Total

		Pass-Through Entities			
Year	Total	Total	Partnership	S Corporation	C Corporation
2012	100.0%	78.4%	34.6%	43.7%	21.6%
2011	100.0%	77.8%	34.3%	43.6%	22.2%
2010	100.0%	77.3%	33.8%	43.5%	22.7%
2009	100.0%	76.5%	33.8%	42.7%	23.5%
2008	100.0%	75.3%	33.2%	43.2%	24.7%
2007	100.0%	74.2%	31.9%	42.2%	25.8%
2006	100.0%	72.9%	30.6%	42.3%	27.1%
2005	100.0%	71.6%	30.3%	41.3%	28.4%
2004	100.0%	70.3%	29.4%	40.9%	29.7%
2003	100.0%	69.0%	28.8%	40.3%	31.0%

During 2012, approximately 78 percent of all business entities that filed U.S. income tax returns were PTEs, with approximately 22 percent filing as C corporations. This contrasts markedly with 2003, when 69 percent of all business entities filed income tax returns as PTEs, with approximately 31 percent filing as C corporations.

The annual percentage growth (or reduction) in the number of entities filing under each form of business is presented in Table 4.4.

TABLE 4.4   *IRS Data Book*, Derived from Table 2—Summary of Number of Business Entity Income Tax Returns—Annual Growth

		Pass-Through Entities			
Year	Total	Total	Partnership	S Corporation	C Corporation
2012	0.4%	1.1%	1.5%	0.8%	−2.2%
2011	0.6%	1.3%	1.9%	0.8%	−1.8%
2010	−1.6%	−0.5%	−1.6%	0.3%	−4.8%
2009	2.5%	4.1%	7.8%	1.3%	−2.4%
2008	6.0%	7.7%	6.8%	8.3%	1.2%
2007	7.2%	9.1%	11.7%	7.2%	2.2%
2006	2.9%	4.7%	4.1%	5.3%	−1.6%
2005	2.7%	4.5%	5.7%	3.7%	−1.8%
2004	3.6%	5.5%	5.9%	5.2%	−0.7%
2003–2012	26.6%	43.7%	52.3%	37.5%	−11.6%

As expected, the 10-year growth in the number of entities filing as a PTE, 43.7 percent, contrasts markedly with the 11.6 percent decrease in the number of C corporations. In addition, we note that there continues to be substantially more S corporations than partnerships in 2012 (4.6 million versus 3.6 million), similar to the 2003 difference in the number of S corporations (3.3 million) and partnerships (2.4 million). During the 10-year period ended 2012, the number of entities filing as a partnership increased by 52.3 percent, and the number of entities filing as an S corporation increased 37.5 percent. Despite the tremendous popularity of LLCs over the last decade, more entities continue to file tax returns as S corporations rather than as partnerships or LLCs. This trend is expected to continue for the foreseeable future.

In the preceding analysis, we have ignored the number of single-member LLCs and sole proprietorships that are PTEs but are disregarded entities for income tax reporting purposes. Such entities do not file separate income tax returns. If these single-member LLCs and sole proprietorships were included, the percentage of PTEs would increase significantly.[7]

CHANGE IN FORM OF ENTITY

Having described the various entity forms and their respective advantages and disadvantages, it would be expected that owners who formed their business as a C corporation may want to change it to a PTE, and that certain types of PTEs may want to change to a different type of PTE. Depending on facts and circumstances, other changes may also be desired. How easy is it to convert from one entity status to another, and what are the tax considerations? Let's find out.

First, let's identify six different types of potential entity changes:[8]

1. C corporation to S corporation
2. C corporation to partnership or LLC
3. S corporation to partnership or LLC
4. Partnership to LLC
5. Partnership or LLC to C corporation
6. S corporation to C corporation

---

[7]Based on IRS estimates, there were approximately 22,614,000 nonfarm federal Forms 1040 Schedule C sole proprietorship tax returns filed during 2008. *Number of Tax Returns, Receipts, and Net Income by Type of Business*, Table 744, http://www.irs.ustreas.gov/taxstats.

[8]I have not included partnership or LLC to S corporation because this is not a conversion that, in general, has merit.

C Corporation to S Corporation

This change in entity form is achieved with the unanimous consent of all C corporation shareholders, and by filing federal Form 2553 on or before the fifteenth day of the third month of the tax year. The corporation must meet all of the requirements of S corporation status described earlier. The tax consequence of this conversion is that if the S corporation later sells appreciated assets that it held as of the conversion date, there may be BIG tax exposure. An additional consideration is that the benefit of net operating loss carryforwards is lost on the conversion to S corporation status, although the net operating loss can be offset against the income recognized in connection with the BIG tax.

C Corporation to Partnership or LLC

This change in entity form is accomplished by having an actual or deemed liquidation of the C corporation, distribution of the corporation's assets to its stockholders, and formation by the stockholders of a new entity into which the distributed assets are contributed. These actions can have adverse tax consequences.

On the date of the actual or deemed liquidation of the C corporation, there is an entity-level tax on the difference between the fair market value of the C corporation's assets and its inside bases. The fair market value of the distributed assets would include assets recorded on the books (i.e., cash, inventory, investments, and property) as well as assets not recorded on the books (i.e., accounts receivable for cash-basis taxpayers, intangible assets such as goodwill). This income tax is imposed at the entity level. Then, upon the distribution of the distributed assets to the stockholders, there may be a gain or loss depending on whether the fair market value of the assets distributed (less the corporation income tax) is greater than the stockholder's basis in the stock. This income tax is imposed at the shareholder level.

For income tax reporting purposes, when such assets are contributed to the new partnership or LLC, they are contributed at the owner's basis.

One other matter worth considering: C corporation net operating losses not applied against the gain (if any) on the deemed liquidation are lost.

S Corporation to Partnership or LLC

This change in entity form is accomplished by liquidating the S corporation, distributing its assets to its stockholders, and having the stockholders form a new entity into which they contribute the distributed assets. When a stockholder of an S corporation sells/distributes his ownership interest in an entity in which the capital account is negative, the negative capital account may result in the recognition of ordinary income, absent carryforwards that could result from the excess of net taxable losses over the stockholder's outside basis.[9] An S corporation's stockholder's capital account may be negative where losses and distributions attributable to the ownership interest exceed net income attributable to, and capital contributions made by, the stockholder.

Another potential tax consequence of this form of conversion is that there are gains/losses recognized depending on the fair market value of the distributed assets as compared to their respective cost bases for income tax reporting purposes. In addition, this conversion may also trigger the BIG tax.

Partnership to LLC

This change in form is often performed to provide limited liability protection to the entity's owners. It is accomplished by checking an election on the federal Form 1065 (U.S. Return of Partnership Income). Company documents need to be updated with appropriate authorizations pursuant to bylaws, partners' agreement, and so on.

Partnership or LLC to C Corporation

When a partner of a partnership or a member of an LLC sells/distributes his ownership interest in the PTE in which the capital account is negative, the negative capital account may result in the recognition of ordinary income, absent carryforwards that could result from the excess of net taxable losses over the owner's outside basis.[10] A partner or member's capital account may be negative where losses and distributions attributable to the ownership interest exceed net income attributable to, and capital contributions made by, the owner.

For income tax reporting purposes, when such assets of the former partnership/LLC are contributed to the new C corporation, they are contributed at the owner's basis.

S Corporation to C Corporation

This change automatically occurs when the S corporation violates permitted stockholder and other S corporation eligibility rules or when an election is made by the corporation's stockholders. An S corporation may change to

---

[9]An S corporation stockholder's outside basis is increased by his or her loans to the company.

[10]A partner or member's outside basis is increased by the amount of partnership debt, both recourse and nonrecourse.

C corporation status when (1) there is a new equity investor that does not want the business to be a PTE, (2) the company plans on raising additional equity from venture capital or public sources, or (3) the company inadvertently fails to qualify for S corporation status.

As noted herein, from the perspective of overall tax cost reduction, limiting owners' personal liability, offering flexible/variable ownership benefits, and so on, the entity form decision is very important. The entity form decision requires careful consideration of many different factors and clearly impacts the rights, privileges, economic returns, and ultimately the value of an ownership interest. If an owner chooses to change the business entity form from C corporation to PTE, from PTE to C corporation, or from one form of PTE to another, it might result in significant adverse tax consequences with significant valuation implications as well.

CHAPTER 5

Income Approach and Value to the Holder

Internal Revenue Service Revenue Ruling 59–60 directs business appraisers to consider the following factors when valuing the stock of closely held corporations:

a. The nature of the business and the history of the enterprise from its inception.

b. The economic outlook in general and the condition and outlook of the specific industry in particular.

c. The book value of the stock and the financial condition of the business.

d. The earning capacity of the company.

e. The dividend-paying capacity.

f. Whether or not the enterprise has goodwill or other intangible value.

g. Sales of the stock and the size of the block of stock to be valued.

h. The market price of stocks of corporations engaged in the same or similar line of business having their stocks actively traded in a free and open market, either on an exchange or over-the-counter.[1]

Factors to consider when applying the income approach are presented in Revenue Ruling 59–60, § 4.02, which states that "[p]rimary consideration should be given to the dividend-paying capacity of the company rather than to dividends actually paid in the past."[2] The Revenue Ruling continues thus:

In the final analysis, goodwill is based upon earning capacity. The presence of goodwill and its value, therefore, rests upon the excess of net earnings over and above a fair return on the net tangible assets. While the element of goodwill may be based primarily on earnings,

---

[1]Rev. Rul. 59–60, 1959-1 C.B. 2031, § 4.01.
[2]*Id.* § 4.02(e).

such factors as the prestige and renown of the business, the owner-ship of a trade or brand name, and a record of successful operation over a prolonged period in a particular locality, also may furnish support for the inclusion of intangible value.[3]

VALUE TO THE HOLDER VERSUS VALUE TO THE BUYER

When applying the income approach, it is important to recognize that the conclusion of value may be different depending on the purpose or standard of value applied in connection with the appraisal. In addition, the degree of control of the subject may also have an impact on value because absent the ability to assert influence or control, the owner of a business ownership interest may have limited ability to affect the future cash flows. When valuing a noncontrolling interest, the pretax cash flows may not be much different in the hands of the hypothetical (or specific) seller than in the hands of the hypothetical (or specific) buyer. This is true whether or not the subject interest is a minority ownership interest in a C corporation or a PTE.

On the other hand, if the subject interest can exercise influence or the prerogatives of control, then the present value of future pretax cash flows generated for the benefit of the subject interest may be very different in the hands of a seller or a buyer. A seller or a buyer may offer the business different (1) synergies, (2) depth of expertise, (3) sources of capital, (4) cost of capital, and so forth.

The holder of an ownership interest in a business may enjoy a very different effective income tax rate than the hypothetical buyer. For example, the holder may be a qualifying owner of a business operating as an S corporation, whereas the hypothetical buyer may be a C corporation (which would automatically terminate the S corporation election). The holder may have a different overall effective income tax rate than the buyer due to other sources of income, expenses, and deductions.

Finally, the holder may have a different cost of capital than the buyer. If the buyer has greater (1) sources of working capital and/or (2) access to debt and/or equity capital than the holder, then the buyer's potentially lower cost of capital may yield a greater value than the company's value in the hands of the holder. Thus, when valuing an ownership interest based on a value to the holder assumption, it is not the selling price that could be realized from the sale to a hypothetical buyer that is relevant (unless there is an intention to sell, near term); rather, it is the value of the ownership interest in the hands of the owner that matters.

---

[3] *Id.* § 4.02(f).

When valuing an ownership interest based on a value to the buyer (investment value) assumption, it is not the pretax cash flows, income tax rate, or cost of capital of the seller that matters; it is the value of the ownership interest in the hands of the buyer that matters. When preparing a business appraisal under the value to the holder assumption, it is important to properly match (1) pretax normalized cash flows, (2) the applicable income tax rate, and (3) the applicable cost of capital to the appropriate buyer/seller valuation assumption.

JURISDICTIONAL ISSUES

Value to the holder assumptions vary by state. In some jurisdictions, the value to the holder is equivalent to fair value and should be employed in matrimonial dissolutions, dissenting shareholder/partner/member disputes, and other circumstances. In other jurisdictions, fair value can be interpreted very differently from value to the holder, that is, pro rata share of fair market value or whatever the court thinks is fair and equitable under the circumstances. It is advisable to confirm the jurisdictional interpretation of fair value and the value to the holder assumption with counsel before employing it on a valuation engagement.

DELAWARE OPEN MRI RADIOLOGY ASSOCIATES, P.A. v. HOWARD B. KESSLER[4]

It is essential to understand relevant case law when applying the value to the holder assumption because the courts are ultimately the final arbiters of competing valuation theory. When considering the issue of tax-affecting PTEs under the value to the holder assumption, reference is made to the 2006 decision *Delaware Open MRI Radiology Associates, P.A. v. Howard B. Kessler.*[5]

The parties involved in *Delaware Open MRI* were radiologists who formed an S corporation to capture additional revenues by owning MRI centers. Due to a split in the underlying radiology practice, majority and minority stockholder groups were formed. The majority stockholder group

---

[4]Many of the principles and methodologies discussed in this chapter applicable to the analysis of *Delaware Open MRI Radiology Associates, P.A. v. Howard B. Kessler,* including the MDMM, are derived from and reprinted with permission from Eric J. Barr, "Pass-Through Entity Valuations and 'Value to the Holder': A New Perspective," *Value Examiner* (Sept./Oct. 2012).

[5]898 A.2d 290 (Del. Ch. 2006).

TABLE 5.1   Delaware MRI—Business Appraiser's Tax-Affecting Assumptions

	C Corporation	S Corporation
Pretax income	$ 100	$ 100
Corporate tax rate	40	—
Available earnings	$ 60	$ 100

(respondents) forced a squeeze-out merger, and the minority stockholder group (petitioners) filed suit in 2004, claiming that they did not receive fair value for their shares in the S corporation that owned the MRI centers.[6]

In *Delaware Open MRI*, the Court of Chancery of Delaware considered the testimony of two valuation analysts. Both analysts relied on the discounted cash flow method due to the recent and expected growth of the subject business. However, respondent's valuation analyst imposed a 40 percent corporation income tax rate, and the petitioner's valuation analyst imposed a 0 percent corporation income tax rate.[7] The positions taken by each valuation analyst are presented in Table 5.1, which is derived from a chart in the case opinion itself.[8]

The valuation conclusion derived by applying a 40 percent tax rate results in earnings subject to capitalization of 60 percent; the valuation conclusion derived by applying a 0 percent tax rate results in earnings subject to capitalization of 100 percent. The difference between the two tax-affecting adjustments is very substantial—and illustrates the PTE conundrum. Here, one valuation analyst concluded that because an income tax will be paid at the owner level via distributions to stockholders, a 40 percent tax-affecting adjustment is required. In substance, this analyst treated the earnings of the S corporation as if it were the earnings of a C corporation. The other valuation analyst concluded that because no tax is incurred at the entity level of an S corporation, no tax-affecting adjustment is appropriate.

The following are the facts and circumstances specific to this case, the court's application of the fair value standard of value, the theories and reasoning advanced by the court, and the court's conclusions with respect to how best to address the PTE conundrum in this instance.

The court concluded the following:

1. Petitioners should be awarded their pro rata share of the subject company's appraisal value on the valuation date. This value was referred to as

---

[6]*Id.* at 299.
[7]*Id.* at 326.
[8]*Id.* at 330.

fair value and is more of a jurisprudential concept than an interpretation of the Delaware appraisal statute.[9]

2. "[I]t would be highly misleading" to (1) determine the value of a market-based acquisition of an S corporation by comparison to C corporations and (2) "then assume that the S corporation would be sold at a higher price because of its [PTE] tax status."[10] The court was "not trying to quantify the value at which Delaware Radiology would sell to a C corporation"; it tried "to quantify the value of Delaware Radiology as a going concern with an S corporation structure and award the [petitioners] their pro rata share of that value."[11] This conclusion was based on Delaware law, which states that a "petitioner is 'entitled to be paid for that which has been taken from him.'"[12]

3. Petitioners were "involuntarily deprived of the benefits of continuing as stockholders in a profitable S corporation—benefits that [included] the favorable tax treatment that [potentially] accompanies S corporation status."[13] For the reasons described in Chapter 3 and as acknowledged by the court, the stockholders of the S corporation paid lower income taxes than they would have if the company operated as a C corporation.

The court adhered to the reasoning of prior decisions that recognized that an S corporation structure can produce a material increase in economic [interest]. That reasoning [supports] not only [court decisions] [in] the *Adams*, *Heck*, and *Gross* cases in the U.S. Tax Court,[14] but an appraisal decision of [the same Delaware Court of Chancery], which coincidentally also involved a radiology [practice]. The opinion *In re Radiology Associates* noted that "under an earnings valuation analysis,

---

[9]*Id.* at 310.

[10]*Id.* at 327.

[11]*Id.*

[12]*Id.* (quoting *Tri-Cont'l Corp. v. Battye*, 74 A.2d 71, 72 (Del. 1950)). The standard of value in this case was fair value as defined under Delaware law.

[13]*Id.*

[14]In *Estate of Adams v. Commissioner*, T.C.M. 2002-80, 83 T.C.M. (CCH) 1421, T.C.M. (RIA) para. 54,696, 2002 Tax Ct. LEXIS 84 (Mar. 28, 2002), *Estate of Heck v. Commissioner*, T.C.M. 2002-34, 83 T.C.M. (CCH) 1181, T.C.M. (RIA) para. 54,639, 2002 Tax Ct. LEXIS 38 (Feb. 5, 2002), and *Gross v. Commissioner*, T.C.M. 1999-254, 78 T.C.M. (CCH) 201, T.C.M. (RIA) para. 99,254, 1999 Tax Ct. LEXIS 290 (July 29, 1999). The U.S. Court of Appeals affirmed the decision of the Tax Court, 272 F.3d 333 (6th Cir. 2001), each discussed in detail in Chapter 9; the U.S. Tax Court rejected the inclusion of a 40 percent tax-affecting adjustment when valuing a PTE for estate and gift tax reporting purposes under the fair market value standard of value.

what is important to an investor is what the investor ultimately can keep in his pocket."[15]

4. No evidence was presented to the court indicating that the business would convert to C corporation status in the foreseeable future.[16]

5. The business was "highly profitable" and "distribute[d] income well in excess of the stockholder level taxes its stockholders [would] pay" on the income of Delaware Open MRI taxed on their personal income tax returns.[17]

The court concluded that the second appraiser's 0 percent tax-affecting adjustment was improper, stating thus:

> Assessing corporate taxes to a shareholder at a personal level does not affect the primary tax benefit associated with an S corporation, which is the avoidance of a dividend tax in addition to a tax on corporate earnings. This benefit can be captured fully while employing an economically rational approach to valuing an S corporation that is net of personal taxes. To ignore personal taxes would overestimate the value of an S corporation and would lead to a value that no rational investor would be willing to pay to acquire control. This is a simple premise—no one should be willing to pay more than the value of what will actually end up in her pocket.[18]

The court's analysis fully recognized the PTE premium resulting from the double taxation of C corporation earnings due to the dividend tax on distributions. The court then analyzed how best to quantify the PTE premium.

Ultimately, the court concluded that a 29.4 percent effective corporation tax rate was appropriate in the circumstances.[19] The court assumed the following in connection with its calculations, based on the testimony of the two valuation analysts:[20]

1. A perpetual effective combined federal and state C corporation income tax rate of 40 percent

---

[15]*Delaware Open MRI*, 898 A.2d at 327–28 (quoting *In re Radiology Assocs.*, 611 A.2d 485, 495 (Del. Ch. 1991)) (some citations omitted).
[16]*Id.* at 326.
[17]*Id.*
[18]*Id.* at 328–29 (citations omitted).
[19]*Id.* at 330.
[20]*Id.* at 329.

2. One hundred percent of available earnings to be perpetually distributed in cash in the year earned
3. A perpetual effective combined federal and state individual income tax rate of 40 percent on ordinary income
4. A perpetual effective combined federal and state individual tax on qualifying dividend income of 15 percent

The court's calculations are presented in Table 5.2, which are derived from a table in the case opinion.[21]

The court accepted the inputs provided by the two valuation analysts to calculate the amount that was ultimately available to the stockholders after corporation and individual income taxes. The court accepted valuation analyst #1's assumptions that (1) the C corporation would continue to pay federal and state income taxes at a combined effective tax rate of 40 percent, and (2) the stockholder of a C corporation would continue to pay a tax on dividends received at the federal tax rate of 15 percent. The court also accepted valuation analyst #2's assumptions that (1) the S corporation shareholders would pay federal and state individual income taxes at a combined effective tax rate of 40 percent, and (2) $60 is the amount available

TABLE 5.2   Delaware MRI Experts' Conclusions

	Valuation Analyst #1 C Corporation	Valuation Analyst #2 S Corporation	Court Findings
Pretax income	$ 100	$ 100	$ 100
Combined federal and state C corporation tax rate	40.0% [1]	0.0%	29.4% [5]
After-tax company earnings [2]	60	100	71
Dividend/income tax rate	15.0% [3]	40.0% [4]	15.0%
Available after corporation and individual income taxes	$ 51	$ 60	$ 60

Notes:
[1] Assumed effective combined federal and state C corporation income tax rate (at maximum marginal rates).
[2] Assumed that 100% of available earnings will be distributed in cash in year earned.
[3] Assumed effective combined federal and state tax on dividend income.
[4] Assumed effective combined federal and state individual income tax rate.
[5] Implied effective combined federal and state C corporation income tax rate.

---

[21]*Id.* at 330; see also Eric J. Barr, "Pass-Through Entity Valuations and 'Value to the Holder': A New Perspective," *Value Examiner* (Sept./Oct. 2012), at 16, 17.

after corporation and individual income taxes assuming S corporation status. "In its decision, the court mathematically determined [the] 29.4 percent effective corporation tax rate (a plug) in order to produce the desired available after-tax amount" ($60).[22]

Table 5.2 shows that the amount available to the stockholders after individual income taxes as an S corporation, $60, exceeds the amount that is available to the stockholders assuming a 40 percent effective corporation income tax rate (federal and state) and a 15 percent qualified dividend tax rate, $51. The $9 benefit of being taxed as an S corporation over the amount that the stockholders would receive as a C corporation is of real value to the S corporation stockholders—it is not a hypothetical benefit.

The court in *Delaware Open MRI* valued the subject interest under the value to the holder assumption by using after-tax company earnings of $71 and dividing it by a capitalization rate. The capitalization rate used by the court was derived using the build-up method from after-tax public company data. Hence, the court consistently matched hypothetical after-tax C corporation earnings of the S corporation (before individual income taxes) with a capitalization rate derived from after-tax net earnings of public C corporations (before individual income taxes) in deriving its conclusion of value.[23]

BERNIER v. BERNIER

In its 2012 decision, the Appeals Court of Massachusetts, in *Bernier v. Bernier*,[24] also applied the methodology utilized in *Delaware Open MRI*. *Bernier* was a matrimonial dissolution matter that involved the valuation of two supermarkets that were operated as S corporations. The lower court stated that "where valuation of assets occurs in the context of divorce, and where one of the parties will maintain, and the other be entirely divested of, ownership of a marital asset after divorce, the judge must take particular care to treat the parties not as arm's-length hypothetical buyers and sellers in a theoretical open market, but as fiduciaries entitled to equitable distribution of their marital assets." The court applied the concept of "value to the holder" in this Massachusetts matrimonial matter, similar to *Delaware Open MRI*.[25]

In *Bernier*, after applying applicable year's (2000) tax rates and utilizing the *Delaware Open MRI* methodology, the mathematically derived effective

---

[22]Barr, supra at 17.

[23]*Id.*

[24]82 Mass. App. Ct. 81 (2012).

[25]Barr, supra note at 17 (internal citation omitted). "In *Bernier*, the court referred to its use of value to the holder as fair market value." *Id.* at 17, n.2.

corporation tax rate was zero percent. The court concluded that "a zero percent tax affecting rate does not necessarily lead to an inequitable result. There is a distinction to be drawn between failing to tax affect at all the earning of the supermarkets because an S corporation does not pay federal taxes at the entity level and utilizing a zero percent tax affecting rate arrived at through application of all applicable rates, as ordered."[26]

LIMITATIONS OF *DELAWARE OPEN MRI* AND *BERNIER*

The courts' reported decisions in *Delaware Open MRI* and *Bernier* did not address changes that would need to be made to the model presented in Table 5.2 in the event that facts and circumstances under the "value to the holder" assumptions were different. For example:

- Both decisions utilized maximum statutory federal tax rates (2004 for *Delaware Open MRI* and 2000 for *Bernier*) as presented in experts' reports. Both decisions were completely silent as to the *actual* individual income taxes paid by S corporation shareholders on PTE earnings.
- States have different corporation and individual tax rates; therefore, one effective individual or corporation income tax rate cannot apply to each and every state.
- Certain states or localities (New York City, for example) do not recognize S corporation status.
- Certain states or localities impose unincorporated business taxes on partnership or limited liability company income (e.g., New York City).
- Not all companies and individuals earn levels of taxable income that place them in the highest federal statutory income tax rate.
- The amount of earnings retained in a business significantly impacts the after-tax returns to the owner. It cannot be assumed that substantially all earnings will always be distributed.[27]

What is the impact of changing any of these assumptions? Obviously, a change in income tax rates (all other things being unchanged) would change the amount of after-tax income that is available to a business owner. Therefore, businesses that operate in states (or during years) with higher income tax rates would generate lower after-tax cash flows.[28]

---

[26]*Id.* at 17.
[27]*Id.* at 17–18.
[28]*Id.* at 18.

What is the impact on the value of a PTE when a business retains instead of distributes its profits? By definition, the owners of a PTE recognize 100 percent of the business's taxable income whether or not there is a distribution from the business. If a business distributes all of its profits, then the owner is paying income taxes on profits actually received. On the other hand, if a business does not distribute any of its profits, the owner is still personally responsible for paying out-of-pocket the income taxes related to business earnings. This places the owner of a PTE in a distinct and significant economic disadvantage relative to an owner of a C corporation when earnings are not distributed.[29]

Many businesses are unable to distribute all of their profits. Cash is often retained in a business for capital expenditures, repayment of interest-bearing debt, expansion plans, working capital needs, and many other reasons. Income retention is a highly sensitive assumption when estimating after-tax return on investment because any income retained by a PTE reduces its dividend-paying capacity. There often is an inverse relationship between earnings retained in the business and after-tax returns to the equity owner (however, in some instances, the income retained in a business can greatly accelerate revenue, net income growth, and value). It is important to note that many of the tax benefits of owning a PTE relative to a C corporation disappear when pretax income retention is 60 to 65 percent. It logically follows that if a business expects to have income retained at a level that causes the owner to lose the benefit of a PTE premium relative to actual C corporation rates, the pass-through election may be terminated. However logical it might be in certain circumstances to terminate the PTE election, in practice this does not appear to be a common occurrence.

THE MODIFIED DELAWARE MRI MODEL

"I have modified the *Delaware [Open] MRI* model (but not the inputs) utilized by the Court of Chancery of Delaware to address" the limitations described in the preceding paragraphs.[30] The revised model, referenced herein as the Modified Delaware MRI Model (MDMM), follows the format given in Table 5.3.[31]

---

[29]Any future distributions of previously taxed income will occur tax-free to the owners of a PTE.
[30]Barr, supra at 18.
[31]*Id.*

TABLE 5.3 Modified Delaware MRI Synopsis

	PTE and Individual Rates	Derivation of C Corporation Tax Rate
Normalized pretax cash basis income	$ 100 [1]	$ 100 [1]
State/local UBT/S corporation taxes	0.0% [2]	N/A
Income before federal corporation income taxes	100	100
Combined federal and state C corporation tax rate	N/A	29.4% [6]
Available company earnings	$ 100	$ 71
Available company earnings	$ 100	$ 71
Pretax earnings retained %	0.0% [3]	0.0% [7]
Distributable company earnings	$ 100	$ 71 [8]
State and local income taxes— individual	— [4]	— [9]
Federal income taxes—individual	40.0% [5]	15.0% [10]
Individual income taxes	$ 40	$ 11
Available to owner/invested capital— after corporation and individual income taxes	$ 60	$ 60

Notes:
[1] Can be either pretax income to equity or pretax income to invested capital.
[2] May not be applicable depending on the tax jurisdiction. Presumed $0 in *Delaware MRI*.
[3] Presumed $0 in *Delaware MRI*. This could be a significant amount depending on specific facts and circumstances, requiring a detailed analysis of working capital, capital expenditures, and other cash flow requirements.
[4] Based on state of residence of shareholder/member.
[5] Court applied 40% presumed combined federal and state individual income tax rate.
[6] This is a derived percentage that is needed to make the column foot.
[7] Earnings retained as a percent (%) of pretax income. The dollar amount retained as a C corporation should match the amount retained in the business as a PTE.
[8] Use this amount for estimate of value under Income Approach.
[9] Assumed to be 0% in *Delaware Open MRI*.
[10] *Delaware Open MRI* applied maximum federal statutory qualified dividend rate.

The preceding table can also be expressed as follows:

Normalized pretax income – Entity-level tax on S corporation pretax income – Income retained in business – Individual income taxes on S corporation income

=

Normalized pretax income – C corporation income taxes – Income retained in business – Dividend tax

This formula simplifies to the following:

Entity-level tax on S corporation pretax income + Individual income taxes on S corporation income

=

C corporation income taxes + Dividend tax

The interaction of the S corporation and individual and implied C corporation tax rates can also be expressed algebraically as follows:[32]

$$PTIs - Ts - IR - Ti = PTIs - Tc - IR - Td$$

and

$$Ts + Ti = Tc + Td$$

where:

PTIs is the pretax income of PTE
Ts is the federal and state entity-level income tax rated imposed on the PTE
Ti is combined federal and state individual income taxes on the PTE
IR is income retained in the PTE
Tc is the combined federal and state C corporation income tax (implied by the MDMM)
Td is the combined federal and state tax on dividends distributed by the PTE

It logically follows that when $Ts = \$0$, this formula simplifies to the following:

$$Ti = Tc + Td$$

Table 5.4 expands the above *Delaware Open MRI* synopsis to include (1) common-size data and (2) the following algebraic abbreviations.

---

[32]*Id.* at 20.

TABLE 5.4   Modified Delaware MRI Synopsis, Including Common-Size Data

	PTEs and Individual Rates			Derivation of C Corporation Tax Rate		
	Amount		Percent	Amount		Percent
Normalized pretax cash basis income	$ 100.0	PTIs	100.0%	$ 100.0	PTIs	100.0%
State/Local UBT/S corporation taxes	—	Ts	0.0%	N/A		N/A
Income before federal corporation income taxes	100.0		100.0%	100.0		100.0%
Combined federal and state C corporation tax rate	N/A		N/A	29.4	Tc	29.4%
Available company earnings	$ 100.0		100.0%	$ 70.6		70.6%
Available company earnings	$ 100.0	IR	100.0%	$ 70.6	IR	70.6%
Pretax earnings retained %	—		0.0%	—		0.0%
Distributable company earnings	$ 100.0		100.0%	$ 70.6		70.6%
State and local income taxes—individual	—		0.0%	—		0.0%
Federal income taxes—individual	40.0		40.0%	10.6		10.6%
Individual income taxes	$ 40.0	Ti	40.0%	$ 10.6	Td	10.6%
Available to owner/invested capital—after corporation and individual income taxes	$ 60.0		60.0%	$ 60.0		60.0%

The MDMM algebraic formula confirms the findings in Table 5.4: $PTIs$ ($100) $-$ Ts ($0) $-$ IR ($0) $-$ Ti ($40) $=$ $PTIs$ ($100) $-$ Tc ($29.4) $-$ IR ($0) $-$ Td ($10.6), calculating to $60 = $60.

It also follows that Ts ($0) $+$ Ti ($40) $=$ Tc ($29.4) $+$ Td ($10.6), calculating to $40 = $40.

FLEXIBILITY OF THE MDMM

As noted in Chapters 2 and 3, tax laws, tax brackets, and tax rates change, often substantially. Vastly different implied C corporation rates should result when tax rates change. Is the MDMM flexible enough to adjust to such changes?

As previously stated, $Ts + Ti = Tc + Td$. Therefore, when (1) $Ts = 0, (2) $IR = 0, and (3) $Ti = Td$, Tc must equal zero. These were the assumptions employed in *Bernier* and *Gross v. Commissioner*. In order for Tc to be greater than zero, the effective combined federal and state individual tax rate must be greater than the effective combined federal and state tax rate on dividends.

"This conclusion begs the question: How often does it occur that the effective combined federal and state individual tax rate is not greater than the effective combined federal and state tax rate on . . . dividends?"[33]

As discussed in Chapter 3, since 1953 (except for the period 2003–2013) the federal individual tax rate on qualifying dividends has never been less than the maximum statutory federal individual income tax rate. Table 5.5

TABLE 5.5   Maximum Statutory Federal Tax Rates

| Year | Individual | | Corporate |
	Taxable Income [1]	Qualified Dividends [2]	Taxable Income
1981	50.00%	70.00%	46.00%
1982	50.00%	50.00%	46.00%
1983	50.00%	50.00%	46.00%
1984	50.00%	50.00%	46.00%
1985	50.00%	50.00%	46.00%
1986	50.00%	50.00%	46.00%
1987	38.50%	38.50%	40.00%

---

[33]Barr, supra at 20.

1988	28.00%	28.00%	34.00%
1989	28.00%	28.00%	34.00%
1990	28.00%	28.00%	34.00%
1991	31.00%	31.00%	34.00%
1992	31.00%	31.00%	34.00%
1993	39.60%	39.60%	35.00%
1994	39.60%	39.60%	35.00%
1995	39.60%	39.60%	35.00%
1996	39.60%	39.60%	35.00%
1997	39.60%	39.60%	35.00%
1998	39.60%	39.60%	35.00%
1999	39.60%	39.60%	35.00%
2000 [4]	39.60%	39.60%	35.00%
2001	39.10%	39.10%	35.00%
2002	38.60%	38.60%	35.00%
2003	35.00%	15.00%	35.00%
2004 [5]	35.00%	15.00%	35.00%
2005	35.00%	15.00%	35.00%
2006	35.00%	15.00%	35.00%
2007	35.00%	15.00%	35.00%
2008	35.00%	15.00%	35.00%
2009	35.00%	15.00%	35.00%
2010	35.00%	15.00%	35.00%
2011	35.00%	15.00%	35.00%
2012	35.00%	15.00%	35.00%
2013	39.60%	23.40% [3]	35.00%

Notes:

[1] Maximum marginal rates may be greater depending on case-specific facts and circumstances. For example, a phase-out of itemized deductions and exemptions, self-employment taxes, and alternative minimum taxes can result in a maximum federal marginal tax rate that is greater than the maximum statutory rates noted above.

[2] During the period 1981–1986, $750 to $1500 of dividends were exempt if reinvested in utilities.

[3] Includes 3.8% Medicare surtax.

[4] The year 2000 is the valuation date of *Bernier v. Bernier.*

[5] The year 2004 is the valuation date of *Delaware Open MRI.*

presents a comparison of maximum statutory federal tax rates for individuals and corporations, for each year in the period 1981–2013, using data derived from Tables 2.8–2.12.

It therefore logically follows that for tax years 1936–1939 and 1953–2002, (1) when the maximum statutory individual federal tax rate on dividends was not less than the maximum statutory federal individual income tax rate, (2) where there was no income retained in the business, and (3) assuming no entity-level PTE income tax, 0 percent should be the effective C corporation tax rate when valuing PTEs using the MDMM under the "value to the holder" assumption. This result is consistent with the findings in *Gross*, which involved the 1992 valuation of a PTE ownership interest, and other cases discussed in Chapter 9.

CHAPTER 6

Inputs to Modified Delaware MRI Model

hapter 5 described the model used by the courts in *Delaware Open MRI*, which has been modified to incorporate factors not relevant to that case but that impact the model's utilization. The modified version of the *Delaware Open MRI* calculation requires the following inputs:

1. Normalized pretax income
2. Entity-level taxes on PTE income, that is, unincorporated business taxes and corporation income taxes on S corporation pretax income
3. Income retained in the business not subject to distribution
4. PTE owner's effective federal income taxes on pass-through income
5. PTE owner's effective state and local income taxes on pass-through income
6. Owner's effective federal and state dividend taxes on C corporation income available for distribution

With these six inputs, the effective combined federal and state C corporation income tax rate can be derived. This chapter describes the factors to be considered when determining each of these inputs.

NORMALIZED PRETAX INCOME

Normalized pretax income may differ from tax-reported or GAAP-reported pretax income insofar as normalized pretax income

1. Eliminates nonrecurring or extraordinary items
2. Removes errors in the calculation of reported income and expenses

3. Reconciles the classification of similar transactions during different periods of time for comparison
4. Adjusts for changes or inconsistencies in accounting and/or income tax methods

The purpose of such normalization adjustments is to convert reported pretax income and expenses of the subject interest to an economic basis that is indicative of the future cash flows of the subject interest.

Additional adjustments may be required depending on the degree of control attributable to the subject interest because a controlling interest enjoys certain prerogatives that noncontrolling or minority interests do not.

The following is a list of some of the rights that go with control shares that minority shares often do not have:

1. Appoint or change operational management.
2. Appoint or change members of the board of directors.
3. Determine management compensation and perquisites.
4. Set operational and strategic policy and change the course of the business.
5. Acquire, lease, or liquidate business assets, including plant, property, and equipment.
6. Select suppliers, vendors, and subcontractors with whom to do business and award contracts.
7. Negotiate and consummate mergers and acquisitions.
8. Liquidate, dissolve, sell out, or recapitalize the company.
9. Sell or acquire treasury shares.
10. Register the company's equity securities for an initial or secondary public offering.
11. Register the company's debt securities for an initial or secondary public offering.
12. Declare and pay cash and/or stock dividends.
13. Change the articles of incorporation or by-laws.
14. Set one's own compensation (and perquisites) and the compensation (and perquisites) of related-party employees.
15. Select joint venture partners and enter into joint ventures and partnership agreements.
16. Decide what products and/or services to offer and how to price those products/services.
17. Decide what markets and locations to serve, enter into, and discontinue serving.
18. Decide which customer categories to market to and which not to market to.

19. Enter into inbound and outbound license or sharing agreements regarding intellectual properties.
20. Block any or all of the above actions.[1]

In contrast, a minority interest in a closely held entity is characterized by a lack of control, among other things. That is, the minority owner does not have the same control over the 20 factors noted previously that a controlling shareholder would have.

When valuing a controlling interest, certain additional adjustments may be appropriate with respect to reasonable compensation of the owner, nonbusiness expenses, operational efficiencies, and so on. A minority interest may not be able to make such changes. Case-specific facts and circumstances will dictate what normalization adjustments are appropriate.

Normalized pretax income (PTI) can be determined on a cash basis or an accrual basis. If PTI is determined on an accrual basis, then an adjustment for income retained in the business for working capital requirements (discussed below) is likely required. Normalized pretax income can also be calculated on the basis of earnings available to equity owners or earnings available to invested capital (owners' equity plus interest-bearing debt that is part of the company's capital structure).

ENTITY-LEVEL INCOME TAXES ON PASS-THROUGH EARNINGS

There are certain local jurisdictions that do not recognize the pass-through status of S corporations, partnerships, or LLCs and impose an entity-level income tax on PTE pretax income. For example, New York City imposes a C corporation income tax on S corporation taxable income. New York City also imposes an unincorporated business tax on partnership and LLC taxable income. Such entity-level income taxes reduce the PTI available to retain in the business, as well as the earnings that pass through to owners as taxable income. Thus, it is important to be certain of the jurisdictional tax requirements to avoid an overstatement of PTI and a resulting overstated conclusion of value, if not addressed properly.

---

[1]Shannon P. Pratt, Robert F. Reilly, and Robert P. Schweihs, *Valuing a Business: The Analysis and Appraisal of Closely Held Companies*, 4th ed. (New York: McGraw-Hill, 2000), p. 385.

INCOME RETAINED IN THE BUSINESS

Even though the owner(s) of a PTE will pay the income tax expense incurred with respect to the earnings of the PTE, it does not logically follow that the entity will distribute all of its earnings. A PTE may retain some portion of its PTI due to anticipated future needs, or it may be contractually prohibited from making distributions due to restrictive bank debt requirements. The following is a partial list of the reasons that a PTE would not distribute all of its PTI to owners:

1. Working capital requirements
2. Capital expenditures
3. Business acquisitions
4. Purchase of an ownership interest
5. Hiring of additional staff
6. Settlement of litigation
7. Debt service
8. Restrictive covenants in loan documents
9. Uninsured claims
10. Deferred maintenance and repairs
11. Research and development
12. Geographic and/or product line expansion
13. Software development/purchase
14. Development of e-commerce solutions
15. Website upgrade

Consequently, the valuation analyst must consider whether all of a PTE's PTI will be available for distribution to its owners. Failing to include an appropriate adjustment for these items could overstate the after-tax earnings available to the equity owners, perhaps substantially, and result in an overstatement of value. Although a "retained-income" adjustment reduces the cash available for distribution to the owners, it does not result in an adjustment to the taxable income that passes through to the owners. The taxable earnings that pass through to the owners are separate and distinct from any income-retention adjustment.

As the amount of income retained in a business increases, the distributable cash available to the owners decreases. Accordingly, there is an inverse relationship between income retained and distributable cash available to the owners. Let's quantify the impact of income retained in a business on the value of a business by examining two relatively straightforward hypothetical examples. In both examples, assume (1) a value to the holder assumption, (2) no sources of taxable income for the owner other than the PTE flow-through,

TABLE 6.1   Analysis: 5 Percent Retained and FIT Rate of 10 Percent

	Actual PTE and Individual Tax Rates	Derivation of C Corporation Tax Rates
Normalized pretax cash basis income	$ 1,000	$ 1,000
Entity-level income tax on normalized pretax income	0%	0%
Corporation income before C corporation income taxes	1,000	1,000
C corporation tax rate	—	10%
Available corporation earnings	$ 1,000	$ 900
Available corporation earnings	$ 1,000	$ 900
Pretax earnings retained	50	50
Distributable corporation earnings	950	850
Federal dividend tax rate	—	0%
Effective federal individual income taxes	10%	—
Available after corporation and individual income taxes	$ 850	$ 850

(3) no entity-level income tax on normalized pretax business income, and (4) no individual state income taxes. In the first example, income retained in the business is equal to 5 percent of normalized pretax income, and the effective federal individual income tax rate is 10 percent (Table 6.1); in the second example, income retained in the business is 40 percent of normalized pretax income, and the effective federal individual income tax rate is 40 percent (Table 6.2).

Based on the 5 percent/10 percent assumptions shaded in Table 6.1, the C corporation income tax rate is also 10 percent. Accordingly, the valuation performed under the income approach would be based on $850 of distributable corporation earnings. Let's see what happens when these assumptions change.

In the second example, a 40 percent/40 percent assumption is used. As a result of the higher effective federal individual income tax rate, the federal dividend tax rate increases to 23.8 percent (20% plus the Medicare surcharge of 3.8%). Consequently, the effective C corporation income tax rate is 34 percent, and distributable corporation income is now $262—a substantial decrease from $850 in the previous example. These two simple examples show how dramatically distributable corporation earnings and the effective C corporation income tax rates are impacted by changes in pretax earnings retained in the business and by changes in the effective federal income tax rate.

TABLE 6.2 Analysis: 40 Percent Retained and FIT Rate of 40 Percent

	Actual PTE and Individual Tax Rates	Derivation of C Corporation Tax Rates
Normalized pretax cash basis income	$ 1,000	$ 1,000
Entity-level income tax on normalized pretax income	0%	0.0%
Corporation income before C corporation income taxes	1,000	1,000
C corporation tax rate	—	33.8%
Available corporation earnings	$ 1,000	$ 662
Available corporation earnings	$ 1,000	$ 662
Pretax earnings retained %	400	400
Distributable corporation earnings	600	262
Federal dividend tax rate	—	23.8%
Effective federal individual income taxes	40%	—
Available after corporation and individual income taxes	$ 200	$ 200

Table 6.3 illustrates the effective C corporation income tax rate changes under different income retention and federal individual income tax rates, based on the previous examples. As expected, the larger the percentage of pretax income retained and the larger the federal individual income tax rate, the larger the C corporation income tax rate.

TABLE 6.3 Sensitivity Analysis—Effective C Corporation Tax Rates

		Effective Federal Individual Income Tax Rates			
		10%	20%	30%	40%
	5%	10%	7%	15%	23%
	10%	10%	8%	16%	24%
	15%	10%	9%	17%	26%
Income Retained	20%	10%	9%	18%	28%
	25%	10%	10%	20%	29%
	30%	10%	11%	21%	31%
	35%	10%	12%	22%	32%
	40%	10%	13%	23%	34%

TABLE 6.4 Sensitivity Analysis—Distributable Corporation Earnings

		Effective Federal Individual Income Tax Rates			
		10%	20%	30%	40%
	5%	850	882	800	722
	10%	800	824	739	656
	15%	750	765	677	591
Income Retained	20%	700	706	616	525
	25%	650	647	554	459
	30%	600	588	493	394
	35%	550	529	431	328
	40%	500	471	369	262

In Table 6.4, it is shown that the larger the percentage of pretax income retained and the larger the federal individual income tax rate, the smaller the amount of distributable corporation earnings subject to capitalization.

EFFECTIVE FEDERAL AND STATE INCOME TAX RATES ON PASS-THROUGH INCOME

The effective federal and state input would appear to be easy to calculate. Yet there are many different schools of thought on the most appropriate way to derive this input. Let's identify some of the more commonly considered methods of calculating the input for the effective federal and state income tax rates under the value to the holder standard of value and critique them.

Maximum Federal and State Individual Statutory Income Tax Rates

The reasons for rejecting using maximum federal and state individual income tax rates should be obvious based on the analyses contained in Chapters 2 and 3: It is very rare to have an effective tax rate equal to the statutory income tax rate for individual or married taxpayers in the maximum income bracket. Different levels of income will dictate different effective federal and state income tax rates.

Using 40, 0, 29.4, or Some Other Fixed Percent

There is no one-rate-fits-all solution, hence using 40, 0, 29.4, or some other fixed percent in all situations is incorrect. We have seen the courts reject assumed 40 percent and 0 percent C corporation income tax rates in some circumstances and have heard their very legitimate reasons for rejecting these approaches.[2] Moreover, the 29.4 percent rate applied in *Delaware Open MRI* was only intended to apply to the facts and circumstances in that case, including, among other things, 2004 tax law and no income retained in the subject business. We know based on Chapter 3 that effective federal income tax rates can vary significantly as PTI increases from low levels of income to larger levels of income.

Application of Nominal Statutory Rates for Each Income Bracket

Applying nominal statutory rates for each income bracket is appealing as it is easily derived by calculating the federal and state income tax expense that would result in a given year using normalized pretax income, nominal statutory rates for each income bracket, and the applicable individual filing status. The resulting total federal and state income tax divided by normalized pretax income yields the effective federal and state income tax rate under this approach.

The problem with this approach is that it allocates the entire tax benefit of the lower income brackets to normalized PTI and no portion to other taxable income of the PTE owner. For example, if the tax benefit of these lower income brackets is $100,000, there is no justification for applying this benefit solely to the PTE without allocating any portion of it to other sources of income, such as wages. Applying this method would tend to understate the effective federal income tax input.

Overall Effective Income Tax Rates Indicated on the Owner's Individual Income Tax Returns

At first glance, applying the overall effective income tax rates indicated on the owner's individual income tax return has appeal because the owner's tax returns present an indisputable indication of the income tax cost of the owner's pass-through earnings. However, this approach is also flawed for the following reasons:

1. There are many circumstances where the business is paying for perquisites of the owner and such perquisites are not being recognized as

---

[2]For example, in *Delaware Open MRI*, the court rejected both 40 percent and 0 percent income tax inputs.

taxable income on the owner's income tax return, yet they are included as part of normalized PTI. In this situation, relying on the tax expense reported on the owner's federal and state income tax returns would understate and not provide a true indication of the normalized tax cost of the PTE ownership interest.

2. If PTE-reported taxable income and reported wages differ from normalized PTI and reasonable compensation, the resulting effective federal and state income tax rates may be materially incorrect.

3. A taxpayer's income tax returns may include nonrecurring items that need to be removed.

4. If a business owner has itemized deductions, dependents, loss carryforwards, and other items that reduce his taxable income, why should such items impact the effective income tax incurred on a PTE's PTI? For example, if one business owner has 10 children and his income tax expense is accordingly reduced, should this reduction in tax cost increase the value of his business? Of course not. It simply reduces the cost of raising the family. Similarly, if a business owner is able to deduct $100,000 of real estate taxes and mortgage interest costs on her individual income tax return, does this increase the value of her business? Again, no. It may decrease the cost of home ownership and thereby possibly impact the value of the property, but it does not increase the value of the business.

Accordingly, this is not an appropriate way of calculating the owner's effective federal income tax rate on pass-through earnings.

"With and Without" Method

The "with and without" method recalculates the taxpayer's federal and state income tax liability based on known and knowable future tax laws, rates, and brackets. The calculation incorporates (1) all recurring items reflected on the taxpayer's historical federal and state income tax returns except for reported historical income that flows through from the PTE and historical PTE wages/guaranteed payments; (2) owner's reasonable compensation; and (3) normalized PTI. This is the "all-in" or "with" federal and state income tax calculation. The next step is to calculate the federal and state income tax "without" normalized PTI (3), but with items (1) and (2). The difference in the federal and state income taxes calculated under the "with and without" method is the total income tax attributable to the PTE.

This methodology, although somewhat cumbersome, takes into consideration the impact of the alternative minimum tax, itemized deduction phase-outs,[3] self-employment taxes, the itemized tax deduction benefit on the federal income tax return of PTE state income taxes, and so on. **It effectively calculates the incremental federal and state income tax to the holder resulting from normalized PTI.** If the ownership interest in the business was sold, the annual income tax amount saved can be determined by this "with and without" approach. This method is conceptually sound because it calculates the actual amount of incremental income taxes associated with the holder's ownership interest in the PTE, and does not have any of the shortcomings of the other factors identified.

Implied in this approach is that the valuation analyst can access the holder's historical tax returns. What should the valuation analyst do if an owner's tax returns are not available? The valuation analyst should attempt to "obtain sufficient relevant data to afford a reasonable basis for conclusions, recommendations or positions." A member must consider scope limitations that impact the level of reliance on the information received.[4]

When owner tax returns are not available, the valuation analyst may consider the appropriateness of:

1. Reasonably estimating the effective federal and state income tax rates based on all known facts and disclosing the relevant assumptions in the valuation report
2. Performing a sensitivity analysis to quantify the potential impact of hypothetical assumptions
3. Disclosing the nature and potential impact of the scope limitation
4. Considering other options

The choice of how to proceed on a valuation engagement in the absence of owner tax returns is ultimately a fact-sensitive decision to be made by the analyst.

Another issue to consider when valuing a PTE is the effective federal and state tax rates that should be used when employing the discounted cash flows method (DCF). If the subject company's earnings are changing, or if it is known that income tax rates are going to change, the effective federal and

---

[3]For tax years beginning after December 31, 2012, an individual whose adjusted gross income exceeds a threshold amount ($300,000 for married filing jointly during 2013) must reduce the amount of allowable itemized deductions by the lesser of (1) 3 percent of the excess of adjusted gross income over the threshold amount, or (2) 80 percent of allowable itemized deductions.

[4]National Association of Certified Valuators and Analysts, NACVA Professional Standards §§ 1.2(f), 3.5 (January 1, 2008). Similar performance requirements are contained in the professional standards of the American Institute of Certified Public Accountants (AICPA) and the American Society of Appraisers.

state individual income tax rates for each period may not be the same. Separate calculations of effective federal and state individual income tax rates for each year in the projection period may be required under the DCF method.

DIVIDEND TAX RATES

Since 2003, federal dividend tax rates have been much lower than federal individual income tax rates. Under current tax law (commencing in 2013):

1. "The maximum rate of tax on qualified dividends is 0% on any amount that otherwise would be taxed at a 10% or 15% rate; 15% on any amount that otherwise would be taxed at rates greater than 15% but less than 39.6%; and 20% on any amount that otherwise would be taxed at a 39.6% rate."[5]
2. A 3.8 percent *net investment income tax (NIIT)* is imposed by IRC Section 1411 commencing January 1, 2013. The NIIT will be assessed on individuals, estates, and trusts. Individual taxpayers with a modified adjusted gross income (MAGI) exceeding an annual threshold amount (for 2013, the annual threshold amount is $250,000 for those filing jointly, or surviving spouse, $200,000 for head of household and single, and $125,000 for those filing married filing separately) are subject to NIIT. The NIIT is 3.8 percent of the lesser of net investment income or the excess of MAGI over the threshold amount.[6] This 3.8 percent tax is also referred to as the Medicare Surcharge on dividends.

The manner in which valuation analysts calculate effective state and local dividend tax rates is also a matter of some controversy. The following are several methods used to calculate the C corporation dividend tax input under the MDMM.

Applying Statutory Federal Dividend Tax Rates and Effective State Income Tax Rates

It is relatively easy to determine the statutory federal dividend tax rate based on the taxpayer's maximum income tax bracket. The state dividend tax rate is often assumed to match the effective state income tax rate above. With these

---

[5]Internal Revenue Service, Publication 550, "Investment Income and Expenses," http://www.irs.gov/pub/irs-pdf/p550.pdf.
[6]Internal Revenue Service, "Questions and Answers on the Net Investment Income Tax," http://www.irs.gov/uac/Newsroom/Net-Investment-Income-Tax-FAQs.

two inputs, shouldn't it be easy to solve for the C corporation dividend tax input correctly and easily? Well, not really.

There are a couple of problems with this approach:

1. It does not take into consideration the applicable state income tax deduction benefit, the impact on the alternative minimum tax calculation, itemized deduction phase-outs, exemption phase-out, and so on, that will be reflected on the federal income tax return for the state dividend tax.
2. The state income tax is based on 100 percent of PTI, whether or not distributed. The state and federal dividend tax is based on PTI after reductions for C corporation income taxes and income retained in the business. Accordingly, the federal and state *income* tax rate is based on a larger amount of taxable income than the federal and state *dividend* tax. In states with progressive tax rates, this will result in an overstatement of the state dividend tax input.

Accordingly, this approach will tend to overstate the dividend tax input and understate the C corporation income tax rate.

Using the "With and Without" Method

Similar to what was described earlier with respect to the derivation of the individual effective income tax inputs, a "with and without" calculation should be performed. The "with" should include an estimate of the dividend that will be paid, that is, PTI less C corporation income taxes less income retained. Alternatively, the approach that I find most efficient is to start with the amount available after corporation and individual income taxes ($850 and $200 in the preceding examples) and estimate the dividend tax using an iterative process. The following two examples illustrate this approach.

Example 1: With Income Retained   The following example illustrates the derivation of the MDMM inputs assuming the following:

1. The valuation date is January 1, 2013.
2. There is a value to the holder assumption.
3. The controlling interest is 100 percent.
4. The subject business is a New Jersey and federal S corporation.
5. The normalized PTI is $1,200,000.
6. The income retained equals 5 percent of normalized PTI.
7. The owner's reasonable compensation is $150,000.
8. The owner has no other sources of income and has itemized deductions of $50,000 of mortgage interest and $30,000 of real estate taxes.
9. The owner's filing status is married filing jointly, with two dependent children.

TABLE 6.5 Example 1: Derivation of Effective Federal and State Individual Income Tax Rate (in thousands)

	With S Corporation Income	Without S Corporation Income	Difference Amount	Effective Tax Rate
Wages	$ 150	$ 150		
S corporation income	1,200	—		
Total income and adjusted gross income	1,350	150		
Itemized Deductions				
Real estate taxes	30	30		
State income taxes	103	5		
Mortgage interest	50	50		
Subtotal	183	85		
3% AGI floor	(31)	—		
	152	85		
Personal exemptions	—	16		
Federal taxable income	$ 1,198	$ 49		
Total Income Taxes				
Federal [1]	$ 422	$ 7	$ 415	34.6%
State (NJ)	103	5	98	8.2%
Total	$ 525	$ 12	$ 513	42.8%
S corporation income			$ 1,200	100.0%

Note: [1] Includes regular tax; alternative minimum tax; and high income HI, Medicare, and other taxes.

Our first step is to calculate the effective federal and state individual income tax rate needed for the MDMM under the "with and without" method. There are a number of individual income tax programs that are available for sale that would enable the valuation consultant to incorporate these assumptions and project the tax consequence of "with and without" calculations. Using a reliable tax software program, the federal ($415,000) and state ($98,000) individual income tax inputs are calculated as indicated in Table 6.5. Using this information, the analysis shown in Table 6.6 is prepared.

All that is needed to complete the calculation is the federal and New Jersey dividend tax amounts. With these inputs, distributable corporation

TABLE 6.6 Example 1: Derivation of Income Available After Corporation and
Dividend Taxes (in thousands)

	Actual PTE and Individual Tax Rates		Derivation of C Corporation Tax Rates	
Normalized pretax cash basis income	$ 1,200	100.0%	$ 1,200	100.0%
Entity-level PTE income tax on normalized pretax income	—	0.0%	—	0.0%
Corporation income before C corporation income taxes	1,200	100.0%		0.0%
C Corporation taxes	—	0.0%	?	
Available corporation earnings	*$ 1,200*	*100.0%*	*?*	
Available corporation earnings	$ 1,200	100.0%	?	
Pretax earnings retained	60	5.0%	60	5.0%
Distributable corporation earnings	*$ 1,140*	*95.0%*	*?*	
Federal dividend taxes			?	
NJ dividend taxes			?	
Effective federal individual income taxes	$ 415	34.6%		
Effective NJ individual income taxes	98	8.2%		
Total individual income taxes	*$ 513*	*42.8%*	*—*	*0.0%*
Available after corporation and individual income taxes	*$ 627*	*52.3%*	*$ 627*	*52.3%*

Note: Includes regular tax; alternative minimum tax; and high income HI, Medicare,
and other taxes.

earnings, available corporation earnings, and the C corporation tax can be
mathematically derived.

By utilizing an iterative process to determine the correct C corporation
dividend amount, the calculations in Table 6.7 can be derived.

Assuming distributable corporation income (dividend income) of
$897,000, the federal ($199,000) and state dividend tax ($71,000) amounts
noted in Table 6.7 now match the amounts noted in Table 6.8. The calculated
C corporation tax under the MDMM is 20.3 percent in this example.

TABLE 6.7 Example 1: Derivation of Effective Federal and State Tax on Dividend Income (in thousands)

	With C Corporation Dividend	Without C Corporation Dividend	Difference Amount	Difference Effective Tax Rate
Wages	$ 150	$ 150		
C corporation dividend	897	—		
Total income and adjusted gross income	1,047	150		
Itemized Deductions				
Real estate taxes	30	30		
State income taxes	76	5		
Mortgage interest	50	50		
Subtotal	156	85		
3% AGI floor	(22)	—		
	134	85		
Personal exemptions	—	16		
Federal taxable income	$ 913	$ 49		
Total Income Taxes				
Federal [1]	$ 206	$ 7	$ 199	22.2%
State (NJ)	76	5	71	7.9%
Total	$ 282	$ 12	$ 270	30.1%
C corporation dividend			$ 897	100.0%

Note: [1] Includes regular tax; alternative minimum tax; and high income HI, Medicare, and other taxes.

Example 2: With No Income Retained   Let's see the impact on the C corporation tax assuming the same facts as in the previous example with one exception— no income is retained in the business.

The S corporation individual income tax inputs are not impacted by the retaining of earnings. Accordingly, the individual income tax inputs are unchanged, and the amount available after corporation and individual income taxes should increase by $60,000 to $687,000 (from $627,000).

However, the amount of distributable corporation earnings and the dividend tax will both increase by the elimination of the $60,000 retained income. By again using an iterative process, the calculations as shown in Table 6.9 can be made.

TABLE 6.8 Example 1: Derivation of Effective C Corporation Tax (in thousands)

	Actual PTE and Individual Tax Rates		Derivation of C Corp Tax Rates	
Normalized pretax cash basis income	$ 1,200	100.0%	$ 1,200	100.0%
Entity-level PTE income tax on normalized pretax income	—	0.0%	—	0.0%
Corporation income before C corporation income taxes	1,200	100.0%	1,200	100.0%
C corporation income taxes	—	0.0%	243	20.3%
Available corporation earnings	$ 1,200	100.0%	$ 957	79.8%
Available corporation earnings	$ 1,200	100.0%	$ 957	79.8%
Pretax earnings retained %	60	5.0%	60	5.0%
Distributable corporation earnings	$ 1,140	95.0%	$ 897	74.8%
Federal dividend tax rate [2]			$ 199	16.6%
NJ dividend tax rate [2]			71	5.9%
Effective federal individual income taxes [1]	$ 415	34.6%		
Effective NJ individual income taxes [1]	98	8.2%		
Total individual income taxes	$ 513	42.8%	$ 270	22.5%
Available after corporation and individual income taxes	$ 627	52.3%	$ 627	52.3%

Notes:

[1] Based on 2013 Federal and NJ individual income tax rates.
Federal individual income taxes includes regular tax, alternative minimum tax, high income HI, Medicare, and other taxes. See Table 6.5.

	With K-1 Income	Without K-1 Income	Difference
Federal individual income tax	$ 422	$ 7	$ 415
NJ individual income tax	103	5	98
Totals	$ 525	$ 12	$ 513

[2] Same assumptions as #1 above, except that instead of K-1 income we assume inclusion and exclusion of dividend income (see Table 6.7):

	With Dividend Income	Without Dividend Income	Difference
Federal individual income tax	$ 206	$ 7	$ 199
NJ individual income tax	76	5	71
Totals	$ 282	$ 12	$ 270

[3] Calculated combined federal and NJ corporation income tax rate.

117

TABLE 6.9   Example 2: Derivation of Effective Federal and State Tax on Dividend Income (in thousands)

	With C Corporation Dividend	Without C Corporation Dividend	Difference Amount	Difference Effective Tax Rate
Wages	$ 150	$ 150		
C Corporation dividend	984	—		
Total income and adjusted gross income	1,134	150		
Itemized Deductions				
Real estate taxes	30	30		
State income taxes	84	5		
Mortgage interest	50	50		
Subtotal	164	85		
3% AGI floor	(25)	—		
	139	85		
Personal exemptions	—	16		
Federal taxable income	$ 995	$ 49		
Total Income Taxes				
Federal [1]	$ 225	$ 7	$ 218	22.2%
State (NJ)	84	5	79	8.0%
Total	$ 309	$ 12	$ 297	30.2%
C Corporation dividend			$ 984	100.0%

Note: [1] Includes regular tax; alternative minimum tax; and high income HI, Medicare, and other taxes.

As noted in Table 6.9, if it is assumed that the dividend amount increases to $984,000 without any income retained (as compared with $897,000 with $60,000 of income retained), the dividend tax increases to $297,000 (as compared with $270,000). As more dividend income is taxed at the higher state rate (due to the progressivity of New Jersey state income taxes), the state dividend tax rate and the total dividend taxes as a percent of dividend income increase.

In Table 6.10, the C corporation tax is calculated using the facts assumed in Table 6.9.

TABLE 6.10 Example 2: Derivation of Effective C Corporation Tax (in thousands)

	Actual PTE and Individual Tax Rates		Derivation of C Corporation Tax Rates	
Normalized pretax cash basis income	$ 1,200	100.0%	$ 1,200	100.0%
Entity-level PTE income tax on normalized pretax income	—	0.0%	—	0.0%
Corporation income before C corporation income taxes	1,200	100.0%	1,200	100.0%
C corporation taxes	—	0.0%	(216)	−18.0%
Available corporation earnings	$ 1,200	100.0%	$ 984	82.0%
Available corporation earnings	$ 1,200	100.0%	$ 984	82.0%
Pretax earnings retained	—	0.0%	—	0.0%
Distributable corporation earnings	$ 1,200	100.0%	$ 984	82.0%
Federal dividend taxes			$ 218	18.2%
NJ dividend taxes			79	6.6%
Effective federal individual income taxes	$ 415	34.6%		
Effective NJ individual income taxes	98	8.2%		
Total individual income taxes	$ 513	42.8%	$ 297	24.8%
Available after corporation and individual income taxes	$ 687	57.3%	$ 687	57.3%

(*continued*)

TABLE 6.10 (*Continued*)

Notes:

[1] Based on 2013 federal and NJ individual income tax rates.
Federal individual income taxes includes regular tax; alternative minimum tax; and high income HI, Medicare, and other taxes. See Table 6.5.

	With K-1 Income	Without K-1 Income	Difference
Federal individual income tax	$ 422	$ 7	$ 415
NJ individual income tax	103	5	98
Totals	$ 525	$ 12	$ 513

[2] Same assumptions as #1 above, except that instead of K-1 income we assume inclusion and exclusion of dividend income (see Table 6.9):

	With Dividend Income	Without Dividend Income	Difference
Federal individual income tax	$ 225	$ 7	$ 218
NJ individual income tax	84	5	79
Totals	$ 309	$ 12	$ 297

[3] Calculated combined federal and NJ corporation income tax rate.

As illustrated in the preceding tables, the C corporation income tax rate decreases to 18 percent without any income retained in the business (from 20.3% with 5% of PTI retained in the business). This reduction in C corporation income tax rates is due to the increase in the dividend tax as a percentage of distributable corporation income. These findings are consistent with our analysis earlier in this chapter, which indicates the lower the amount of income retained in a PTE, the lower the C corporation tax.

SUMMARY

When applying the MDMM, different inputs will yield different valuation conclusions. In my experience, the different valuation conclusions presented by plaintiff's and defendant's experts in a contested PTE valuation matter often result from differing inputs. The old adage, "garbage-in, garbage-out," definitely applies when calculating a business's value using the MDMM. This chapter provides guidance to valuation analysts in connection with the development of proper, supportable inputs to the MDMM, using approaches that will help to justify their PTE valuation conclusions, methodology, and assumptions.

CHAPTER 7

Income Approach and Investment Value

Investment value is defined for real estate transactions as "the specific value of an investment to a particular investor or class of investors based on individual investment requirements; distinguished from market value, which is impersonal and detached."[1] This definition of investment value also holds true for business ownership interests.

Individual investment requirements may be different depending on the buyer. Keeping with our real estate analogy, different home buyers will have different priorities. Buyer priorities may include economic status of a community, safety/crime issues, access to mass transportation or highway, quality of school system, ethnic mix/diversity, houses of worship, shopping, restaurants, appearance of neighborhood, trends in home values, and other non-controllable factors. Selecting a particular home in a neighborhood often involves deciding on busy/quiet street, condition of home (tear-down versus fix-up versus move-in condition), curb appeal, home features (number of bedrooms, size of kitchen, property size), and location on the street (corner home, cul-de-sac).

The process of choosing an industry and company to invest in is similar to the process of buying a home. An informed buyer will evaluate non controllable factors, such as expectations of the economic, technological, life cycle, and other risk factors associated with a target industry; general economic conditions; access to labor, transportation, customers, suppliers, and capital; barriers of entry (and exit) from a particular industry; and other factors. Company-specific factors include expected economic returns (i.e., synergistic benefits, elimination of a competitor, return on investment); intangible value such as customer list, product mix, labor force in place, trademarks, research

---

[1]*The Dictionary of Real Estate Appraisal*, 3rd ed. (Appraisal Institute: Chicago, 1993), p. 190.

and development, and so on; appreciated tangible assets (i.e., real estate); and emotional ties to a target (i.e., favorite product, sports team, family ties).

Investment value can be measured by the risk-adjusted discounted net cash flow that a particular investor would expect a company to earn in the way that a particular investor would operate it. For a potential acquirer, investment value should include the standalone value of the subject company plus any revenue increases or cost savings that the buyer would expect to achieve as a result of the synergies between the companies.[2]

MEASURING INVESTMENT VALUE

The process of measuring investment value under the income approach is similar to the process of measuring value to the holder under the income approach. Whether applying the capitalization of earnings method or the discounted cash flows method, the valuation analyst will need to quantify the following key variables:

1. Normalized pretax income (to either equity or invested capital) and income retained in the business (used to convert pretax income to pretax cash flows)
2. Applicable income taxes
3. Discount/capitalization rates

A discussion of each of the three factors impacting investment value under the income approach follows.

Normalized Pretax Income and Income Retained in the Business

As noted, different buyers of businesses (or business interests) have different motivations. When measuring investment value to a particular buyer, it is important to understand the motivations, plans, benchmarks, budgets/projections/forecasts, planned investment holding period, and so on, of the buyer. This holds true whether valuing a controlling or noncontrolling interest. Although a buyer of a controlling interest would typically have a greater ability to affect decision making and the future cash flows of a business ownership interest, this is not always the case. In certain situations, a noncontrolling investor may also have significant influence (e.g., angel investors,

---

[2]Jay Fishman, Shannon Pratt, and William Morrison, *Standards of Value: Theory and Applications* (Hoboken, NJ: John Wiley & Sons, 2007).

venture capital, investment bankers, or other strategic investors). Case-specific facts and circumstances will dictate the impact of the investor on normalized pretax income of the subject interest.

The valuation analyst must also consider the impact of the purchase of a business ownership interest on the acquirer. For example, if acquiring certain key products, technologies, personnel, trademarks, research and development, and other assets yields synergistic benefits to the acquirer's business, such benefits also need to be considered as part of investment value. Enhanced operational efficiencies should also be considered, for example, where redundant costs (i.e., personnel, rent, and occupancy costs) can be eliminated. Venture capital investors often focus on certain industries; pick and choose seemingly winning products, personnel, and so on from their portfolio of companies; and then consolidate/combine/reconfigure the ownership structures of their investments to create a single entity with greater value than the sum of the individual companies precombination. Hence, investment value and normalized pretax cash flows may be vastly different depending on the facts and circumstances of the hypothetical/identified buyer.

Income Taxes

The income tax expense associated with the normalized pretax income of the acquired ownership interest must also be considered. Accordingly, the valuation analyst must have an informed understanding of the likely acquirer of the subject ownership interest under the investment value assumption. In some instances, the likely purchaser may be an owner/manager; in other instances, a large privately/publicly held company may be the purchaser. Facts and circumstances will dictate who the likely purchaser will be.

If the subject interest expects to enjoy the benefits of PTE status after the transaction, then the MDMM methodology described in Chapters 5 and 6 can be employed. If the subject interest is not expected to provide the successor owner the benefits of PTE status post-acquisition, then a "with and without" analysis with respect to the tax cost to the acquirer, assuming C corporation income tax rates, can be employed.

Discount/Capitalization Rates

The acquirer's cost of debt and equity capital may be different from (or similar to) the subject business. Facts and circumstances will dictate if there is a difference, as well as the amount of such difference.

Let's consider the following example, where the acquirer is a large, publicly owned company with access to equity and debt markets and has depth of management, a diversified product mix, and so forth. This buyer will likely have a lower cost of debt and equity capital than a small, privately owned PTE because the PTE may have limited access to debt and equity capital; have a less diversified product line; be dependent on a few officers, customers, and suppliers; be more geographically concentrated, and so forth. The factors presented for the PTE in this example increase the riskiness and cost of debt and equity of the privately owned PTE. Accordingly, in this example, the PTE's discount/capitalization rates may be greater than the buyer's discount/capitalization rates.

Another example to consider is where an individual is the likely buyer and will be actively involved on a day-to-day basis in the operation of the business (similar to the seller of the business). The successor owner in this instance will likely have risk factors that are very similar to the predecessor owner. In this example, the cost of debt and equity capital of the buyer may approximate that of the seller.

DEAL STRUCTURE

Business transactions are structured to reflect the interests and concerns of the respective parties. In some instances, the acquirer purchases the net assets of a target. Such assets would (1) include those assets desired by the acquirer and (2) exclude assets not wanting to be sold by the current owner. For example, personal or nonoperating assets can be excluded from an asset sale. Ownership interests in subsidiary companies, intangible assets, and past-due accounts receivable are other examples of assets that may be excluded from an asset sale.

Alternatively, the acquirer can purchase the PTE's equity ownership interests. This approach transfers all assets, liabilities, commitments, and contingencies from seller to buyer. Different income tax and business consequences may result from purchasing net assets rather than equity. A discussion of these different consequences follows.

Purchasing Assets

When purchasing assets, the governing legal document should specify the purchase price of each asset acquired (including goodwill and other intangible assets) and liabilities assumed. A buyer may have more legal protection against the business's "sins of the past" when buying assets. Such past sins may include unpaid payroll tax liabilities and ongoing litigation, which should remain the seller's problems.

One tax advantage associated with purchasing assets rather than equity interests is that the acquirer's tax basis is "stepped up" to the purchase price.

As a result, accounts receivable, inventory, and other assets, when converted to cash, generate no taxable income to the extent of the buyer's purchase price. Additional depreciation expense can be recognized on property and equipment having a stepped-up tax basis. For income tax reporting purposes, goodwill can be recognized, amortized, and deducted on a straight-line basis over a 15-year period. The ability to deduct goodwill and other intangible asset amortization expenses can be especially meaningful and could impact the economics of a transaction.

How material is the income tax benefit of the goodwill deduction when purchasing an ownership interest in a LLC or partnership? Table 7.1 presents a calculation of the present value (assumed discount rate of 20%) of the buyer's income tax benefit (assumed combined federal and state effective tax rate of 40%) of goodwill ($150,000).[3]

TABLE 7.1 Tax Benefit of Deducting Goodwill Amortization

Year	Annual Tax Deduction	Effective Tax Rate	Annual Benefit of Tax Deduction	20% Discount Rate Factor	Present Value Benefit of Goodwill Amortization Tax Deduction	
					Annual	Cumulative
1	$ 10,000	40%	$ 4,000	0.9129	$ 3,651	$ 3,651
2	10,000	40%	4,000	0.7607	3,043	6,694
3	10,000	40%	4,000	0.6339	2,536	9,230
4	10,000	40%	4,000	0.5283	2,113	11,343
5	10,000	40%	4,000	0.4402	1,761	13,104
6	10,000	40%	4,000	0.3669	1,467	14,572
7	10,000	40%	4,000	0.3057	1,223	15,795
8	10,000	40%	4,000	0.2548	1,019	16,814
9	10,000	40%	4,000	0.2123	849	17,663
10	10,000	40%	4,000	0.1769	708	18,370
11	10,000	40%	4,000	0.1474	590	18,960
12	10,000	40%	4,000	0.1229	491	19,452
13	10,000	40%	4,000	0.1024	410	19,861
14	10,000	40%	4,000	0.0853	341	20,202
15	10,000	40%	4,000	0.0711	284	20,487
	$ 150,000		$ 60,000		$ 20,487	
	100.0%		40.0%		13.7%	

---

[3]Eric J. Barr, "Are Limited Liability Companies Worth More Than S Corporations?," *Business Valuation Update* 2, no. 3 (Dec. 2012).

TABLE 7.2 Investor Goodwill Recoupment Analysis

Tax Rates	Discount Rates					
	10%	15%	20%	25%	30%	35%
20%	10.6%	8.4%	6.8%	5.8%	5.0%	4.4%
25%	13.3%	10.5%	8.5%	7.2%	6.2%	5.5%
30%	16.0%	12.5%	10.2%	8.6%	7.5%	6.6%
35%	18.6%	14.6%	12.0%	10.1%	8.7%	7.7%
40%	21.3%	16.7%	13.7%	11.5%	9.9%	8.8%
45%	23.9%	18.8%	15.4%	12.9%	11.2%	9.8%
50%	26.6%	20.9%	17.1%	14.4%	12.4%	10.9%
55%	29.3%	23.0%	18.8%	15.8%	13.7%	12.0%
60%	31.9%	25.1%	20.5%	17.3%	14.9%	13.1%

Table 7.1 indicates that over 15 years, an investor recoups 13.7 percent of their investment in goodwill because of tax benefits (using a 40% effective combined federal and state income tax rate and a discount rate of 20%).[4]

Table 7.2 indicates the investor's recoupment percentage assuming different (1) effective combined federal and state income tax rates, and (2) discount rates. As expected, the recoupment percentage increases when (1) the effective combined federal and state income tax rate increases, or (2) the discount rate decreases.[5]

The formula to calculate the present value of the tax benefit associated with the goodwill amortization deduction is as follows:[6]

$$\sum_{i=1}^{15} \frac{GW \times Tr \times 1/15}{(1+K)^i}$$

where:

GW = Goodwill amount
Tr = Combined effective federal and state income tax rate
K = Discount rate

---

[4]Eric J. Barr, "Are Limited Liability Companies Worth More Than S Corporations?," *Business Valuation Update* 2, no. 3 (Dec. 2012).
[5]Ibid., no. 4 (Dec. 2012).
[6]Ibid., no. 3 (Dec. 2012).

The tax deduction benefit of amortizing goodwill and other intangible assets can substantially decrease the after-tax purchase cost of net assets.

Purchasing Equity

Purchasing the equity of a PTE involves purchasing (1) S corporation common stock, (2) partnership interests (sometimes referred to as *units*), or (3) LLC member interests. The price paid for the equity ownership interest (buyer's outside basis) may exceed the owner/member/partner's equity of the acquired entity (company's inside tax basis). There could be a materially different tax result if the subject interest is an equity interest in an LLC or partnership compared to an S corporation or a C corporation. Where the subject interest is an equity ownership interest in an LLC or partnership, the acquirer could make an election under IRC Section 754.[7] This election would enable the acquirer to record an adjustment to the internal tax basis of the assets acquired based on the purchase price. The purchaser would then be able to allocate the purchase price to each of the assets and liabilities acquired, including goodwill.

Where the interest being sold is the capital stock of an S corporation or a C corporation, no such election is available without adverse tax consequences. Accordingly, the taxable basis of the assets of the acquired company (inside basis) remains unchanged, and the buyer does not receive any immediate tax benefit from the goodwill acquired.[8]

When purchasing the equity of a PTE, the aforementioned "sins of the past" remain with the entity acquired. Accordingly, a buyer may be assuming additional risks when purchasing equity that are avoided when purchasing assets.

Complex Capital Structures

Sometimes ownership interests in partnerships and LLCs are acquired that provide special allocations of income and expense. Such special allocations can be based on lines of business, revenue/net income thresholds, preferred returns, participation rights, conversion features, and so on. In some respects,

---

[7]For tax reporting purposes, purchasing the equity of a sole proprietorship is no different from buying net assets.

[8]The buyer of an S corporation or a C corporation will have an outside basis that is greater than the inside basis of the company. Ultimately, such excess basis will provide a tax benefit in the form of a lower capital gain (or higher capital loss) on disposal of the business; Eric J. Barr, "Are Limited Liability Companies Worth More Than S Corporations?," *Business Valuation Update* 2, no. 3 (Dec. 2012).

complex partner/member ownership interests may be similar to the rights of preferred shareholders of C corporations. In other instances, special ownership interests can be used to facilitate a combination/joint venture of different PTEs. Greater rights, benefits, and value can be ascribed to certain noncontrolling ownership interests in a PTE with a complex capital structure than to other noncontrolling interests. A discussion of the issues associated with valuating ownership interests in companies with complex capital structures is featured in Chapter 13 of this book.

CHAPTER 8

Income Approach and Fair Market Value

In Chapter 1, *fair market value* (*FMV*) was defined as

> [t]he price at which the property would change hands between a willing buyer and a willing seller when the former is not under any compulsion to buy and the latter is not under any compulsion to sell, both parties having reasonable knowledge of relevant facts. Court decisions frequently state in addition that the hypothetical buyer and sell are assumed to be able, as well as willing, to trade and to be well informed about the property and concerning the market for such property.[1]

This definition can be illustrated in Chart 8.1, where the balance point of the two parties on the seesaw is FMV.

CHARACTERISTICS OF FMV

FMV is distinguishable in many respects from value to the holder and value to the buyer:

1. FMV assumes a willing buyer and a willing seller, both under no compulsion to effect a transaction; value to the holder and value to the buyer do not assume a lack of compulsion.

---

[1]Rev. Rul. 59–60, 1959-1 C.B. 2031, § 2.02 (as defined in § 20.2031-1(b) of the Estate Tax Regulations (81.10 of the Estate Tax Regulations 105) and § 25.2512-1 of the Gift Tax Regulations (section 86.19 of the Gift Tax Regulations 108).

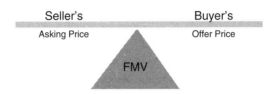

CHART 8.1 Fair Market Value Is the Balance Point

2. FMV assumes hypothetical parties to a transaction; neither value to the holder nor value to the buyer assumes hypothetical parties. In fact, in many instances under value to the holder and value to the buyer, the parties are known.
3. FMV assumes reasonable knowledge of relevant facts; value to the holder and value to the buyer do not require this assumption.
4. FMV is defined as a price; neither value to the holder nor value to the buyer is defined as a price. Value and price are different. Warren Buffett has sagely noted that "price is what you pay, value is what you get."[2] Anyone paying for poorly performed automobile repairs understands the difference between price and value.
5. Under FMV, the perspectives of two parties must be considered: the hypothetical seller and the hypothetical buyer. Under value to the holder and value to the buyer, only one perspective is considered.

Let's analyze the perspectives of the two parties under FMV: the hypothetical seller and the hypothetical buyer.

Value to the Hypothetical Seller

The informed hypothetical holder, under no compulsion to sell, would not agree to a price that was less than the value of the subject interest in the hands of the seller. Why would a business owner with an asset worth $10 million, fully informed and under no compulsion to sell, dispose of that asset for less than $10 million? Therefore, the floor value under FMV is the value of the subject interest to the hypothetical holder.

Chapters 5 and 6 discussed the factors that need to be considered under the MDMM in order to determine a PTE's value to the holder. Once value to the hypothetical holder is determined, the floor value on the left side of the seesaw is known.

---

[2]Warren Buffett, "About Investing: Know the Difference Between Price and Value," in Janet Lowe, *Warren Buffett Speaks: Wit and Wisdom from the World's Greatest Investor* (Hoboken, NJ: John Wiley & Sons, 2007).

Value to the Hypothetical Buyer

The informed hypothetical buyer, under no compulsion to purchase the subject interest, would not agree to a price that was more than the value of the subject interest in the hands of the buyer. Why would a fully informed investor, under no compulsion to buy, pay $15 million for an asset that was only worth $10 million? It is therefore unrealistic to assume that the ceiling value under FMV can be more than investment value to the hypothetical buyer of the subject interest.

Chapter 7 discussed that in order to determine a PTE's investment value, it is necessary to determine whether assets or equity are to be purchased and if the subject business will continue to enjoy the benefits of PTE status after the proposed transaction. In addition, Chapter 7 discussed the need to quantify the following:

1. Pretax cash flows of the subject interest to the buyer post-transaction should be determined. This amount may be less than, equal to, or more than normalized historical cash flows of the seller, depending on the degree of control over operations exercisable by the subject interest, as well as other factors.
2. If the acquirer is assumed to enjoy the benefits of the PTE status of the subject interest, then the buyer's individual income and dividend tax expense and C corporation income tax cost should be quantified, and the MDMM should be applied. It should *not* be automatically assumed that the buyer's marginal income and dividend tax rates will be the same as the holder's rates.
3. If the acquirer will not enjoy the benefits of the PTE status of the subject interest, then the buyer's incremental C corporation income taxes as a result of the transaction should be quantified and utilized in connection with the valuation of the subject interest.
4. The buyer's discount/capitalization rate must be determined to complete the valuation calculation.

Each of these factors can change materially on a case-by-case basis, where different facts and circumstances may apply. None, some, or all of these factors (to a buyer) may match the factors utilized in connection with the value to the hypothetical holder. There may be instances, for example, where (1) the value resulting from lower cash flows is offset by lower capitalization rates, (2) higher tax-affecting adjustments are offset by lower capitalization rates, or (3) greater cash flows are offset by higher tax-affecting adjustments. Once value to the buyer is determined, the ceiling value on the right side of the seesaw is known.

DETERMINING FMV

Once the floor and ceiling values have been determined, the next step is to select the price (or range of prices) that represents FMV. This analysis requires consideration of different factors, including the following:

1. **The supply of alternative investment opportunities as of the valuation date.** There may be many comparable business ownership interests (for example, pizza restaurants, gas stations, hardware stores, certified public accounting firms) available for sale at the valuation date. This lowers the negotiating leverage of the holder/seller, and vice versa if there are fewer comparable business ownership interests for sale.
2. **The number of qualified buyers seeking to make an investment in the subject interest as of the valuation date.** This may also be impacted by general economic and/or industry conditions, the availability of private equity or debt financing, exchange rates, and other factors. The more qualified buyers, the greater the negotiating leverage of the holder/seller, and vice versa.
3. **Trends in pricing of similar ownership interests.** A pattern of increasing values and prices of companies in a particular industry may increase demand for and, ultimately, the price realized in connection with a transaction, and vice versa.

Once these and other relevant factors are analyzed and the relative negotiating leverage of each party determined, the valuation analyst can make an informed decision as to FMV. A conclusion about FMV can be a specific price or a range of prices.

There are valuation analysts who mix and match (1) cash flows, (2) tax rates, and (3) discount/capitalization rates of sellers and buyers to determine FMV. For example, the cash flows of the seller and the income tax rate and capitalization rate of the buyer may be utilized to determine FMV under the income approach. Although there may be instances where this process coincidentally achieves the proper result (like a broken clock that is correct twice a day), it is conceptually inconsistent with the definition of FMV articulated earlier.

There are also some business appraisers who do not tax-affect PTE earnings under FMV for the reasons set forth in Chapter 5. There are other business appraisers who do not tax affect PTE earnings because of their interpretation of different court decisions in connection with estate and gift valuations under the FMV standard of value. These cases are analyzed in Chapter 9.

EXAMPLE OF FAILING TO CONSIDER FLOOR AND CEILING VALUES

The following is a case that illustrates the consequences of failing to consider floor and ceiling values, and the reconciliation of these two values, in connection with a determination of the FMV of a business ownership interest.

This example involved the 2011–2012 valuation of a controlling ownership interest in a privately held company. The need for the valuation resulted from the dissolution of a lengthy marriage. The couple had accumulated a substantial marital estate, including a controlling interest in the subject company. Both husband and wife worked in the business.

The subject company was purchased by the couple for $355 million in 2004. Since that time, annual revenues grew from approximately $150 million in 2004 to $246 million in 2011, an increase of 64 percent over a seven-year period (or an average revenue growth of $14 million per year). Operating income grew from (negative $19 million) in 2004 to positive $33 million in 2011, an average annual increase of approximately $7.4 million. Such growth justified an increase in value from 2004 through 2011, but how much? Plus, the company had significant intangible value attributable to its brand and location; it also had significant value due to its real property.[3]

As it turns out, there was an independent appraisal of the company that was reported in *Forbes* magazine. Based on its analysis of all relevant factors, including eight comparable transactions of similar companies in the same business, *Forbes* reported that the subject company had a fair market value of $800 million in 2011. The $800 million was approximately double the $399 million value it had estimated for the subject company back in 2004 and approximately 225 percent of its original purchase price.[4]

By now, you may have already guessed that the divorcing couple is Frank and Jamie McCourt, and the subject company is the Los Angeles Dodgers.

At $800 million, reported *Forbes*, the Dodgers were the third most valuable baseball franchise in 2011, right behind the New York Yankees and Boston Red Sox.[5]

As events unfolded in 2011, the Dodgers and the McCourts were experiencing financial difficulties. The McCourts had lived a very expensive, well-publicized lifestyle. They had withdrawn funds from the Dodgers,

---

[3]MLB Team Values: The Business of Baseball, *Forbes*, http://www.forbes.com/lists/2011/33/baseball-valuations-11_Los Angeles Dodgers-33867.
[4]Ibid.
[5]Ibid.

causing the Dodgers to go deeply into debt. Ultimately, there was a June 2011 bankruptcy filing for the Dodgers, and Major League Baseball took control of the team.[6]

In October 2011, Mrs. McCourt entered into a final divorce settlement agreement with her husband. It was reported that she settled for a cash payment of $130 million. Her decision to accept this cash settlement was applauded by legal professionals. "I think this may be a strategically sensible decision for her," said Scott Altman, a law professor at the University of Southern California. "If Frank McCourt gets $130 million out of bankruptcy, it's hers. It reduces her risk because she doesn't have to share proceeds from the bankruptcy case."[7]

After settling with his wife, Frank McCourt agreed to sell the Dodgers as a result of an agreement reached with Major League Baseball. A process was put in place to auction the team to the highest bidder.[8]

The potential buyers of the Dodgers knew what had been reported by *Forbes*. But when the potential buyers performed their analyses, their findings were astonishingly different—apparently there was hidden value associated with the renewal of television contracts, which had been previously overlooked. Blackstone Group was the investment bank that handled the transaction. Blackstone received three bids: two competing bids in the range of $1.5 billion, and the winning bid of $2.15 billion received in March 2012. The bankrupt Dodgers sold for $2.15 billion! The previous record sale for a major league baseball team was $845 million in 2009, for the Chicago Cubs.[9]

What lessons can we learn from this? I offer the following:

1. Understand the financial motivations of the seller and the buyer of the subject interest.
2. Consider all applicable valuation approaches and methodologies.
3. Consider the number of bona fide potential buyers.
4. Consider the negotiating leverage of buyer(s) and seller.

---

[6]Ken Gurnick and Barry M. Bloom, "Dodgers File for Bankruptcy Protection," June 27, 2011. http://losangeles.dodgers.mlb.com/news/article.jsp?ymd=20110627&content_id=21068838&c_id=la.

[7]*Huffington Post*, "McCourt Divorce Settlement: Jamie No Longer Wants Control of the Dodgers," October 18, 2011, http://www.huffingtonpost.com/2011/10/17/mccourt-divorce-settlemen_n_1015600.html.

[8]Scott Kendrick, "Dodgers Fans Can Finally Celebrate: McCourt Will Sell Team," SeeNews Online, November 2, 2011, http://seenews.net/dodgers-fans-can-finally-celebrate-mccourt-will-sell-team.

[9]Matthew Futterman, "$2 Billion Dodgers Price Tag Shatters Records," *Wall Street Journal*, March 29, 2012, http://online.wsj.com/new/articles/SB10001424052702303404704577308483250633906.

5. If you choose not to incorporate the facts and circumstances that may cause the value to a prospective buyer to exceed value to the holder, be prepared to justify your reasoning. This is especially true when the appraiser's going-concern premise of value applies highest and best use.

These steps may tend to blur the line between investment value and fair market value. However, they may be necessary if you wish to avoid the valuation variances that occurred in the 2012 sale of the Los Angeles Dodgers.

CHAPTER 9

Fair Market Value Court Decisions

Business appraisers wisely seek guidance from the courts and other authoritative sources when addressing the PTE conundrum. However, the courts have issued what appears to be conflicting opinions when addressing the issue of tax-affecting PTEs. Further confusing the issue, the IRS has a nonauthoritative guide that accepts tax affecting, yet it has also litigated for *not* tax affecting. What are the lessons to be learned from court decisions and the IRS?

I believe that the starting point for relying on any decision of the court is gaining a proper interpretation of the facts and circumstances impacting the case and the court's reasoning and conclusions in each situation. Let's analyze the IRS's position and the courts' decisions with respect to several cases involving the fair market value standard of value.

Each year, the television networks endlessly promote the NCAA basketball tournament's buildup to the Sweet Sixteen, the Elite Eight, and the Final Four. The IRS is also a promoter, although in the tax arena instead of the basketball arena; it promotes and has often referred to six cases in which the courts have applied a 0 percent tax rate when valuing an ownership interest in a PTE. The six cases are *Gross v. Commissioner*,[1] *Estate of Heck v. Commissioner*,[2] *Wall v. Commissioner*,[3] *Estate of Adams v. Commissioner*,[4]

---

[1]T.C.M. 1999-254, 78 T.C.M. (CCH) 201, T.C.M. (RIA) para. 99,254, 1999 Tax Ct. LEXIS 290 (July 29, 1999). The U.S. Court of Appeals affirmed the decision of the Tax Court, 272 F.3d 333 (6th Cir. 2001).
[2]T.C.M. 2002-34, 83 T.C.M. (CCH) 1181, T.C.M. (RIA) para. 54,639, 2002 Tax Ct. LEXIS 38 (February 5, 2002).
[3]T.C.M. 2001-75, 81 T.C.M. (CCH) 1425, 2001 Tax Ct. LEXIS 97 (March 27, 2001).
[4]T.C.M. 2002-80, 83 T.C.M (CCH) 1421, T.C.M. (RIA) para. 54,696, 2002 Tax Ct. LEXIS 84 (March 28, 2002).

TABLE 9.1   *IRS Data Book*, Table 2—Summary of Number of Returns (in thousands)

Year	Total	Estate Tax	Gift Tax
2012	276	27	249
2011	219	11	208
2010	259	29	230
2009	292	47	245
2008	298	46	252
2007	303	50	253
2006	314	58	256
2005	343	66	277
2004	322	73	249
2003	379	92	287
Totals	3,005	499	2,506

Robert Dallas v. Commissioner,[5] and *Gallagher v. Commissioner*.[6] These six cases represent a limited subset of the many estate and gift tax returns that involve the valuation of PTE ownership interests.[7]

NUMBER OF FEDERAL ESTATE AND GIFT TAX RETURNS

As noted in Table 9.1, the IRS has had more than three million estate and gift tax returns from which to select cases for audit during the 10 years ended 2012.[8]

Let's examine the fact patterns that existed in the previously referenced six cases that caused the IRS to challenge the tax-affecting approaches of the taxpayer. In particular, let's analyze the following:

1. Purpose of valuation
2. Standard of value
3. Controlling versus noncontrolling (minority) interest
4. Date of valuation

---

[5] T.C.M. 2006-212, 2006 WL 2792684 (T.C. September 28, 2006).
[6] T.C.M. 2011-146 (June 28, 2011).
[7] The valuation consultant may also consider other relevant case law, and where appropriate, consult with counsel regarding the interpretation of such case law and statutes.
[8] Table 9.1 contains data from the 2003–2012 annual *IRS Data Books*, Table 2, Number of Returns Filed, by Type of Return, available at www.irs.gov.

5. Date of court's decision
6. Form of PTE
7. Amount of annual taxable income versus annual distributions
8. Valuation approach
9. Expectation, or lack thereof, that the business entity would be sold
10. Expectation, or lack thereof, that the business entity would lose its status as a PTE

GROSS V. COMMISSIONER[9]

Gross involved the valuation of 1992 gifts of less than 1 percent of the common stock of an S corporation, Pepsi Cola Bottlers, Inc. (G&J), to the children of G&J's owners. The standard of value was fair market value on the date that the gift was made.[10]

G&J's predecessor entity was formed in the 1920s by two married couples. The business was incorporated in 1969 and elected S corporation status in 1982. There were no plans to sell the company or change its S corporation status. In fact, the shareholders' agreement contained provisions restricting the transfer of any ownership interests that jeopardized the S corporation status of G&J. By the time of the gifts in 1992, the founders were deceased and ownership of G&J had passed through, 50 percent to each founders' relatives.[11]

On the date of the gift, "G&J was the third largest independent bottler of Pepsi-Cola products [and] . . . had an exclusive franchise agreement to distribute these products within several geographic territories." The company was highly profitable and from 1988 to 1992, "enjoy[ing] steady increases in its operational income, total income, and distribution to shareholders. In addition, G&J's shareholder distributions nearly totaled the company's entire income for each of these years."[12]

The taxpayer and the IRS both engaged experts that employed the income approach. The taxpayer's expert utilized a 40 percent income tax rate to tax-

---

[9]Portions of this case summary are from http://www.lexis.com/research/retrieve with respect to Walter L. Gross Jr. and Barbara H. Gross (9902239); Calvin C. Linnemann and Patricia G. Linnemann (99-2257), *Petitioners-Appellants v. Commissioner of Internal Revenue*, Respondent-Appellate; Nos. 99-2239/99-2257 U.S. Court of Appeals for the Sixth Circuit, 272 F.3d 333, 2001 U.S. Appellate LEXIS 24803, Federal Appendix 0405P (6th Cir.); 57 Federal Register Evidence Service (Callaghan) 1042. Argued October 27, 2000; decided and filed November 19, 2011.
[10]Treas. Reg. 25-2512-2(a).
[11]*Gross v. Commissioner*, 272 F.3d.
[12]Ibid.

TABLE 9.2   *Gross v. Commissioner*—Business Appraisers' Tax-Affecting
Assumptions

	Appraiser 1	Appraiser 2
Pretax income	100.0%	100.0%
Corporate tax rate	40.0%	0.0%
Available earnings	60.0%	100.0%

affect the earnings of G&J; the IRS's expert applied a 0 percent income tax rate.
The IRS's position was that the earnings of G&J should not be tax affected for
valuation purposes under the fair market value standard of value in the subject
instance.[13] Table 9.2 reflects the positions of the two experts.

The effect of these different positions is that one expert capitalized the
60 percent amount to derive his conclusion of value; the other expert capitalized the 100 percent amount, yielding a very substantial difference in value.

The taxpayer's expert claimed that a 40 percent tax-affecting adjustment
was appropriate for the following reasons:[14]

1. It was the generally accepted practice of business appraisal at that time.
2. "[T]he use of a 0% tax affect ha[d] not been published or submitted for peer review."
3. "[T]here are costs or trade-offs in electing S corporation status which tax affecting is intended to address." Examples of such trade-offs included the claim "that S corporations sacrifice growth opportunities and capital appreciation in exchange for current income."
4. "S corporation shareholders were at risk that the corporation might not distribute enough of its income . . . through dividends to cover the shareholders' tax obligations."
5. "S corporations [are] 'committed' to distributing enough income to [their] shareholders to cover their tax liabilities and this 'imbedded cost' must be recognized."
6. "[T]ax affecting was necessary in order to protect against the danger that an S corporation might lose its 'S' status."
7. "[T]ax affecting was necessary to compensate for the disadvantages G&J faced as an S corporation in raising capital."
8. "The IRS itself ha[d] implicitly endorsed the policy of tax affecting in valuing stock of S corporations. In support of this claim," two internal IRS documents were presented that "mention[ed] making adjustments for

---

[13]*Gross v. Commissioner*, 272 F.3d.
[14]Ibid.

taxes of S corporations. The *IRS Valuation Guide for Income, Estate and Gift Taxes: Valuation Training for Appeals Officers* states at pages 7–14: "S corporations lend themselves readily to valuation approaches comparable to those used in valuing closely held corporations. You need only adjust the earnings from the business to reflect estimated corporate income taxes that would have been payable had the Subchapter S election not been made." In addition, the *IRS Examination Technique Handbook* provides:

> If you are comparing a Subchapter S corporation to the stock of similar firms that are publicly traded, the net income of the former must be adjusted for income taxes using the corporate tax rates applicable for each year in question, and certain other items, such as salaries. These adjustments will avoid distortions when applying industry ratios such as price to earnings."

9. The IRS had previously accepted the 1988 tax affecting of gifts of G&J stock.
10. The IRS "should not have discretion to treat taxpayer in a manifestly unfair and inequitable manner, especially given the fact that the IRS ha[d] not adopted uniform rules or regulations banning tax affecting S corporations."

The appeals court rejected each of the arguments advanced by the taxpayer's expert because of case-specific facts and other reasons, as follows:[15]

1. The taxpayer's expert acknowledged under oath that (a) there was a growing controversy within the business appraisal community surrounding the issue of tax affecting at the time of the gift, and (b) if he had to value the gifted stock of G&J as of the date of trial, "he would give further consideration as to whether he would use the [same] method." The Commissioner argued that tax affecting was not the generally accepted practice within the business appraisal community at the time of the gift in 1992.
2. As the U.S. Supreme Court recognized in *Daubert v. Merrell Dow Pharmaceuticals, Inc.*, "in some instances well-grounded but innovative theories will not have been published. . . . Some propositions, moreover, are too particular, too new, or of too limited interest to be published. . . . The fact of publication (or lack thereof) in a peer reviewed journal thus will be a relevant, though not dispositive, consideration in assessing

---

[15]*Gross v. Commissioner*, 272 F.3d.

the scientific validity of a particular technique or methodology on which an opinion is premised."[16]

3. As a "theoretical matter" and "as a matter of economic theory," tax affecting was inappropriate to offset risks #3–6 cited by the taxpayer's expert.

4. "[T]he evidence on the record indicated that G&J distribute[d] substantially all of its income to the shareholders and found that this fact, combined with G&J's strong growth record[,] made it unlikely that the corporation would be unable to distribute sufficient income to cover shareholder tax liabilities."

5. "[I]t was illogical to tax affect an S corporation's income without facts or circumstances that established the likelihood that its S corporation status would be lost." Furthermore, there were "restrictive agreements [in place] that would preempt any transfers that would jeopardize G&J's S corporation status[,] and . . . there was no indication in the record that G&J planned to terminate this practice."

6. Any potential impediment to G&J's ability to raise capital should impact the company's cost of capital.

7. The IRS documents referenced by the taxpayer's expert were "intended for internal IRS use only," "designed specifically for training purposes only," and "[u]nder no circumstances [were to] be used or cited as authority for setting or sustaining a technical position." The taxpayer's expert acknowledged these limitations. (The court did acknowledge, however, that the IRS documents "reflect[ed] a certain acceptance of tax affecting as a valid method of valuation.")

8. Given the amount of time between the 1988 gifts and the 1992 gifts at issue, and in the absence of any specific regulation or policy that specifically approved tax affecting, it did not follow that its acceptance of tax affecting with respect to the 1988 gifts created a precedent for the 1992 gifts.

9. There was no evidence that the taxpayer was being treated in a manifestly unfair and inequitable manner.

The Commissioner's expert "testified that it would be unreasonable to subtract hypothetical corporate income taxes from G&J's projected future taxable income because the company did not (and was not expecting in the future to) pay any income taxes." The court accepted this testimony and applied a 0 percent tax-affecting adjustment.[17] There is no evidence in the

---

[16]509 U.S. 579, 593–94 (1993) (internal citation omitted by *Daubert* Court).
[17]*Gross*, 272 F.3d.

record that an alternative tax-affecting rate between 0 and 40 percent was considered.

ESTATE OF HECK V. COMMISSIONER

Heck involved the valuation of a minority equity ownership interest in F. Korbel & Brothers, Inc. (Korbel), an S corporation. The valuation was performed for estate tax reporting purposes, and the valuation date (the date of death, in this instance) was February 15, 1995. The standard of value applied to the subject interest was fair market value.[18]

The common stock of Korbel at the valuation date was held by the following:[19]

Decedent (Richie Heck)	630 shares	39.6%
Gary Heck	830 shares	52.2%
Trust for benefit of two grandchildren of decedent	130 shares	8.2%
Total	1,590 shares	100.0%

The business of Korbel began in 1860, and the corporate entity was formed in 1903. During 1986, Korbel elected to be taxed as an S corporation. As of the valuation date, Korbel produced champagne (70% of total sales), brandy (27% of total sales), and still wine (3% of total sales). Korbel was historically very profitable and generated revenues of $82,758,000 and net income of $11,955,000 in 1994. Korbel's December 31, 1994, audited balance sheet indicated shareholders' equity of $73,870,000. Korbel also had significant land holdings, of which "1,099 acres were not used in Korbel's business activities." Such land was valued at $2,000 per acre.[20]

Korbel had an agreement with Brown-Forman Corp. (Brown-Forman) that provided Brown-Forman exclusive worldwide distribution rights. This agreement also provided thus:

Right of First Refusal

In the event any member of the Heck family desires to sell his or her shares of stock in KORBEL to a person who is not a lineal descendant of ADOLF L. HECK [decedent's husband], he or she shall notify

---

[18]*Estate of Heck v. Commissioner*, T.C.M. 2002-34 (February 5, 2002).
[19]Ibid.
[20]Ibid.

BROWN-FORMAN, in writing, giving the name of the prospective purchaser, a copy of the offer to purchase, the number of shares and the price per share. BROWN-FORMAN shall have thirty (30) days from receipt of such notice to elect to purchase and pay for the said stock at the price stated for cash. If BROWN-FORMAN does not purchase such stock within said 30 day period, it may be sold to the stated person at the stated price without any further obligation to BROWN-FORMAN, meaning that BROWN-FORMAN shall not have any further right to purchase any of the KORBEL stock sold. If KORBEL has a prospective purchaser for 50% or more of KORBEL stock who is not a lineal descendant of ADOLF L. HECK and BROWN-FORMAN does not exercise its prior right to purchase said stock, then BROWN-FORMAN shall have no further first right of refusal to buy that stock of Korbel at any time.[21]

The taxpayer's expert and the Commissioner's expert both acknowledged that the presence of this agreement and the inability of a purchaser of decedent's minority interest to influence dividend distributions, which would be at the discretion of the controlling shareholder, reduced the value of the subject interest. Such reductions in value were incorporated into each expert's discounts for lack of control and lack of marketability.[22]

The two experts disagreed over many issues in connection with the valuation of the decedent's equity ownership interest in Korbel. Such differences of opinion included the applicability of the market approach, assumptions incorporated into the discounted cash flow analysis, discounts for lack of control and marketability. However, both experts agreed that the cash flows to equity derived from their respective discounted cash flow analyses should not be tax affected for federal income tax reporting purposes;[23] hence, there was no contesting of this particular issue for the court to decide.

WALL V. COMMISSIONER

Prior to 1992, John E. Wall owned 100 percent of the common stock of Demco, Inc., an S corporation, (i.e., Mr. Wall "owned all 1,200 issued and outstanding shares of Demco's voting common stock and all 12,000 issued and outstanding shares of Demco's nonvoting stock"). On January 1, 1992, gifts of shares of Demco nonvoting common stock were made to 20

---

[21] *Estate of Heck v. Commissioner*, T.C.M. 2002-34 (February 5, 2002).
[22] Ibid.
[23] Ibid.

irrevocable trusts; such gifts were attributed 50 percent to Mr. Wall and 50 percent to Mr. Wall's wife. The 20 irrevocable trusts consisted of two irrevocable trusts for each of Mr. and Mrs. Wall's 10 children: one trust was known as an "annual exclusion" trust, and one was known as a "nonvoting stock" trust.[24]

The gifts consisted of 443 shares of "Demco nonvoting . . . stock to each of the annual exclusion trusts and 495 shares of . . . Demco non-voting . . . stock to each of the nonvoting stock trusts." In total, 9,380 shares of nonvoting stock (78.17% of the nonvoting common stock, or 71.06% of all common stock) were gifted. After the gifts, Mr. Wall owned 1,200 shares (100%) of Demco's voting common stock and 2,620 shares (21.83%) of Demco's nonvoting common stock. Even though Mr. Wall's retained ownership interest in all of Demco's common stock was only 28.94 percent, he maintained control of Demco through his ownership of 100 percent of Demco's voting stock.[25]

"Demco is a direct mail distributor and manufacturer of office supplies, furniture, and accessories. . . . Demco started [its] business in 1906 as part of the Democrat Printing Company of Madison, Wisconsin." By 1978, Demco was a subsidiary of a publicly owned company. In 1978, Demco's management (including Mr. Wall, who was then president and chief executive officer of Demco) acquired Demco's stock in a leveraged buyout. There were six transactions in Demco common stock that occurred between 1978 and the gifts in 1992. Of the six transactions, three occurred more than five years before the date of the gift, and three occurred more than two years before the date of the gift and involved the redemption of stock from Demco employees. The redemption price for each of the redemption transactions was determined through individual negotiations. "The redemption price actually paid was only slightly higher than [the] book value" of the stock at the time of the transaction, which was the price pursuant to the buy–sell agreement. Demco's capital stock "before the redemptions consisted of 1,800 shares of voting common stock," of which 600 voting shares were redeemed. Hence, each stock redemption involved noncontrolling, nonmarketable ownership interests.[26]

In connection with the valuation of the ownership interests gifted by Mr. Wall, Mr. Wall's expert applied a 34 percent income tax rate as a normalization adjustment. The 34 percent income tax rate was based on Demco's average income from 1987 to 1992. Mr. Wall's valuation expert argued for a tax-affecting normalization adjustment because (1) "many potential buyers

---

[24] *Wall v. Commissioner*, T.C.M. 2001-75 (March 27, 2001).
[25] Ibid.
[26] Ibid.

of S corporations are C corporations," and (2) a C corporation would be unable to maintain the S corporation status of Demco following an acquisition. Accordingly, the fair market value of the gifted interests should be tax affected using C corporation tax rates.[27]

The valuation experts for Mr. Wall and the commissioner both employed the income approach and the market approach to produce their conclusions of value. However, as noted in the following quoted text, the court identified problems with both experts' application of the income approach and put little weight on it:

> Ms. Walker [Mr. Wall's expert] testified that in theory, income-based approaches should produce more accurate determinations of value, because they attempt to value directly the future income streams flowing from an investment. She also testified, however, that many assumptions must be made to employ such approaches and the results are highly sensitive to the assumptions used. Most importantly, if the subject company's future income is unpredictable, then income-based methods will produce inaccurate appraisals of the company's value.
>
> We conclude that as of the date of the gifts, it was very difficult to predict Demco's future income. It appears that as of that date Demco's management had predicted only 1 year of future results. Due to the lack of a long-range forecast, Ms. Walker did not even attempt to predict Demco's future revenues. Instead, she used an average of Demco's historical and forecasted results to create a measure she described as Demco's "normalized" free cash-flow, and assumed this would grow at a constant rate. In this connection, we note that one of the leading treatises on business valuations cautions that historical averages or pure extrapolations from those averages are usually inadequate bases for an income-based analysis; an analyst should use such averages only if she can explain why they are a reasonable proxy for future expectations. Given the fluctuations in Demco's net income, the difficulties being experienced by Demco's major customer groups, and the unsettled economic conditions around the time of the gifts, it appears less likely than usual that Demco's past results could have served to predict its future results. We also note that Ms. Walker's original report relied entirely on a market-based approach; her revised report added an income-based approach

---

[27] *Wall v. Commissioner*, T.C.M. 2001-75 (March 27, 2001). Mr. Wall's valuation expert testified that appraisers disagree on whether it is appropriate to tax affect the income of an S corporation.

only in response to respondent's criticism of her original report. For all these reasons, we conclude that Ms. Walker's income-based approach is entitled to little weight.

Although Mr. Schroeder[28] at least attempted to predict Demco's future income, his income-based analysis suffers from the same flaws as Ms. Walker's. Mr. Schroeder's predictions, like Ms. Walker's extrapolations, were based to a great extent on Demco's average past performance. In addition, Mr. Schroeder did not explain or justify very well either his assumptions about future changes in Demco's performance or his choice of discount rates. We also note that although Ms. Walker had little criticism of Mr. Schroeder's guideline company approach—or couched that criticism in terms of reasonable professional differences—she identified several more serious problems with Mr. Schroeder's income-based approach. For all these reasons, we conclude that Mr. Schroeder's income-based analysis, like Ms. Walker's, is entitled to little weight.[29]

Tax-affecting S corporation income was ultimately not an issue decided in *Wall* because the court placed little weight on the income approach.

ESTATE OF ADAMS V. COMMISSIONER

The subject interest in *Adams* was a 61.59 percent interest in Waddell Sluder Adams & Co., Inc. (WSA), valued in 1995 for estate tax reporting purposes. All of WSA's outstanding shares were voting shares on the valuation date. "WSA ha[d] been an S corporation since the early 1970s." WSA operated as a retail insurance agency (5 percent of revenues) and managing general insurance agency (95 percent of revenues).[30]

The PTE valuation issue presented to the court in *Adams* was whether the taxpayer, the Estate of William G. Adams, used inappropriate discount and capitalization rates. This issue is different from the other three cases noted earlier, which involved whether to tax-affect the PTE's cash flows when applying the income approach. In *Adams*, the valuation expert for the estate tax affected the discount rate and capitalization rate, and the opposing expert for the Commissioner did not.[31]

---

[28]Mr. Schroeder was the Commissioner's valuation expert.
[29]*Wall v. Commissioner*, T.C.M. 2001-75 (March 27, 2001).
[30]*Estate of Adams v. Commissioner*, T.C.M. 2002-80 (March 28, 2002).
[31]Ibid.

Both sets of experts developed capitalization rates using the buildup method, and they both agreed to a capitalization rate of 20.53 percent (before tax-affecting adjustment) that was presented to the court. The estate's expert then tax affected the capitalization rate, increasing it from 20.53 to 31.88 percent.[32] For the reasons noted ahead, the Commissioner's expert and the court disagreed.

The net cash flow and the capitalization rate used to compute the fair market value of the WSA stock should have the same tax character, that is, before tax or after corporate tax.

The estate contends that Shriner's[33] estimates of WSA's prospective net cash flows are before corporate tax. The estate also contends that Shriner properly converted the capitalization rate from an after corporate tax rate to a before corporate tax rate to match estimated prospective net cash flows and that the conversion increased his capitalization rate from 20.53 percent to 31.88 percent. We disagree with the estate on both points.

We disagree that Shriner's estimates of WSA's prospective net cash flows are before corporate tax because it is appropriate to use a zero corporate tax rate to estimate net cash flow when the stock being valued is stock of an S corporation. WSA is an S corporation, and its cash flows are subject to a zero corporate tax rate. Thus, Shriner's estimates of WSA's prospective net cash flows are after corporate tax (zero corporate tax rate) and not before corporate tax as the estate contends.

We disagree that Shriner properly converted the capitalization rate because there was no need to do so. The parties agree that Shriner's estimated capitalization rate (before he converted it to before corporate tax) is an after tax rate. Thus, as in *Gross*, the tax character of Shriner's estimate of WSA's prospective net cash flows matches that of the unconverted capitalization rate because both are after corporate tax. It follows that Shriner should not have converted the capitalization rate from after corporate tax to before corporate tax because the tax character of both his estimated net cashflows for WSA and unconverted capitalization rates is after corporate tax.

We conclude that Shriner improperly increased the capitalization rate from 20.53 percent to 31.88 percent.[34]

---

[32]*Estate of Adams v. Commissioner*, T.C.M. 2002-80 (March 28, 2002).
[33]Shriner is the valuation expert for the estate.
[34]*Estate of Adams v. Commissioner*, T.C.M. 2002-80 (March 28, 2002).

ROBERT DALLAS V. COMMISSIONER

Dallas involved the valuation of November 29, 1999, and 2000 transactions aggregating 55 percent of the nonvoting series B common stock of Dallas Group of America, Inc. (DGA). Such transactions involved the sale by the controlling shareholder (Robert Dallas) of the subject interests to two trusts for cash and notes. One trust was for the benefit of son Robert Dallas II, president of DGA, and one trust was for the benefit of son David Dallas, chief executive officer of DGA. Each trust received 27.5 percent of the nonvoting series B common stock of DGA. As of the date of the 1999 and 2000 transactions, both sons had been employed by DGA (or its predecessor entity) for more than 20 years. The Commissioner "determined that the transactions were bargain sales and thus were gifts."[35]

After the transactions, the 25,078 shares of series B stock were owned as follows (percent amounts are rounded):[36]

Robert Dallas	1,878 shares	7.5%
Robert Dallas II	4,644 shares	18.5%
David Dallas	4,644 shares	18.5%
Trust for benefit of Robert Dallas II	6,956 shares	27.7%
Trust for benefit of David Dallas	6,956 shares	27.7%
Totals	**25,078 shares**	**100.0%**

The notes that were received as payment from Robert Dallas's sons as trustees of the trusts included share-adjustment clauses. Such clauses effectively stated that if it is finally determined in any IRS proceeding that the value per share is less than the amount per share designated by the agreement, there will be an adjustment to the shares issued, and the trusts will not have to pay more for the purchased shares.[37]

A discussion of the history and background of DGA is pertinent to the discussion at issue here: "In 1959, [Robert Dallas] and Thomas Skeuse . . . formed Reagent Chemical & Research, Inc. (Reagent)[,] [which] initially processed elemental sulfur and later distributed hydrochloric acid. In the 1970s, Reagent expanded" its line of business to include manufacturing and distributing ammonium chloride and synthetic magnesium silicate.

---

[35]*Robert Dallas v. Commissioner*, T.C.M. 2006-212 (September 28, 2006).
[36]Ibid.
[37]Ibid.

In February 1989, the ammonium chloride and synthetic magnesium silicate divisions of Reagent were spun off into DGA. Robert Dallas received the stock of DGA in exchange for his ownership interest in Reagent.[38]

Substantially all of the company's revenues were generated from its ammonium chloride (29 percent of total sales) and magnesium silicate (70 percent) divisions during 1999 and 2000. As of September 1999, DGA supplied (1) approximately 90 percent of the ammonium chloride used in the United States and Canada and (2) was "the only manufacturer of synthetic magnesium silicate in the Western Hemisphere." DGA was profitable and paid enough dividends to its shareholders to pay the PTE income tax.[39]

In connection with the valuation of the subject interest, the taxpayer engaged two valuation consultants, and both reduced net earnings by a tax-affecting adjustment; one utilized a 35 percent tax adjustment, and one utilized a 40 percent tax adjustment. The Commissioner's valuation consultant did not tax affect. As a result, the taxpayer's valuation consultants concluded that the per-share value of the subject interest was approximately 40 percent less than the value determined by the Commissioner's valuation consultant.[40]

The taxpayer's experts tried to justify the use of a tax-affecting adjustment by arguing the following:[41]

1. "[A]fter a sale, the corporation will lose its S corporation status."
2. The "shareholder[s] [are] liable for income tax[es] on S corporation profits even if those profits are not distributed to the shareholder."
3. They have "always tax-affected S corporation income."
4. "[A]n informal poll at a recent conference showed 90 to 95 percent of responding appraisers tax-affect S corporation income."
5. "[T]he American Society of Appraisers (ASA) Board of Review rejects any application for certification if the candidate submits test answers or reports for review that do not tax-affect S corporation income."
6. "[A]ll bankers, investment bankers, and business brokers use tax-affecting in estimating the value of S corporation stock."
7. The firm of one of the experts tax-affects "employee stock ownership plans (ESOP) that [are] submit[ed] to the Department of Labor."

---

[38]*Robert Dallas v. Commissioner*, T.C.M. 2006-212 (September 28, 2006).
[39]Ibid.
[40]Ibid.
[41]Ibid.

The Court disagreed, noting thus:[42]

1. "There is no evidence in the record that DGA expects to cease to qualify as an S corporation" at any time.
2. "DGA has a history of distributing enough earnings for shareholders to pay their individual income tax liabilities on DGA's earnings," and "[t]here is no evidence that DGA intends to change [this] practice."
3. "We give little weight to [expert]'s testimony about an informal poll at an unidentified conference held on a date not stated on the record."
4. The expert "admitted that the ASA has never issued an official directive or recommendation on tax-affecting S corporations' earnings."
5. The opposing expert "submitted a report to the board of the ASA that did not tax-affect," and his report was not rejected.
6. "[T]here is no evidence that the Department of Labor's definition of value is similar to the definition of fair market value in this case."

The Court "conclude[d] that there is insufficient evidence to establish that a hypothetical buyer and seller would tax-affect DGA's earnings and that tax-affecting DGA's earnings is not appropriate."[43]

GALLAGHER V. COMMISSIONER

This case involved the valuation of 3,970 units of Paxton Media Group, LLC (PMG), owned by the estate of Louise Paxton Gallagher for estate tax reporting purposes. "As of the valuation date [(July 5, 2004, which was the decedent's date of death)], decedent's estate was PMG's largest single unit holder, holding 15 percent of [PMG]'s 26,439 . . . units."[44]

PMG was formed in 1896 and was a privately held and family-owned newspaper publishing company. "[B]y July 2004, PMG published 28 daily newspapers, 13 paid weekly publications, and a few specialty publications, and owned and operated a television station. . . . PMG serves primarily small and mid-sized communities in the southeastern and midwestern United States."[45]

"On December 26, 1996, PMG elected to become an S corporation. . . . On the same day, PMG executed a shareholder agreement to protect its 'S'

---

[42]*Robert Dallas v. Commissioner*, T.C.M. 2006-212 (September 28, 2006).
[43]Ibid.
[44]*Gallagher v. Commissioner*, T.C.M. 2011-146 (June 28, 2011).
[45]Ibid.

election by restricting the sale of stock." As of the valuation date, "there was no plan to discontinue the 'S' election."[46]

PMG's equity was $74 million as of December 28, 2003, according to PMG's audited financial statements. During 2004, PMG was very profitable and generated revenues of $169 million and net income of $48 million.[47]

One of the disputed adjustments was the 39 percent tax-affecting adjustment used by the taxpayer's valuation expert in connection with calculating future cash flows under the discounted cash flow method. The taxpayer's valuation consultant "assumed a 40-percent marginal tax rate in calculating the applicable discount rate." However, the court found no explanation for employing either tax rate and for ignoring the benefits associated with S corporation status. The court agreed with the Commissioner's valuation consultant and applied a 0 percent tax-affecting adjustment.[48]

ANALYSIS OF CASES

Each of these six cases involved tax affecting as well as many other issues. They all very clearly and consistently articulate the court's position with respect to tax affecting a PTE under the fair market value standard. As stated in *Gross*,

> We believe that the principal benefit that shareholders expect from an S corporation election is a reduction in the total tax burden imposed on the enterprise. The owners expect to save money, and we see no reason why that savings ought to be ignored as a matter of course in valuing the S corporation.[49]

This point of view pervades all six cases. As summarized in Table 9.3, regardless of the type of tax (estate or gift taxes), the type of interest (controlling or noncontrolling), the valuation date, and the form of the PTE, in all six instances there was no tax-affecting adjustment.

We further note that the courts did not always address whether the following four questions impacted their decision:

1. Was the subject ownership interest active or passive?
2. Was there an expectation that the subject entity would remain a PTE?

---

[46]*Gallagher v. Commissioner*, T.C.M. 2011-146 (June 28, 2011).
[47]Ibid.
[48]Ibid.
[49]*Gross v. Commissioner*, 272 F.3d 333 (6th Cir. 2001).

TABLE 9.3 Summary of Findings—Fair Market Value PTE Court Decisions

	Gross	*Heck*	*Wall*	*Adams*	*Dallas*	*Gallagher*
1. Purpose	Gift	Estate	Gift	Estate	Gift	Estate
2. Standard of value	FMV	FMV	FMV	FMV	FMV	FMV
3. Noncontrolling or Controlling	NC	NC	NC	C	NC	NC
4. Date of valuation	1992	1995	1992	1995	1999	2004
5. Date of court's decision	2001	2002	2001	2002	2006	2011
6. Form of PTE	S Corp	S Corp	S Corp	S Corp	S Corp	LLC
7. Valuation approach	Income	Income	Income	Income	Income	Income
8. Income tax rate	0%	0%	0%	0%	0%	0%
9. Tax-affecting decided by	Court	Both parties	Not decided	Court	Court	Court

3. Was there a buy–sell agreement in place that limited the rights of the holder?
4. Was there an expectation that the subject company or the subject interest would be sold?

More important, the courts never indicated that an alternative to the all-or-nothing tax-affecting methodology was considered. The courts knew that there was a benefit of overall tax reduction for a company that was a PTE, and that this benefit should have been quantified and considered as part of the PTE income tax adjustment.

There is no issue that the courts have the authority to wholly or selectively accept or reject the testimony of an expert. As stated in *Wall*:

We are not bound by the formulas and opinions proffered by an expert witness and will accept or reject expert testimony in the exercise of sound judgment. Where necessary, we may reach a determination of value based on our own examination of the evidence in the record. Moreover, while we may accept the opinion of an expert in its entirety, we may be selective in the use of any part of such opinion or reject the opinion in its entirety. Finally, because valuation necessarily results in an approximation, the figure at which we arrive need not be directly attributable to specific testimony if it is within the range of values that may properly be arrived at from consideration of all the evidence.[50]

It is significant that the court's reasoning in each of these cases was entirely consistent with the reasoning in the court's decision in *Delaware Open MRI*—so why were the decisions so different? The reason is that five of these fair market value cases (all but *Gallagher*) had valuation dates prior to the 2003 reduction in the dividend tax, when the application of the MDMM would result in a 0 percent effective corporation income tax (see *Bernier*). The valuation date in *Delaware Open MRI* was 2004, after the 2003 reduction in the dividend tax. The different tax laws and different tax rates necessitated different results! Accordingly, these five cases support and do not contradict the conceptual underpinning of *Delaware Open MRI* and *Bernier*.[51]

---

[50]*Wall v. Commissioner*, T.C.M. 2001-75 (March 27, 2001).
[51]The reported decision in *Gallagher* did not indicate whether the impact of the change in dividend tax rates was considered.

CHAPTER 10

The Market Approach

The market approach is one of three generally accepted approaches to value. Under the market approach, indications of value can be obtained by analyzing transactions of ownership interests of companies in the same or similar lines of business. Like the income approach, it is referenced in IRS Revenue Ruling 59–60, as well as in other valuation standards, such as those of the Appraisal Standards Board and the AICPA. This chapter addresses the underlying theory and authoritative support for the market approach, the process of applying the market approach in connection with determining the value of an ownership interest in a PTE, and the normalization adjustments that need to be considered under the market approach with respect to applying PTE valuation inputs. The market approach considers the price at which transactions occur between buyers and sellers. Accordingly, the market approach is very relevant if the standard of value is fair market value.[1]

REVENUE RULING 59–60

Revenue Ruling 59–60, § 4, lists eight factors that "are fundamental and require careful analysis in each case." Included in this list of factors are two examples of the market approach, specifically (1) prior "sales of the stock and the size of the block of stock to be valued," and (2) "[t]he market price of the stocks of corporations engaged in the same or a similar line of business having their stocks actively traded in a free and open market, either on an exchange or over the counter."[2]

---

[1]Shannon P. Pratt, *The Market Approach to Valuing Businesses*, 2nd ed. (Hoboken, NJ: John Wiley & Sons, 2005), xxxiii.
[2]Rev. Rul. 59–60, 1959-1 C.B. 237, § 4.01.

Prior Sales of the Stock and the Size of the Block to Be Valued

Revenue Ruling 59–60 states thus:

> Sales of stock of a closely held corporation should be carefully investigated to determine whether they represent transactions at arm's length. Forced or distress sales do not ordinarily reflect fair market value nor do isolated sales in small amounts necessarily control as the measure of value. This is especially true in the valuation of a controlling interest in a corporation. Since, in the case of closely held stocks, no prevailing market prices are available, there is no basis for making an adjustment for blockage. It follows, therefore, that such stocks should be valued upon a consideration of all the evidence affecting the fair market value. The size of the block of stock itself is a relevant factor to be considered. Although it is true that a minority interest in an unlisted corporation's stock is more difficult to sell than a similar block of listed stock, it is equally true that control of a corporation, either actual or in effect, representing as it does an added element of value, may justify a higher value for a specific block of stock.[3]

Market Price of the Stock of Corporations Engaged in the Same or a Similar Line of Business

Revenue Ruling 59–60 strongly advocates the guideline public company method:

> As a generalization, the prices of stocks which are traded in volume in a free and active market by informed persons best reflect the consensus of the investing public as to what the future holds for the corporations and industries represented. When a stock is closely held, is traded infrequently, or is traded in an erratic market, some other measure of value must be used. In many instances, the next best measure may be found in the prices at which the stocks of companies engaged in the same or a similar line of business are selling in a free and open market.[4]

---

[3] Rev. Rul. 59–60, 1959-1 C.B. 237, § 4.02(g).
[4] Ibid., § 3.03.

Revenue Ruling 59–60 also discusses comparable companies:

Section 2031(b) of the Code states, in effect, that in valuing unlisted securities the value of stock or securities of corporations engaged in the same or a similar line of business which are listed on an exchange should be taken into consideration along with all other factors. An important consideration is that the corporations to be used for comparisons have capital stocks which are actively traded by the public. In accordance with section 2031(b) of the Code, stocks listed on an exchange are to be considered first. However, if sufficient comparable companies whose stocks are listed on an exchange cannot be found, other comparable companies which have stocks actively traded in on [*sic*] the over-the-counter market also may be used. The essential factor is that whether the stocks are sold on an exchange or over-the-counter there is evidence of an active, free public market for the stock as of the valuation date. In selecting corporations for comparative purposes, care should be taken to use only comparable companies. Although the only restrictive requirement as to comparable corporations specified in the statute is that their lines of business be the same or similar, yet it is obvious that consideration must be given to other relevant factors in order that the most valid comparison possible will be obtained. For illustration, a corporation having one or more issues of preferred stock, bonds or debentures in addition to its common stock should not be considered to be directly comparable to one having only common stock outstanding. In like manner, a company with a declining business and decreasing markets is not comparable to one with a record of current progress and market expansion.[5]

APPRAISAL STANDARDS BOARD STANDARDS

The Uniform Standards of Professional Appraisal Practice states thus:

In developing an appraisal of an interest in a business enterprise or intangible asset, an appraiser must collect and analyze all information necessary for credible assignment results.

a. An appraiser must develop opinion(s) and conclusion(s) by use of one or more approaches that are necessary for credible assignment results.

---

[5]Rev. Rul. 59–60, 1959-1 C.B. 237, § 4.02(h).

    b. An appraiser must, when necessary for credible assignment results, analyze the effect on value, if any, of: . . .

        iv. Past sales of capital stock or other ownership interests in the business enterprise or intangible asset being appraised;

        v. Sales of capital stock or other ownership interests in similar business enterprises;

        vi. Prices, terms, and conditions affecting past sales of similar ownership interests in the asset being appraised or a similar asset.[6]

AICPA STATEMENT ON STANDARDS FOR VALUATION SERVICES

In 2007, the AICPA issued its Statement on Standards for Valuation Services No. 1: Valuation of a Business, Business Ownership Interest, Security, or Intangible Asset (SSVS 1), whose purpose is to "establish[] standards for AICPA members . . . who are engaged to, or as part of another engagement, estimate the value of a business, business ownership interest, security, or intangible asset."[7]

SSVS 1 states that

> [i]n developing the valuation, the valuation analyst should consider the three most common valuation approaches:
>
> > Income (Income-based) approach
> > Asset (Asset-based) approach (used for businesses, business ownership interests, and securities) or cost approach (used for intangible assets)
> > Market (Market-based) approach[8]

---

[6]Appraisal Standards Board, Uniform Standards of Professional Appraisal Practice, at Standards R. 9-4 (2013–2014).

[7]Consulting Services Executive Committee, American Institute of Certified Public Accountants, Statement on Standards for Valuation Services No. 1: Valuation of a Business, Business Ownership Interest, Security, or Intangible Asset, para. 1 (June 2007) (emphasis omitted).

[8]Ibid., para. 31 (emphasis omitted).

In addition, SSVS 1 states thus:

Three frequently used valuation methods under the market approach for valuing a business, business ownership interest, or security are:

Guideline public company method
Guideline transactions method
Guideline sales of interests in the subject entity, such as business ownership interests or securities[9]

Accordingly, in order for a valuation to be performed in conformity with IRS rulings and authoritative valuation standards, the valuation analyst should consider the applicability of the market approach. In the following sections, we discuss the two methods referenced in SSVS 1, namely, the guideline public company method and the guideline transactions method.

GUIDELINE PUBLIC COMPANY METHOD

Applying the guideline public company method when performing a valuation of a PTE involves a three-step process:

1. Find sufficiently comparable publicly traded companies whose ownership interests are actively traded.
2. Identify and quantify appropriate pricing metrics to be applied to the subject interest.
3. Apply the pricing metrics derived from comparable guideline public companies to the normalized financial results of operations of the subject PTE (or PTE ownership interest).

The valuation analyst should be able to identify potentially comparable publicly traded companies by performing a search by North American Industry Classification System (NAICS) or Standard Industry Code (SIC). There are services (i.e., Bloomberg) that facilitate the finding of industry information. When a potentially comparable publicly traded company is identified, the valuation analyst should review the public company's Securities and Exchange Commission (SEC) filings. Important relevant information regarding the company's and industry's business, strengths, weaknesses, opportunities,

---

[9]Consulting Services Executive Committee, American Institute of Certified Public Accountants, Statement on Standards for Valuation Services No. 1: Valuation of a Business, Business Ownership Interest, Security, or Intangible Asset, para. 36 (June 2007) (emphasis omitted).

risk factors, management, trading history, material events, financial position, results of operations, performance trends, and so forth, are available from a reading of the public company's interim and year-end filings with the SEC, as well as from registration statements, Forms 8-K, and other filings.

Armed with this data, the valuation analyst can make an informed judgment, consistent with IRS Revenue Ruling 59–60 and other authoritative and nonauthoritative guidance, as to the comparability of the subject PTE to the public company. Facts and circumstances will dictate the number of guideline public companies needed in order to apply this method; what special consideration is required for any outliers in the sample; whether a public company is actively traded; and whether differences in the magnitude of revenues, product mix, geographic markets, depth of management, financial performance, growth rate, capitalization structure, and other factors support or invalidate the inclusion of a public company for purposes of applying the guideline public company method.

There are many different pricing metrics that valuation analysts consider. Such metrics include price (of common equity or enterprise value) of the last 12 months' revenues; gross profit; operating income; earnings before interest, taxes, depreciation and amortization (EBITDA); earnings before interest and taxes (EBIT); pretax income; net income; free cash flows; net assets; and other financial performance measures. These same metrics can be applied based on year-over-year growth of each category, an average or weighted average of some combination of past years, next year's projected results of operations, and so on. For leveraged public companies, similar combinations of metrics can be applied to derive the price of invested capital. A detailed explanation of how to select comparable guideline public companies and applicable metrics is beyond the scope of this text.

Guideline public company financial statements and their metrics may need to be normalized for valuation purposes. The following are examples of the types of guideline public company normalization adjustments that need to be considered regardless of whether a controlling or noncontrolling interest is being valued:

1. Changes in entities comprising the consolidated guideline public company
2. Changes in accounting methods
3. Nonrecurring events
4. Error corrections impacting prior years

These normalization adjustments potentially impact the following:

1. The comparability of the guideline public company's financial position and results of operations over time

2. The comparability of the guideline public company's financial performance to its peer group
3. The comparability of the guideline public company to the subject
company
4. The reliability of pricing metrics

It is often useful to examine the most recent year's financial statements
and compare the prior period amounts to previously issued financial statements to see if there were any material changes in amounts or footnote
disclosures. By doing this, the valuation analyst may be able to identify
certain events that require further investigation and possibly impact the
selection of pricing metrics. Failing to properly normalize the financial results
of operations of the guideline public company may result in improperly
selecting valuation metrics or calculating an improper amount with respect to
an appropriate metric.

Once comparable public companies are selected and sufficient relevant
data is analyzed, the valuation analyst will (1) select the appropriate metric(s)
and the period to which the metric(s) should be applied, (2) correlate the
financial performance of each guideline public company to its metric(s), and
(3) select the amount for each applicable metric that should be applied to the
subject company. The valuation analyst should be prepared to defend his
selection of guideline public companies, selection of valuation metrics, the
period(s) to which each metric applies, whether price to equity or price to
invested capital metrics is selected, and the amount selected for each metric to
be applied to the subject PTE under the guideline public company method.

GUIDELINE PUBLIC COMPANY METHOD AND PTE
VALUE TO THE HOLDER

Under a value to the holder assumption, when the valuation analyst applies a
valuation multiple to a PTE based on the guideline public company method, it
is assumed that the PTE's owner(s) will receive the same after-tax returns as
the public company's owners. For example, applying a guideline public
company's price-to-revenues multiple of say 100 percent to a PTE assumes
that the risk-adjusted after-tax returns to the owner of the PTE would be the
same as the risk-adjusted after-tax returns of the public company. Under a
value to the holder assumption, a price-to-revenues multiple assumes that
the combination of cost of goods sold, operating expenses, and income taxes
for the public company will approximate that of the PTE. A price-to-gross-
profit multiple assumes that the combination of operating expenses and
income taxes for the public company will approximate that of the PTE.

A price-to-pretax-income multiple assumes that the income taxes to a holder of the guideline public company's stock will approximate that of the PTE. Clearly, as one moves down the income statement, under value to the holder, there are fewer expense items that could deviate as a percent of revenues. This would, at least theoretically, make the price-to-net-income multiple more reliable than the price-to-revenues multiple. But how reliable is even the price-to-pretax-income multiple?

Many of the tax-affecting issues that were discussed under the income approach also apply when valuing a PTE under the guideline public company method. This is because PTEs do not pay entity-level federal corporation income taxes, whereas guideline public companies from which pricing metrics are derived are subject to federal corporation income taxes at the entity level. Accordingly, the PTE conundrum needs to be considered when applying the guideline public company method in connection with value to the holder.

Let's again consider the impact of income taxes on after-tax returns to an owner of a C corporation versus the owner of a PTE, assuming value to the holder. Table 10.1 presents the normalized income statement of a potentially comparable guideline public company and the after-tax returns to an investor in that company.

Assuming an equity valuation of $500 million for the guideline public company, pricing multiples are calculated based on six company-level metrics, and one metric is developed based on the holder's after-tax returns. This example also assumes an effective combined federal and state corporation income tax rate of 40 percent and an effective combined federal and state investor dividend tax rate of 20 percent.

For this analysis, it is also assumed that the subject PTE has valuation multiples equal to 70 percent of the guideline public company's valuation multiples based on an analysis of risk and other factors (but not financial/common-size expense factors). Accordingly, the price-to-revenues multiple should be 1.00 multiplied by 70 percent equals .70, and so on, for the subject PTE. The inputs for the subject PTE assume (1) revenues of $5 million and (2) a normalized common-sized income statement that exactly matches the guideline public company, from the "cost of goods sold" line all the way through to the "pretax income" line (30.8% of revenues).

The results are shown in Table 10.2.

Five of the six company-level multiples indicate a PTE value to the holder of approximately $3.5 million, and one company-level multiple indicates a PTE value to the holder of $5.8 million. The PTE valuation based on investor net income after taxes is $4.371 million.

This example yields vastly different results, but which amount is correct? Should the majority rule? Five of the six company-level multiples indicate that

TABLE 10.1 Analysis of Guideline Public Company Valuation Multiples

	Hypothetical C Corporation		Multiple Assuming Equity Value of $500,000,000	70% of Guideline Public Company Multiples
C corporation results of operations				
Revenues	$ 500,000,000	100.0%	1.00	0.70
Cost of goods sold	200,000,000	40.0%		
Gross profit	300,000,000	60.0%	1.67	1.17
Selling, general, and administrative expenses	100,000,000	20.0%		
EBITDA	200,000,000	40.0%	2.50	1.75
Depreciation and amortization expense	6,000,000	1.2%		
EBIT	194,000,000	38.8%	2.58	1.80
Interest	40,000,000	8.0%		
Pretax income	154,000,000	30.8%	3.25	2.27
Income taxes (40%)	61,600,000	12.3%		
Net income	92,400,000	18.5%	5.41	3.79
Individual income taxes Dividend tax (20%)	18,480,000	3.7%		
Net income, after all taxes	$ 73,920,000	14.8%	6.76	4.73

approximately $3.5 million is the PTE value to the holder. This clustering ordinarily would be a compelling factor in determining PTE value to the holder. On the other hand, the price-to-net-income multiple indicates a value of $5.8 million, and this is the amount of after–corporation taxes but before individual income taxes typically considered in connection with the income approach. This metric takes into consideration any differences between the subject PTE's costs of operations and the guideline public company's cost of operations and, it can be argued, is more appropriate when applying a value to the holder standard of value.

The problem with each of these six company-level multiples is that not one takes into consideration the holder's tax savings benefit of the subject company's PTE status. Since our definition of value is derived from the after-tax risk-adjusted present value of future cash flows to the holder, the PTE tax savings benefit must be considered. The final value derived in the above

TABLE 10.2   Example 1: Guideline Public Company Valuation Multiples Applied to Hypothetical S Corporation

	Hypothetical S Corporation		70% of Guideline Public Company Multiples	
			Multiple	Indicated Value
C corporation results of operations				
Revenues	$ 5,000,000	100.0%	0.70	$ 3,500,000
Cost of goods sold	2,000,000	40.0%		
Gross profit	3,000,000	60.0%	1.17	$ 3,510,000
Selling, general, and administrative expenses	1,000,000	20.0%		
EBITDA	2,000,000	40.0%	1.75	$ 3,500,000
Depreciation and amortization expense	60,000	1.2%		
EBIT	1,940,000	38.8%	1.80	$ 3,492,000
Interest	400,000	8.0%		
Pretax income	1,540,000	30.8%	2.27	$ 3,496,000
Income taxes	—	0.0%		
Net income	1,540,000	30.8%	3.79	$ 5,837,000
Investor income taxes Income tax on pass-through income (40%)	616,000	12.3%		
Investor net income, after all taxes	$ 924,000	18.5%	4.73	$ 4,371,000

example, $4.371 million, is the only one that accomplishes this; it follows then that $4.371 million is the appropriate conclusion of value.

What happens when we modify several of the operating expense amounts of the PTE subject company in the above example? Assuming increases of 5 percent in common-size "cost of goods sold" and "selling, general and administrative expenses," the indicated values of each multiple now are vastly different, as illustrated in Table 10.3.

By simply modifying two of the common-size expenses, the five previously identical valuation amounts of approximately $3.5 million now range from a low of $2.363 million to a high of $3.5 million.

It is not unusual for the subject PTE (or any privately held company) to have a different cost structure than the guideline public companies from

TABLE 10.3 Example 2: Guideline Public Company Valuation Multiples Applied to Hypothetical S Corporation

	Hypothetical S Corporation		70% of Guideline Public Company Multiples	
			Multiple	Indicated Value
C corporation results of operations				
Revenues	$ 5,000,000	100.0%	0.70	$ 3,500,000
Cost of goods sold	2,250,000	45.0%		
Gross profit	2,750,000	55.0%	1.17	$ 3,218,000
Selling, general, and administrative expenses	1,250,000	25.0%		
EBITDA	1,500,000	30.0%	1.75	$ 2,625,000
Depreciation and amortization expense	60,000	1.2%		
EBIT	1,440,000	28.8%	1.80	$ 2,592,000
Interest	400,000	8.0%		
Pretax income	1,040,000	20.8%	2.27	$ 2,361,000
Income taxes	—	0.0%		
Net income	1,040,000	20.8%	3.79	$ 3,942,000
Investor income taxes Income tax on pass-through income (40%)	416,000	8.3%		
Investor net income, after all taxes	$ 624,000	12.5%	4.73	$ 2,952,000

which valuation metrics and multiples are derived. Consequently, a valuation analyst may frequently find that applying guideline public company multiples based on different income statement line items yields very different results. In this example, as in the previous one, the value derived from investor net income after all taxes ($2.952 million, in this case) would arguably indicate a more appropriate PTE value. Revenue, gross profit, EBITDA, EBIT, pretax, and net income valuation multiples can be reverse-engineered assuming a final valuation amount of $2.952 million.

It is worth noting that when more than one guideline public company is considered with respect to the development of applicable valuation metrics, the process by which one selects metrics may change, but the same analysis presented earlier with respect to the final conclusion of value is necessary.

GUIDELINE PUBLIC COMPANY METHOD
AND PTE INVESTMENT VALUE

Value to the holder considers normalized results of operations of the subject interest in the hands of its current owner; investment value considers normalized results of operation of the subject interest in the hands of the buyer. Application of the guideline public company method involves consideration of the subject PTE's historical and projected revenues, expenses, and income taxes, inclusive of synergies, in the hands of the owner. If the buyer has the ability to increase the after-tax cash flows of the subject PTE, that fact must be taken into consideration in applying the guideline public company method and the investment value assumption.

Under value to the holder in the previous series of examples, it was assumed that the subject company multiples were 70 percent of the guideline public company's multiples. Given the potential for synergies with the buyer and the possibility that the buyer has a substantially lower risk profile than the guideline public company, it is possible that the 30 percent discount will be less, perhaps even 0 percent. Facts and circumstances will dictate whether the valuation analyst applies multiples that are greater than, equal to, or less than the guideline public companies when applying the guideline public company method.

Another factor to consider is whether the buyer will be able to enjoy the tax savings and other benefits of the subject company's status as a PTE. If so, then such benefits must be incorporated into the valuation analysis.

Assume the same facts as in the previous example under value to the holder except that (1) revenues increase by 10 percent from $5 million to $5.5 million; (2) the buyer has cost savings synergies that reduce "selling, general and administrative expenses" from 25 percent of revenues to 20 percent; (3) the buyer can take advantage of the subject company's PTE status; and (4) the guideline public company multiples are reduced by 10 percent (not 30%).

As shown in Table 10.4, by modifying three inputs—revenues (increased by 10%); selling, general and administrative expenses (decreased from 25% to 20% of revenues), and the discount applied to the metric multiples (30% discount reduced to 10%)—a substantially different range of values is derived (i.e., $4.278 million to $7.135 million). Under a value to the buyer assumption, the value is $5.344 million (which contrasts with $2.952 million under the value to the holder assumption). This analysis illustrates the sensitivity of changing even a few inputs when applying the guideline public company method.

If the same facts as in the previous example are assumed except that the buyer will not be able to enjoy the benefits of PTE status and will have an

TABLE 10.4 Example 3: Guideline Public Company Valuation Multiples Applied to Hypothetical S Corporation

	Hypothetical S Corporation		90% of Guideline Public Company Multiples	
			Multiple	Indicated Value
C corporation results of operations				
Revenues	$ 5,500,000	100.0%	0.90	$ 4,950,000
Cost of goods sold	2,475,000	45.0%		
Gross profit	3,025,000	55.0%	1.50	$ 4,538,000
Selling, general, and administrative expenses	1,100,000	20.0%		
EBITDA	1,925,000	35.0%	2.25	$ 4,331,000
Depreciation and amortization expense	60,000	1.1%		
EBIT	1,865,000	33.9%	2.32	$ 4,327,000
Interest	400,000	7.3%		
Pretax income	1,465,000	26.6%	2.92	$ 4,278,000
Income taxes	—	0.0%		
Net income	1,465,000	26.6%	4.87	$ 7,135,000
Investor income taxes Income tax on pass-through income (40%)	586,000	10.6%		
Investor net income, after all taxes	$ 879,000	16.0%	6.08	$ 5,344,000

effective C corporation federal and state income tax of 40 percent (same as the guideline public company), then the investment value of the ownership interest decreases from $5.344 million to $4.282 million, as shown in Table 10.5.

GUIDELINE PUBLIC COMPANY METHOD AND PTE FAIR MARKET VALUE

Many valuation analysts apply guideline public company multiples to the normalized historical results of operations of the PTE subject company when deriving FMV. This application of the guideline public company method assumes that the hypothetical buyer will be unable to utilize the benefit of the subject company's PTE status and that prior transactions involving the

TABLE 10.5 Example 4: Guideline Public Company Valuation Multiples Applied to Hypothetical S Corporation

	Hypothetical C Corporation		90% of Guideline Public Company Multiples	
			Multiple	Indicated Value
C corporation results of operations				
Revenues	$ 5,500,000	100.0%	0.90	$ 4,950,000
Cost of goods sold	2,475,000	45.0%		
Gross profit	3,025,000	55.0%	1.50	$ 4,538,000
Selling, general, and administrative expenses	1,100,000	20.0%		
EBITDA	1,925,000	35.0%	2.25	$ 4,331,000
Depreciation and amortization expense	60,000	1.1%		
EBIT	1,865,000	33.9%	2.32	$ 4,327,000
Interest	400,000	7.3%		
Pretax income	1,465,000	26.6%	2.92	$ 4,278,000
Income taxes	586,000	10.7%		
Net income	879,000	16.0%	4.87	4,281,000
Investor income taxes				
Dividend tax (20%)	175,800	3.2%		
Investor income, after all taxes	$ 703,200	12.8%	6.08	$ 4,282,000

guideline public company are relevant with respect to the pricing of the subject PTE. Are these valid assumptions, and are they consistent with the definition of *fair market value*?

As discussed in Chapter 8, the FMV standard of value requires consideration of value to the holder/seller as well as value to the buyer. Relying on transaction prices of a guideline public company is consistent with this concept.

However, the other assumptions employed by implementing the guideline public company method in this manner require further analysis. When applying the guideline public company method, the transactions from which pricing metrics are derived involve noncontrolling minority interests without the ability to impact the normalized results of operations of the public company. When the guideline public company method is applied to a minority interest in a PTE, the buyer may also have limited ability to change the normalized results of operations of the investee. If so, it is logical and appropriate to utilize historical, normalized PTE results of operations under the guideline public company method when applying the FMV standard of value to value a noncontrolling minority interest.

Let's next consider the appropriateness of using the normalized PTE results of operations when valuing a controlling interest under the FMV standard of value. If the subject interest in the PTE enjoys the prerogatives of control and the buyer's after-tax economic return on investment is different from that of the seller, it may be inappropriate to utilize the seller's normalized PTE results of operations for valuation purposes under the guideline public company method. The resulting indication of value would be based on the seller's returns, which may be different from the buyer's returns, or some other mutually agreeable amount. Some might argue that the buyer will not (or should not) pay for synergistic benefits that result from a transaction. Again, facts and circumstances will dictate whether that is true (e.g., consider the example described in Chapter 8 regarding the Los Angeles Dodgers).

The valuation analyst should also investigate the likely population of buyers and determine if there are two groups of hypothetical buyers: one that can take advantage of the pass-through status of the subject ownership interest and one that cannot. If there are buyers who would enjoy the tax and other benefits of the subject PTE, they may have a financial incentive to pay more for the PTE ownership interest than for a C corporation. Under the FMV standard of value, the holder/seller is fully informed and is under no compulsion to sell; accordingly, the hypothetical buyer may be able to enjoy the continued benefits of PTE status and pay more than the valuation multiple of the guideline public company.

GUIDELINE TRANSACTIONS METHOD

There are several useful databases available to the appraiser when attempting to apply the guideline transactions method (e.g., Pratt's Stats, BIZCOMPS, and Done Deals). These databases contain actual transactional data sorted by NAICS/SIC code and may include transactions of PTEs and small and midsize companies that may be more comparable to the subject company from a size and risk perspective than a guideline public company. Hence, it is often considered an appropriate methodology to use, especially when there are a reasonable number of potentially comparable transactions and the indicated valuation multiples are in a close range.

A detailed analysis of the criteria to be considered in connection with the selection of guideline transactions and the applicable metrics to select under this method is beyond the scope of this text. However, the following is a brief discussion of certain issues to consider when applying the guideline transactions method to the valuation of a PTE ownership interest.

Limited Information

When considering the guideline public company method, an appraiser can access a significant amount of information regarding the guideline public company. On the other hand, very little relevant information is generally accessible regarding potential guideline transactions. This limits the appraiser's ability to identify guideline transactions involving companies with similar cost structures, strengths, weaknesses, threats, opportunities, growth, and depth of management as the subject PTE. The source data may also not provide sufficient information about the buyer's synergies or other compensation paid to the seller in the form of salary, covenants not to compete, management fees, above (or below) fair market rentals of property, and other factors.

Guideline Transactions

The valuation analyst should select transactions that are reasonably comparable. Such transactions may occur over an extended period of time (i.e., before, during, and after known recessions). Accordingly, valuation analysts must be mindful of the business cycle's impact on the transaction price. Recessions can also impact certain parts of the country differently than others. The geographic impact of a recession should also be considered when analyzing transaction prices.

Other issues to consider when analyzing guideline transactions are differences in size (i.e., revenues of the sold company far greater or less than those of the subject company), location (i.e., foreign versus domestic), and profitability (i.e., profitable versus unprofitable).

Normalized versus Historical Data

A valuation analyst will normalize the historical results of operations of a subject company for valuation purposes. Such normalization adjustments often materially impact the historically reported results of operations and can convert a reported tax or GAAP loss into substantial net income, and vice versa. Normalized financial statements provide a truer picture of the economic financial position and results of operations of a business.

It is unknown the extent to which reported historical results of operations of the guideline transaction companies have been normalized. It is inconsistent to apply valuation multiples derived from historical data of guideline transaction companies to the normalized data of the subject company; doing so may yield difficult-to-justify valuation conclusions.

Purchase Price Allocation

The guideline transaction data may indicate whether a transaction involves a sale of equity or assets, as well as the nature of the assets and liabilities included in the sale. As different companies have different mixes of assets and liabilities, the valuation analyst should be able to allocate the purchase price between tangible and intangible assets. The valuation analyst needs to carefully consider whether appreciated assets have been included in the transaction (i.e., real estate) and, if so, adjust the valuation metrics accordingly.

Number of Transactions

A sufficient number of potentially comparable transactions should be considered before relying on the guideline transactions method. The number of transactions necessary in order to rely on the guideline transactions method is a matter of the analyst's professional judgment based on facts and circumstances. Fewer transactions are needed when the valuation multiples converge and the transactions involve companies that are similar to one another as well as the subject company. More transactions are needed when this is not the case.

Facts and circumstances will dictate an appraiser's ability to rely on the guideline transactions method when valuing a PTE.

CHAPTER 11

Individual State Income Taxes

In Chapters 4 and 5, individual state income taxes were identified as an input needed to apply the MDMM. The potentially significant impact of this input is often overlooked when valuing PTEs. Individual state income taxes, depending on the state and amount of taxable income, can range from 0 percent to more than 10 percent. Moreover, certain cities (i.e., New York City) impose additional income taxes on individuals. Such state and local income taxes reduce business owners' after-tax cash flows and the value of a business ownership interest. This chapter discusses individual state income tax rates for all 50 states and Washington, D.C. (collectively, individual state income tax rates), identifies those parts of the country having the highest individual state income taxes, and illustrates the sensitivity of taxable income on individual state income taxes.

STATUTORY INDIVIDUAL STATE INCOME TAX RATES

There is a wide range in state individual income tax rates throughout the United States. In addition, many states define *taxable income* differently than the federal government defines the term.[1] Table 11.1 is a summary of 2013 maximum individual income tax rates by state, based on data contained in https://tax.thomsonreuters.com/wp.ttps/Checkpoint_State_Local_Tax_2013.

"Clearly, the business [appraiser] should avoid applying the same combined federal, state, and local income tax rate to all valuations. To do so would effectively ignore the impact of such widely differing state tax rates."[2]

---

[1]Eric J. Barr, "The Impact of State and Local Income Taxes on Pass-Through Entity Valuations," *Value Examiner* (July/August 2013), at 14.
[2]Ibid., at 15.

TABLE 11.1 Summary of 2013 Maximum State Income Tax Rates

- Seven states have no individual income taxes: Alaska, Florida, Nevada, South Dakota, Texas, Washington, and Wyoming.

- Thirteen states have maximum individual income tax rates ranging from 1 to 5 percent: Alabama (5%), Arizona (4.54%), Colorado (4.63%), Illinois (5%), Indiana (3.4%), Kansas (4.9%), Michigan (4.25%), Mississippi (5%), North Dakota (3.99%), New Hampshire (5%), New Mexico (4.9%), Pennsylvania (3.07%), and Utah (5%).

- Nineteen states have maximum individual income tax rates ranging from 5.1 to 7.5 percent: Arkansas (7%), Connecticut (6.7%), Delaware (6.75%), Georgia (6%), Idaho (7.4%), Kentucky (6%), Louisiana (6%), Massachusetts (5.25%), Maryland (5.75%), Missouri (6%), Montana (6.9%), Nebraska (6.84%), Ohio (5.925%), Oklahoma (5.25%), Rhode Island (5.99%), South Carolina (7%), Tennessee (6%), Virginia (5.75%), and West Virginia (6.5%).

- Washington, D.C. (8.95%) and nine states have maximum individual income tax rates ranging from 7.6 to 9.9 percent: Iowa (8.98%), Maine (7.95%), Minnesota (7.85%), North Carolina (7.75%), New Jersey (8.97%), New York (8.82%), Oregon (9.9%), Vermont (8.95%), and Wisconsin (7.75%).

- Two states have maximum individual income tax rates of 10 percent or greater: California (12.3%) and Hawaii (11%).[3]

EFFECTIVE INDIVIDUAL STATE INCOME TAX RATES

Chapters 2 and 3 described the wide discrepancy between federal income tax rates in the maximum income bracket and effective federal rates for married filing jointly taxpayers with $10,000, $100,000, and $1 million of CPI-adjusted taxable income. Does this wide discrepancy also hold true for state income taxes? Let's find out.

Table 11.2 presents the 2013 state (but not city/local) income tax expense for each of the 50 states plus Washington, D.C., of a married filing jointly taxpayer with $10,000, $100,000, and $1 million of taxable income. Not included in the following table are the federal income tax benefits, if any, associated with such state income tax expenses. The federal income tax benefit of the state income tax deduction needs to be considered and quantified on a case-by-case basis, as it may be impacted by itemized deduction phase-out, alternative minimum taxes, and other factors.

---

[3]Eric J. Barr, "The Impact of State and Local Income Taxes on Pass-Through Entity Valuations," *Value Examiner* (July/August 2013), at 14–15.

TABLE 11.2 2013 State Income Tax Expense Assuming S Corporation K-1 Income of $10,000, $100,000, and $1,000,000

State	State Income Tax Expense Assuming S Corporation K-1 Income of			Effective State Income Tax Rate Assuming S Corporation K-1 Income of		
	$10,000	$100,000	$1,000,000	$10,000	$100,000	$1,000,000
AK	—	—	—	0%	0%	0%
AL	80	4,127	32,779	1%	4%	3%
AR	41	5,740	68,740	0%	6%	7%
AZ	3	2,730	42,873	0%	3%	4%
CA	—	3,582	96,055	0%	4%	10%
CO	—	3,704	45,735	0%	4%	5%
CT	—	4,508	67,000	0%	5%	7%
DC	104	6,671	86,063	1%	7%	9%
DE	—	4,985	65,735	0%	5%	7%
FL	—	—	—	0%	0%	0%
GA	190	5,560	59,560	2%	6%	6%
HI	46	6,215	98,273	0%	6%	10%
IA	—	5,626	57,086	0%	6%	6%
ID	—	5,434	72,611	0%	5%	7%
IL	290	4,790	49,790	3%	5%	5%
IN	272	3,332	33,932	3%	3%	3%
KS	—	3,742	47,842	0%	4%	5%
KY	104	5,343	59,343	1%	5%	6%
LA	20	2,845	36,991	0%	3%	4%
MA	525	5,250	52,500	5%	5%	5%
MD	12	4,204	55,093	0%	4%	6%
ME	—	5,237	77,407	0%	5%	8%
MI	89	3,914	42,164	1%	4%	4%
MN	—	5,181	90,769	0%	5%	9%
MO	—	4,443	58,443	0%	4%	6%
MS	166	4,620	49,620	2%	5%	5%
MT	16	4,774	66,874	0%	5%	7%
NC	—	6,018	76,073	0%	6%	8%
ND	—	1,179	28,735	0%	1%	3%
NE	—	4,196	67,320	0%	4%	7%
NH	—	—	—	0%	0%	0%
NJ	140	2,750	72,658	1%	3%	7%
NM	—	3,512	47,994	0%	4%	5%
NV	—	—	—	0%	0%	0%
NY	—	4,805	67,445	0%	5%	7%
OH	43	3,143	51,395	0%	3%	5%
OK	—	4,112	51,362	0%	4%	5%
OR	—	7,241	95,769	0%	7%	10%

(continued)

TABLE 11.2   (*Continued*)

State	State Income Tax Expense Assuming S Corporation K-1 Income of			Effective State Income Tax Rate Assuming S Corporation K-1 Income of		
	$10,000	$100,000	$1,000,000	$10,000	$100,000	$1,000,000
PA	307	3,070	30,700	3%	3%	3%
RI	—	3,048	57,662	0%	3%	6%
SC	—	5,116	68,116	0%	5%	7%
SD	—	—	—	0%	0%	0%
TN	—	—	—	0%	0%	0%
TX	—	—	—	0%	0%	0%
UT	—	4,870	50,000	0%	5%	5%
VA	43	5,041	56,791	0%	5%	6%
VT	—	3,472	82,148	0%	3%	8%
WA	—	—	—	0%	0%	0%
WI	—	5,723	71,710	0%	6%	7%
WV	180	5,115	63,615	2%	5%	6%
WY	—	—	—	0%	0%	0%

These results are summarized in Table 11.3, reflecting much different ranges in effective state income tax rates depending on the level of taxable income.

One would expect that the greater the amount of S corporation K-1 income, the greater the individual state income tax expense. Except for states with no income tax, this assumption is proven true in the above analyses.

TABLE 11.3   Frequency of Effective State Income Tax Rates Assuming S Corporation K-1 Income of $10,000, $100,000, and $1,000,000

	$10,000	$100,000	$1,000,000
0%	39	9	9
1%	5	1	0
2%	3	0	0
3%	3	8	4
4%	0	10	3
5%	1	15	9
6%	0	6	8
7%	0	2	10
8%	0	0	3
9%	0	0	2
10%	0	0	3
Totals	51	51	51

Another factor to consider when analyzing state income taxes for purposes of the MDMM input is that not all states impose individual income taxes on C corporation dividend income at the same rate as ordinary income. For example, New Hampshire and Tennessee have no individual income tax on S corporation pass-through income, yet both impose an individual income tax on dividend income. This could potentially complicate the analysis.

Taking into consideration city and local income taxes, "*Forbes* magazine listed the following U.S. cities as having the highest 2012 state and local income taxes on $1 million of income":[4]

1. New York City, New York
2. Honolulu, Hawaii
3. Los Angeles, California
4. Portland, Oregon
5. Baltimore, Maryland
6. Washington, D.C.
7. Portland, Maine
8. Burlington, Vermont
9. Minneapolis, Minnesota
10. Wilmington, Delaware

All other things being equal (including pretax cash flows, state and local financial incentives, access to labor, efficient transportation, etc.), the after-tax cash flows of an ownership interest in a business located in one of these 10 cities would be less than if the business were located in another part of the country.

---

[4]"Wolter Kluwer's CCH division calculated the tax bill for a married couple with $1 million in salary, two children, and $110,000 in itemized deductions, living in the largest city in each state." Eric J. Barr, "The Impact of State and Local Income Taxes on Pass-Through Entity Valuations," *Value Examiner* (July/August 2013), at 14, n. 2.

CHAPTER 12

Discounts, Premiums, Bylaws, and State Laws

A PTE ownership interest conveys certain rights and benefits to the holder. The degree of control that the holder of a PTE ownership interest can exercise has a substantial impact on the value of the ownership interest. Similarly, the greater the ease and speed with which a PTE ownership interest can be sold without risk of loss, the greater its value. These two issues—control and marketability—have been discussed at length in other treatises. Although a detailed and comprehensive discussion and analysis of the various factors impacting discounts for lack of control (control premiums) and discounts for lack of marketability (marketability premiums) are beyond the scope of this text, noted ahead are certain discount/premium issues that specifically impact PTEs.

PTE AGREEMENTS

A PTE, like a C corporation, typically defines the rights and responsibilities of all owners of the subject company in an agreement. Such agreements for LLCs, partnerships, and S corporations are referred to as *members' agreements*, *partnership agreements*, and *shareholders' agreements*, respectively. Additional terms and provisions governing the rights and responsibilities of the company and its owners can be found in governing bylaws.

PTE owners have certain voting rights that are defined in the provisions of such agreements. Depending on the agreement, a supermajority (often defined as more than 75% of the voting interests) or a majority (more than 50%) may be required to authorize certain actions. In other words, in some instances, a 30 percent minority interest may be able to block certain company actions (where a 75% vote is required); in other instances, a minimum of 50 percent is required (where a majority vote is required). The more votes required to block an action, the less control can be exercised by a minority interest; conversely, the fewer the number of votes required to block an action, the more control can be exercised by a minority interest. Such agreements may act to effectively transfer value between the different categories of controlling and noncontrolling interests rather than add or diminish value at the entity level. Thus, the discount for lack of control is impacted by the applicable PTE agreement.

The following is a list of major decisions that may require approval of a PTE's owners and are affected by the supermajority/majority vote provisions of the PTE's agreement:[1]

   a. Sale, lease, transfer, mortgage, pledge or other disposition or undertaking of company or subsidiary.

   b. Increase or reduction in capital of company; issue of additional shares in capital of company.

   c. Consolidation, merger or amalgamation of company with any other entity.

   d. Capital expenditures or commitments exceeding specified amount.

   e. Leases of company property having capital value exceeding specified amount.

   f. Borrowing by company or subsidiary which would result in aggregate indebtedness exceeding specified amount.

   g. Loans by company or subsidiary to shareholder or affiliate.

   h. Contracts between company and shareholder or affiliate.

   i. Any transaction out of ordinary course of business of company, including establishment of new business ventures.

   j. Any change in authorized signing officers in respect of legal documentation or any financial institution.

   k. Amendments to articles, bylaws, and other fundamental changes such as amalgamations.

   l. Payment of dividends and profits of company.

   m. Adoption or amendment of budget.

   n. Any agreement by company restricting, or permitting any other party to accelerate or demand payment of company indebtedness upon sale, transfer, or other disposition by shareholder of his or her shares or loan.

   o. Any amendment to any employment contract made between company and one of other parties to agreement, or representatives of one of those other (corporate) parties.

---

[1]Shareholders' Agreement Checklist, Koskie.com, http://www.koskie.com/downloads/files/USAChecklist.pdf (internal citations omitted).

p. Employment by company of any relatives of shareholder or, if a corporate shareholder, its representative.

q. Waiver or appointment of auditor.

r. Other decisions of particular importance having regard to nature of company business.

s. Compensation of directors, officers and key employees.

t. Issue, redemption, hypothecation or purchase of shares.

u. Declaration of dividends and dividend policy.

These issues impact PTE owners more directly than shareholders of C corporations because the taxable income of a PTE passes through to its owners. Accordingly, a PTE's decision to take certain actions may ultimately limit dividend distributions, causing the PTE's owners to be out-of-pocket for the individual income taxes resulting from pass-through taxable income. In contrast, C corporations pay income tax at the entity level and do not subject their shareholders to income tax unless dividend payments are made.

STATE LAW

State law can also impact the rights of owners of PTEs. Certain states have a large body of applicable case law that provides clarity as to how the courts will interpret such laws; other states do not have a large body of relevant case law. Certain states have laws that provide for greater protection of minority interests; other states have laws that provide for greater protection of controlling interests. The valuation analyst needs to be aware of applicable state limitations on the rights of PTE owners that may impact value.

Nevada Senate Bill 350, enacted during 2009, is an example of a state law that restricts the rights of PTE ownership interests.[2] Significantly greater valuation discounts would appear to be available to owners of restricted LLCs and restricted limited partnerships subject to Nevada Senate Bill 350. However, it is uncertain if such increased discounts for lack of control and lack of marketability would be sustained by the courts if challenged by the IRS as there is no case law yet.

NEVADA SENATE BILL 350

Nevada Senate Bill 350 created two new types of business entities: (1) a restricted limited liability company (Restricted LLC) and (2) a restricted

---

[2]S.B. 350 (Nev. 2009).

limited partnership (Restricted LP). Restricted LLCs and Restricted LPs are collectively referred to herein as Restricted PTEs. Restricted PTEs are Nevada LLCs and Nevada limited partnerships that agree to be restricted entities by indicating their restricted nature on their certificate of partnership or certificate of formation, as applicable. This election can be made for new LLCs or new limited partnerships or for existing LLCs or existing limited partnerships that are converting to a Restricted PTE.

Unless otherwise stated in the certificate of partnership or certificate of formation, the Restricted PTE cannot make any distributions to their owners for 10 years from their date of formation. Thus, by operation of the partnership/members' agreement and consistent with Nevada state law, a PTE could be restricted from making any distributions, including income tax reimbursement distributions, for up to 10 years. The length of time selected can be any period but not greater than 10 years. If the agreement is silent on the length of time, 10 years is the default provision under Nevada state law if the statute is cited within the certificate of formation, as indicated in the Nevada Senate Bill:

> **So, why would anyone want to set up a limited partnership (or LLC) that restricts distributions for 10 years?** Internal Revenue Code Section 2704(b) currently states that when valuing a limited partnership interest for gift or estate tax purposes, the liquidation restrictions in the operating agreement will be disregarded if the person transferring the interest in the partnership to a family member and the transferor and members of the transferor's family control the entity immediately before the transfer. The transferred partnership [or member] interest will be valued without considering any applicable restrictions. Since the restrictions in the partnership agreement will be ignored, there will be no valuation discounts. However, under section 2704(b)(3)(B), restrictions imposed under state . . . laws are not considered applicable restrictions. This exception acknowledges that restrictions imposed by state law cannot be ignored. Therefore, the limited partnership [member] arrangement will be a factor in determining estate and gift valuation discounts and can help reduce [gift, estate, and generation-skipping transfer] taxes.[3]

Restricted PTEs under Nevada Senate Bill 350 provide wealth-management protection as well as asset protection. This law protects debtor assets by

---

[3]Neveda [sic] Senate Bill 350, RINA, http://www.rina.com/resource-library/articles/nevada-senate-bill-350 (emphasis in original).

making it more difficult for a creditor to demand that the Restricted PTE make distributions.

Nevada Senate Bill 350 does not include a residency requirement. Accordingly, family limited partnerships and family LLCs from all over the country can presumably take advantage of this law.

An owner of a Restricted PTE has an ownership interest that has less value than an ownership interest in an identical entity that does not impose limits on distributions. The longer the distribution limitation is in effect, the greater the discounts for lack of control and lack of marketability. The magnitude of these discounts will be impacted by the nature and risk inherent within the assets held by the Restricted PTE and by the expected income tax cost associated with holding the ownership interest during the distribution limitation period, among other factors.

As of the writing of this text, no other state has adopted a law similar to that of Nevada Senate Law 350. Presumably, state legislators are waiting to see how the IRS responds. If the IRS respects this law and permits the larger discounts, other states will likely follow.

CHAPTER 13

Valuing Complex PTE Ownership Interests

The value of an ownership interest in a PTE can sometimes be derived by multiplying the entity's equity value by the subject percentage ownership and then applying applicable control and/or marketability discounts/premiums—but not always. That is because ownership interests, like wedding dresses, are often specifically tailored to satisfy the needs and desires of their owners. Some ownership interests, because of preferential allocations of revenues, expenses, proceeds on sale, and so forth, have substantially greater value than interests within the same entity that do not. Such special allocations need to be considered when valuing an ownership interest in a PTE. This chapter analyzes and provides guidance when valuing special allocations of ownership benefits in PTEs with complex capital structures.

REASONS FOR COMPLEX CAPITAL STRUCTURES

C corporations often have complex ownership structures. It is not unusual to identify public companies with multiple classes of preferred and common stock, options, warrants, and phantom stock. These different types of equity provide investors/employees/founders a return on investment commensurate with the risk associated with each round of financing. Higher risk investments (i.e., early stage or angel investments) tend to require greater returns. Such greater returns may be in the form of a larger percentage ownership interest in the company, board of director representation, preferences on liquidation/sale/distributions, participation rights, conversion rights, warrants, and other benefits.

PTEs are also structured to provide different rates of return to different classes of investors. Several examples of special allocations found in PTEs follow:

- **Family Limited Partnerships.** These entities are often formed for family wealth management, asset protection, and estate planning purposes. The general partner or managing member typically enjoys all of the prerogatives of control, often with only a small percentage equity ownership interest.

■ **Employee Ownership.** When a PTE adds an employee into the ownership ranks, there may be special allocations of net income (i.e., the new owner may only share in net income above an agreed-upon threshold).

■ **Strategic Investor.** A strategic investor (i.e., venture capital, investment banking, or industry investor) in a PTE may acquire rights and privileges similar to those provided to preferred stockholders of C corporations.

■ **New Venture.** Different owners may contribute disproportionate amounts of cash and sweat equity into a new venture, resulting in special allocations of future revenues and expenses.

■ **Merger of PTEs.** As part of a combination of two companies, special allocations of future income based on the combined entities' performance may create different classes of ownership and allocations of income (e.g., when two accounting firms or law firms merge).

■ **Oil and Gas Limited Partnerships.** During the 1970s and 1980s, it was common practice to provide limited partners in oil and gas partnerships special allocations of currently deductible expenses (i.e., intangible drilling and development costs), whereas general partners were allocated the capitalized costs (i.e., leasehold rights, tangible completion costs).

■ **Real Estate Limited Partnerships.** Many real estate partnerships are structured to provide the general partner a preferred return on any gain on sale, disproportionate to their capital contribution.

Facts and circumstances will dictate the form and substance of the special rights and privileges of PTE ownership interests.

The value of an ownership interest in a PTE with a complex capital structure cannot be determined by simply multiplying total equity value of the entity by the percentage ownership interest therein, even though the percent ownership interest may be mathematically determinable based on units, shares of stock, and so on. The following discussion details one methodology that can be applied to value ownership interests in PTEs with complex capital structures.

OPTION-PRICING METHOD[1]

When allocating a subject company's total equity value to different ownership interests, the valuation analyst may consider each ownership interest as a

---

[1]This section on the option-pricing method is derived from Eric J. Barr, "Valuation Issues with Complex Ownership Structures," *Value Examiner* (January/February 2012), at 13–17.

right to receive a portion of the proceeds realized from a liquidity event. The value of such interests will vary depending on the amount realized from the liquidity event. For example, the holders of a preferred return may receive 100 percent of the proceeds up to a certain contractually agreed-upon amount (the liquidation preference); thereafter, the holder(s) of preferred interests may participate in the proceeds on the same per-share or per-unit basis as other owners until the holders of preferred interests receive a total return equal to an agreed-upon multiple of the liquidation preference (the participation right). After the participation right is satisfied, the other owners will receive 100 percent of all remaining proceeds.

This example would indicate that there are two amounts at which ownership allocations change. These two amounts would be (1) the liquidation preference amount and (2) the amount at which the nonpreferred partners/members receive 100 percent of all proceeds. However, if the preferred ownership interest also has a conversion right, then it should be assumed that the preferred interest will exercise that conversion right when circumstances justify conversion. This possibility necessitates consideration of a third amount. The three amounts at which ownership percentages change are called *break points*.

In that simple example, there is one class of preferred ownership interests and one other class of ownership interests. However, there can be many different ownership interest combinations. To value each class of equity, one needs to determine each break point and allocate equity value to each break point. The calculation of value at each break point can be determined using the Black-Scholes-Merton (BSM) model, the binomial option-pricing model, or some other appropriate option-pricing model. These are option-pricing models used by valuation analysts to estimate the fair market value of nontraded stock options. The inputs needed for each of these methods include the following:

- Underlying price or equity value of the company
- Exercise price
- Valuation date
- Expiration date
- Volatility
- Risk-free rate
- Dividend yield

The BSM model is relatively easy to calculate and is commonly used. The discussion and the examples that follow assume the selection of the BSM model. However, if there are multiple expected exit values requiring consideration of scenario-based or probability-weighted expected-return outcomes, another option-pricing model may be more appropriate. A detailed analysis of the relative advantages and disadvantages of the BSM and other option-pricing models is beyond the scope of this text.

Let's summarize what has been discussed so far. In order to allocate the fair market value of a company's equity to individual ownership interests when the company has a complex ownership structure, the following steps are necessary:

1. Identify and fully understand all of the subject company's equity interests currently outstanding that are contingently issuable or that can result from the exercise of warrants, options, phantom interests, convertible debt, convertible equity securities, and other instruments.
2. Assume the exercise of all "in-the-money" warrants, options, and so on.
3. Calculate each break point.
4. Obtain all assumptions needed to apply the BSM model (or another model that is more appropriate under the circumstances).
5. Calculate the value of an ownership interest in the subject company at each break point.
6. Allocate each break-point value to the respective ownership interests.

EXAMPLE 1: PREFERRED-MEMBER UNITS

The preceding six steps are illustrated in the following example, involving an LLC. The valuation date is October 31, 2013.

Steps 1 and 2. The subject company has two classes of member interests: 250,000 preferred-member ownership units owned by the founder/president, and 1,200,000 member units owned by employees and family members. There are no contingently issuable member units.

The company's member agreement states that the following rights are owned by the holder(s) of its preferred-member units:

- Liquidation preference of $2.5 million ($10 per unit)
- Participation right to share on a pro rata per-unit basis until the preferred unit holder receives, in total, four times the liquidation preference ($10 million)
- The right to convert any or all of its shares of preferred units into member units on a unit-for-unit exchange basis

Assume that the company has an equity value of $15 million.

Step 3. Calculate the break points for the (1) liquidation preference, (2) participation rights, and (3) residual value to common stock. See Table 13.1.

TABLE 13.1 Derivation of Break Points

	Units Outstanding	Percent of Total	Break Points No. 1 Liquidation Preference [2]	Break Points No. 2 Participation Rights [3]	Break Points No. 3 All to Other Members [4]
Preferred member units	$ 250,000	17.241%	$ 2,500,000	$ 7,500,000	$ —
Member units	1,200,000	82.759%	—	36,000,000	12,000,000
Incremental value (except units)	$ 1,450,000	100.000%	2,500,000	43,500,000	12,000,000
Cumulative value through prior breakpoint				2,500,000	46,000,000
Enterprise value breakpoints			$ 2,500,000	$ 46,000,000	$ 58,000,000
Incremental per unit value [5]					
Preferred member units			$ 10.00	$ 30.00	$ —
Member units			—	$ 30.00	$ 10.00
Cumulative per unit value [6]					
Preferred member units			$ 10.00	$ 40.00	$ 40.00
Member units			—	$ 30.00	$ 40.00

Notes:
[1] It is assumed that there are no member units contingently issuable.
[2] Each preferred unit has $10-per-share liquidation preference.
[3] Each preferred unit has a participation right equal to the value in excess of the liquidation preference on a per-share equivalent basis up to a maximum of 4 times the original issue price per unit ($4 \times \$2,500,000 = \$10,000,000$).
[4] After break point #3, it is assumed that the preferred-member units will convert to member units.
[5] The incremental per-unit value of each class of unit at each break point.
[6] The cumulative per-unit value of each unit class at each break point.

The result of this analysis is that break points occur when equity value equals $2.5 million, $46 million, and $58 million, respectively.

Step 4. The seven assumptions needed to apply the BSM model are as follows:

1. The underlying price of the equity of the subject company ($15 million) is equal to 100 percent of its equity.
2. The exercise prices are the break-point amounts. As noted earlier, separate break-point calculations are prepared and then used in separate BSM models.
3. The valuation date is October 31, 2013.
4. The expiration date is the assumed date of the liquidity event. In this example, assume that the liquidity event will occur five years from the valuation date (October 31, 2018). This is when the company's management predicts a liquidity event, based on owners' expectations. In those instances where the valuation analyst believes that there are multiple liquidity-event dates to be considered, a calculation for each date should be considered. The conclusion of value would be derived using a probability-based weighting of each liquidity date value.
5. Historical volatility can be derived from the observed volatility of public guideline companies, industry benchmarks, and other sources.[2] In this instance, assume a five-year volatility of 45 percent.
6. The risk-free rate is derived from the yield on U.S. Treasury instruments with a term equal to the expiration date utilized in the BSM model. In this example, assume a five-year risk-free rate of 1.31 percent.
7. The company has never declared or paid any dividends in excess of tax-related distributions, so assume a 0 percent dividend yield.

Steps 5 and 6. Then calculate a value of $17.50 per preferred-member unit and $8.85 per member unit under the option-pricing method as shown in Table 13.2.

In this example, the $8.85 fair value of member units is directly proportional to volatility and the length of time until the liquidity event. In other words, high volatility increases the likelihood that the underlying price will increase, and vice versa. Moreover, the longer the period of time until the liquidity event, the greater the likelihood that the underlying price will increase (and vice versa). This is illustrated in Table 13.3, which assumes the same facts as above except that the liquidity event occurs on the valuation date (which assumes 0% volatility and no holding period).

---

[2]See Aaron M. Rotkowski, "Estimating Stock Price Volatility in the Black-Scholes-Merton Model," *Value Examiner* (NACVA; November/December 2011), at 13–19.

TABLE 13.2 Option Pricing Method of Allocating Value to Preferred and Other Member Units Using Black-Scholes Method — 5-Year Liquidity Event Assumption Valuation Date: October 31, 2013

	Breakpoints			
	#1	#2	#3	End
Total Firm Value	$ 15,000,000	$ 15,000,000	$ 15,000,000	$ 15,000,000
Incremental Value of Breakpoint [5]	$ 2,500,000	$ 43,500,000	$ 12,000,000	$ 58,000,000
Breakpoint [5]	$ 2,500,000	$ 46,000,000	$ 58,000,000	
BSM Inputs				
Dividend yield	0.00%	0.00%	0.00%	0.00%
Years to Maturity	5	5	5	5
Risk-Free Rate (Rf) [2]	1.31%	1.31%	1.31%	1.31%
Volatility [3]	45.00%	45.00%	45.00%	45.00%
BSM Calculated Value of Call Option	$ 15,000,000	$ 12,727,474	$ 1,791,419	$ 1,255,141
Follow-on Option [4]	− 12,727,474	− 1,791,419	− 1,255,141	—
Incremental Option Value	$ 2,272,526	$ 10,936,054	$ 536,279	$ 1,255,141

	Breakpoints [5]			
% of Incremental Option Value	#1	#2	#3	End
Preferred Member Units	100.000%	17.241%	0.000%	17.241%
Member Units	0.000%	82.759%	100.000%	82.759%
Total	100.000%	100.000%	100.000%	100.000%

	Breakpoints [6]				Aggregate Equity Value	Units [5]	Per-Unit Value [7]
	#1	#2	#3	End			
Incremental Option Value							
Preferred member units	$ 2,272,526	$ 1,885,527	$ —	$ 216,403	$ 4,374,456	250,000	$ 17.50
Member units	—	9,050,528	536,279	1,038,737	10,625,544	1,200,000	$ 8.85
	$ 2,272,526	$ 10,936,054	$ 536,279	$ 1,255,141	$ 15,000,000	1,450,000	

Notes:
1 Assumes no contingently issuable units.
2 Assumes 5-years to maturity, same as liquidity date assumption.
3 Based on analysis of public guideline companies.
4 Value of option to purchase company at corresponding Breakpoint amount. In other words, 5-year options to purchase the Company
   for $0, $2,500,000, $46,000,000, and $68,000,000 have a value of $15,000,000, $12,727,474, $1,791,419 and $1,255,141, respectively.
   Therefore, the first Breakpoint increment from $0 to $2,500,000 has a value of $15,000,000 less $12,727,474 = $2,272,526.
   The second Breakpoint increment from $2,500,000 to $46,000,000 has a value of $12,727,474 less $1,791,419 = $10,936,054.
   The third Breakpoint increment from $46,000,000 to $58,000,000 has a value of $1,791,419 less $1,255,141 = $536,279.
   The value of a 5-year option to purchase the Company for $58,000,000 is $1,255,141.
5 See Table 13.1.
6 Calculated by multiplying value of Breakpoint increment by allocation percentages above.
7 Calculated by dividing aggregate equity value by number of shares.

EXAMPLE 2: JOINT VENTURE

Another example of special allocations of PTE ownership interests occurs with joint venture agreements. For example, when a joint venture occurs between (1) an operating company requiring working capital, depth of management, marketing, and/or other resources and (2) another business that is seeking vertical integration, product line diversity, overhead

TABLE 13.3   Valuation Date Is Same as Liquidity Event Date

	Total	Preferred Units	Member Units	Not Allocated
Underlying price	$ 15,000,000	$ —	$ —	$ 15,000,000
Liquidity preference	—	2,500,000	—	(2,500,000)
Participation right allocation	—	2,042,500	10,457,500	(12,500,000)
	$ 15,000,000	$ 4,542,500	$ 10,457,500	$ —
Number of units outstanding		250,000	1,200,000	
Fair value per unit		$ 18.17	$ 8.71	

This example results in a value-per-member unit of $8.71, which is less than the $8.85 value derived when there is a five-year holding period with 45 percent volatility.

absorption, and/or other benefits, the financial arrangement between the parties often results in complex profit- (and value-) sharing arrangements. The following is a relatively simple example in which a joint venture LLC is formed with an operating company (minority member) and an owner that provides financial support (majority member). Proceeds on sale/liquidation of the JV are to be allocated as follows:

1. The first $1.5 million of sales proceeds are paid to the minority member.
2. Excess proceeds are allocated 40 percent to the minority member and 60 percent to the majority member.

The following are the seven assumptions employed in applying the BSM model in this example:

1. The underlying price of the equity of the subject company ($5 million) is equal to 100 percent of its equity.
2. The exercise price is the $1.5 million break-point amount.
3. The valuation date is October 31, 2013.
4. The expiration date is the assumed date of the liquidity event. In this example, assume that the liquidity event will occur five years from the valuation date (October 31, 2018).
5. In this instance, assume a five-year volatility of 45 percent.
6. The risk-free rate is derived from the yield on U.S. Treasury instruments with a term equal to the expiration date utilized in the BSM model. In this example, assume a five-year risk-free rate of 1.31 percent.
7. A dividend payout limited to members' tax reimbursement.

TABLE 13.4 Option Pricing Method of Allocating Value to Joint Venture Black-Scholes Method—5-Year Liquidity Event Assumption—Valuation Date: October 31, 2013

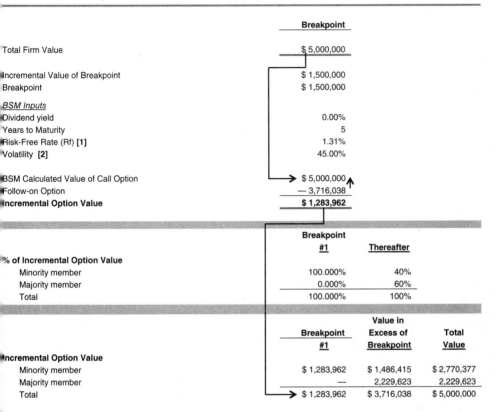

	Breakpoint
Total Firm Value	$ 5,000,000
Incremental Value of Breakpoint	$ 1,500,000
Breakpoint	$ 1,500,000
BSM Inputs	
Dividend yield	0.00%
Years to Maturity	5
Risk-Free Rate (Rf) [1]	1.31%
Volatility [2]	45.00%
BSM Calculated Value of Call Option	$ 5,000,000
Follow-on Option	− 3,716,038
Incremental Option Value	**$ 1,283,962**

	Breakpoint #1	Thereafter
% of Incremental Option Value		
Minority member	100.000%	40%
Majority member	0.000%	60%
Total	100.000%	100%

	Breakpoint #1	Value in Excess of Breakpoint	Total Value
Incremental Option Value			
Minority member	$ 1,283,962	$ 1,486,415	$ 2,770,377
Majority member	—	2,229,623	2,229,623
Total	$ 1,283,962	$ 3,716,038	$ 5,000,000

Notes:
1 Assumes 5-years to maturity, same as liquidity date assumption.
2 Based on analysis of public guideline companies.

TABLE 13.5 Valuation Date Is the Same as the Liquidity-Event Date

	Total	Minority Member	Majority Member
Underlying price	$ 5,000,000	$ —	$ —
Liquidity preference	−1,500,000	1,500,000	—
Participation right allocation	−3,500,000	1,400,000	2,100,000
	$ —	$ 2,900,000	$ 2,100,000

The minority member is allocated approximately $2.77 million of the $5 million total value as of the October 31, 2013, valuation date assuming 45 percent volatility and a five-year liquidity event. Assuming 0 percent volatility and a liquidity-event date on the valuation date, the minority member would realize $2.9 million, as presented in Table 13.5.

EXAMPLE 3: S CORPORATION WITH UNREASONABLE OFFICER/STOCKHOLDER COMPENSATION

S corporations are prohibited from having special allocations of income, losses, and so on. Nevertheless, it is not uncommon for the owners of an S corporation to receive benefits of ownership that are disproportionate to their shareholdings. This may create valuation and, in some instances, legal issues.

Consider the case of an S corporation with two owners: one owns 75 percent of the outstanding shares of common stock and is actively involved in the business, and the 25 percent shareholder is a passive investor not involved in the company. The company is very profitable and has earnings that are far in excess of a reasonable rate of return on its net tangible assets, indicating the existence of intangible assets such as goodwill. As an S corporation, it would appear that both owners should enjoy the benefit of such goodwill and receive annual distributions that are proportional to their respective ownership interest. But what if that were not the case? What if the 75 percent owner received 100 percent of normalized annual cash flows in the form of excess compensation and the minority owner received nothing? Moreover, what if this had occurred during the entire 10-year life of the company? Effectively, the 75 percent owner enjoyed the ongoing benefit of 100 percent of the company's net income, and the 25 percent owner received no current benefit from the S corporation.

These are the facts that I was presented with when I was appointed as a neutral expert to value the majority ownership interest assuming a fair value standard in connection with a New Jersey matrimonial dissolution matter. In this case, there was no shareholder agreement.

First, I valued the subject company on a control basis assuming normalized officer's compensation. I then was left to value the majority ownership interest and considered the arguments in favor of attributing 100 percent of the value of the company to the majority owner:

1. One hundred percent of the normalized historical income of the subject company had historically been received by the majority owner.
2. One hundred percent of future normalized company income was expected to be received by the majority owner until the company was sold.

3. There was no intention of selling the company, so the 100 percent benefit of ownership was expected to continue into the foreseeable future.
4. The minority owner had no intention of selling her shares in the company. Hence, no enterprise-level valuation adjustment could be estimated for any planned redemption.

There were also arguments in favor of attributing 75 percent of the value of the company to the majority owner:

1. It was unclear to me whether the majority owner's receipt of 100 percent of normalized company net income was permissible under applicable state and federal law. I was not qualified to render a legal opinion on this issue and was precluded from obtaining such an opinion.
2. In the event that the company was sold, the majority owner would only receive 75 percent of the proceeds from the sale.
3. The majority owner had no intention of selling his shares in the company.

Based on the facts known and knowable to me at the time of the valuation and based on the scope limitations imposed on my due diligence, I issued a report that indicated a *range* in value of the subject interest of 75–100 percent of the value of the company. I believe that ascribing either 75 percent or 100 percent of the company's value to the majority owner would have placed me in the position of rendering a legal opinion, which I was not prepared or qualified to deliver.

This example highlights the importance of

- Investigating whether there are special allocations of normalized net income, even when valuing ownership interests in S corporations
- Considering the potential impact on the S corporation election if it were determined by a taxation authority that special allocations of company net income effectively created a second class of stock
- Considering the legal issues associated with owners receiving benefits from their ownership interest in PTEs that are disproportionate to their equity holdings
- Considering the valuation impact of owners receiving benefits from their ownership interest in PTEs that are disproportionate to their equity holdings
- Avoiding/limiting opinions on matters where we, as valuation analysts, lack expertise

Checklist

Ralph Waldo Emerson said, "The man who grasps principles can success-fully select his own methods. The man who tries methods, ignoring principles, is sure to have trouble."[1] The accompanying checklist is prepared in the spirit of Emerson's quote; it is intended as a tool to assist with the implementation of the principles presented in this book. It should not be used as a facilitator of rote calculations because an appreciation of PTE principles is necessary in order to understand the context of court decisions and how to apply the methods supporting such court decisions. This is especially true in an environment of frequently changing federal laws, income brackets, and tax rates.

The items in the following checklist are presented in the order of the book's chapters and cover many, but not all, of the issues that need to be considered in connection with the valuation of a PTE ownership interest. Professional judgment, applicable valuation standards, and case-specific facts and circumstances will dictate the additional procedures and considerations required in a given matter.

Printable copies of this checklist in Word format can be accessed at Eric J. Barr, *Valuing PTEs*, www.valuingptes.com.

---

[1]Quotes by Ralph Waldo Emerson, www.searchingwithin.com/reflections/emerson.html.

Valuing PTEs Checklist

	Yes	No	N/A
Introduction			
1. Identify the PTE to be valued.	☐	☐	☐
2. Understand all rights, benefits, and restrictions of the PTE ownership interest to be valued.	☐	☐	☐
3. Define purpose of valuation.	☐	☐	☐
4. Determine date of valuation.	☐	☐	☐
5. Identify and comply with all applicable performance and reporting standards.	☐	☐	☐
6. Access all relevant information needed to perform the valuation.	☐	☐	☐
7. Determine valuation assumption	☐	☐	☐
a. Value to the holder	☐	☐	☐
b. Fair value	☐	☐	☐
c. Investment value	☐	☐	☐
d. Fair market value	☐	☐	☐
e. Liquidation value	☐	☐	☐
f. Other	☐	☐	☐
8. Identify premise of value	☐	☐	☐
a. Going concern	☐	☐	☐
b. Liquidation	☐	☐	☐
9. Consider approaches to value	☐	☐	☐
a. Income approach	☐	☐	☐
b. Market approach	☐	☐	☐
c. Net asset (cost) approach	☐	☐	☐
10. If employing the income approach	☐	☐	☐
a. Capitalization of earnings method	☐	☐	☐
b. Discounted future returns method	☐	☐	☐
11. If employing the market approach	☐	☐	☐
a. Guideline transaction method	☐	☐	☐
b. Guideline public company method	☐	☐	☐
The History of Federal Statutory Tax Rates in Maximum Income Brackets and the Evolution of Different Forms of Business Entities			
1. The Internal Revenue Code was codified in 1926 and then recodified in 1939, 1954, and 1986. Does the valuation analysis apply the Internal Revenue Code of 1986, as amended?	☐	☐	☐
2. The purchasing value of nominal dollars declined during the period 1913–2013 due to inflation. Was this considered in connection with multiperiod analyses of financial data?	☐	☐	☐
3. During the period 1913–2013 (except for the years 1988–1992), federal individual statutory income tax rates in the	☐	☐	☐

maximum income bracket exceeded federal corporation statutory income tax rates in the maximum income bracket. Was this considered and referenced in the valuation analysis?

4. During each of the years 1936–1939 and after 1953 (each □ □ □
   year that there was a federal individual income tax on C
   corporation dividends) for individuals in the maximum
   income bracket, the total of federal C corporation statutory
   income tax rates and federal individual statutory income tax
   rates on C corporation dividends exceeded federal individual
   statutory income tax rates. Was this considered and
   referenced in the valuation analysis?

5. Except for the period 2003–2013, during all years where □ □ □
   there has been a federal individual income tax on C
   corporation dividend income, the applicable individual tax
   rate on dividend income was always at least equal to the
   federal individual income tax rate. Was this considered and
   referenced in the valuation analysis?

6. Federal individual income, dividend, and corporation □ □ □
   income tax rates change, often substantially. Was it known
   or knowable that income tax rates were going to change as
   of the valuation date, and, if so, was this considered and
   referenced in the valuation analysis?

7. The number of income brackets and the range of income □ □ □
   contained in each bracket frequently change. Was it known
   or knowable that income brackets were going to change as
   of the valuation date, and, if so, was this considered and
   referenced in the valuation analysis?

8. Laws governing the calculation of taxable income change. □ □ □
   Was it known or knowable that the calculation of taxable
   income was going to change as of the valuation date, and, if
   so, was this considered and referenced in the valuation
   analysis?

9. Rules favoring business entity forms change. Was it known □ □ □
   or knowable that any such rules were going to change as of
   the valuation date, and, if so, was this considered and
   referenced in the valuation analysis?

Effective Federal Individual and Corporation Income Tax Rates

1. During 1913–2013, only a very small percentage of □ □ □
   taxpayers were impacted by federal individual tax rates in
   the maximum income bracket. Was this considered and
   referenced in the valuation analysis?

2. The same amount of CPI-adjusted taxable income generated □ □ □
   substantially different effective federal individual, C
   corporation, and dividend income tax expenses, depending

(continued)

(Continued)

	Yes	No	N/A
on the year of calculation. Was this considered and referenced in the valuation analysis?			
3. During different years, the amount of tax benefit of operating a business as a PTE or a C corporation could be very different depending on the year and amount of taxable income. Was this considered and referenced in the valuation analysis?	☐	☐	☐
4. Investor after-tax cash flows and value are substantially impacted by entity form, income tax rates, and levels of taxable income. Was this considered and referenced in the valuation analysis?	☐	☐	☐
5. Was the amount of normalized entity-level federal taxable income taken into consideration in determining the income tax inputs used in the valuation analysis?	☐	☐	☐
6. During much of the twentieth century, there were several dozen annual federal individual income brackets that subjected each increment to larger progressive tax rates. There were far fewer income tax brackets for C corporations than for individuals during the period 1913–2013. Thus, more of the taxable income of a C corporation with $1 million of 2012 CPI-adjusted taxable income fell into the maximum income bracket than fell into the maximum individual income bracket as a PTE. Was this considered and referenced in the valuation analysis?	☐	☐	☐

Comparison of Different Entity Forms

	Yes	No	N/A
1. Was the subject business in a start-up phase?	☐	☐	☐
2. If so, did the owners receive a current tax benefit from offsetting PTE tax losses against the owners' other income? Did the valuation analysis explain this benefit?	☐	☐	☐
3. Did the valuation analysis explain the impact of PTE tax loss limitations (i.e., at-risk rules, tax basis) and their potential impact on value?	☐	☐	☐
4. Owners of C corporations, S corporations, limited liability companies, and limited partnerships enjoy limited liability with respect to claims against the business; general partners and sole proprietors do not have limited liability protection. Did the valuation analysis explain the impact of entity form on the owner's liability?	☐	☐	☐
5. PTEs avoid risk of an IRS excess-compensation adjustment. Did the valuation analysis explain the impact of avoiding this adjustment?	☐	☐	☐

6. PTEs avoid the risk of an accumulated earnings tax adjustment. Did the valuation analysis explain the impact of avoiding this penalty tax? ☐ ☐ ☐

7. C corporations are subject to two levels of taxation: one level of taxation occurs at the entity level on any gain on sale of company assets, and the second level of taxation occurs on the distribution of company assets to shareholders. PTEs (other than S corporations that converted from C corporation status and are subject to the BIG tax.) only incur one level of taxation on the gain on sale of company assets, at the owner level. Did the valuation analysis explain the income tax consequence of a sale of the business? ☐ ☐ ☐

8. The purchase of an equity ownership interest in a C corporation, S corporation, LLC, or partnership may have very different tax consequences, which may ultimately impact the after-tax cost of a purchase. Did the valuation analysis explain the impact of entity form on the tax consequences of purchasing a PTE ownership interest? ☐ ☐ ☐

9. Special allocations of income and distributions are permissible for C corporations, LLCs, and partnerships, but not with S corporations. Did the valuation analysis explain the benefits of special allocations? ☐ ☐ ☐

10. S corporations are subject to certain ownership limitations (i.e., number and type of owner); other PTEs and C corporations are not subject to such restrictions. Did the valuation analysis explain the impact of such ownership limitations? ☐ ☐ ☐

11. GAAP-basis C corporation financial statements contain current and deferred income tax assets, liabilities and expenses, and other disclosures. Such balances and disclosures are inapplicable to PTEs. Did the valuation analysis explain the modifications that need to be made to C corporation GAAP-basis financial statements to make them comparable to PTE financial statements? ☐ ☐ ☐

12. PTEs currently account for approximately 78% of all business entities. Was the prevalence of PTE forms of businesses considered in connection with the valuation analysis? ☐ ☐ ☐

13. The number of business entities filing U.S. income tax returns as a PTE increased 43.7% during the period 2003–2012; the number of C corporations filing U.S. income tax returns during this same period decreased 11.6%. Was this increasing trend in the number of PTEs considered in connection with the valuation analysis? ☐ ☐ ☐

(continued)

(*Continued*)

	Yes	No	N/A
Income Approach and Value to the Holder			
1. IRS Revenue Ruling 59–60 specifies eight factors that business appraisers are directed to consider in valuing the stock of closely held corporations. Were such factors considered?	☐	☐	☐
2. Was primary consideration given to dividend-paying capacity rather than dividends actually paid?	☐	☐	☐
3. Were standard of value jurisdictional issues considered?	☐	☐	☐
4. The court in *Delaware Open MRI*, a fair value case, stated that a petitioner is "entitled to be paid for that which has been taken from him." Was this considered and referenced in the valuation analysis?	☐	☐	☐
5. The court in *Delaware Open MRI* concluded that it would be highly misleading to (a) determine the value of a market-based acquisition of an S corporation by comparison to C corporations and then (b) assume that the S corporation would be sold at a higher price because of its PTE status. The court in *Delaware Open MRI* was not trying to quantify the value at which the subject business would sell to a C corporation; it tried to quantify its value as a going concern with an S corporation structure and award the petitioners their pro rata share of that value. Was this considered and referenced in the valuation analysis?	☐	☐	☐
6. The court in *Delaware Open MRI* recognized that no one should be willing to pay more than the value of what will actually end up in their pocket. Accordingly, the court rejected one appraiser's 0% tax-affecting adjustment, based on the 2004 valuation date and applicable income tax law. Was this considered and referenced in the valuation analysis?	☐	☐	☐
7. The court in *Bernier*, where the valuation date was in 2000, relied on the same methodology employed in *Delaware Open MRI* yet applied an effective income tax rate of 0%. Was this considered and referenced in the valuation analysis?	☐	☐	☐
8. The court in *Bernier* drew a distinction between failing to tax affect the earnings of an S corporation because it does not pay federal taxes at the entity level and utilizing a 0% tax-affecting rate arrived at through application of "all applicable rates, as ordered." Was this considered and referenced in the valuation analysis?	☐	☐	☐

9. The tax-affecting model utilized by the courts in *Delaware Open MRI* and *Bernier* did not take into consideration a number of factors that limit its use on other valuation engagements. Was this considered and referenced in the valuation analysis? ☐ ☐ ☐
10. Was the MDMM applied by the valuation analyst for tax-affecting purposes? ☐ ☐ ☐
11. Did the valuation analyst verify that (a) the entity-level tax on PTE pretax income plus individual federal and state income taxes on PTE income equals (b) federal and state income taxes on C corporation pretax income and the federal and state dividend tax on C corporation distributions? ☐ ☐ ☐

Inputs to MDMM
1. Were all of the following inputs considered when applying the MDMM? ☐ ☐ ☐
   a. Normalized pretax PTE income ☐ ☐ ☐
   b. Entity-level taxes on PTE income ☐ ☐ ☐
   c. Income retained in the business and not subject to distribution ☐ ☐ ☐
   d. PTE owner's effective federal income taxes on pass-through income ☐ ☐ ☐
   e. PTE owner's effective state and local income taxes on pass-through income ☐ ☐ ☐
   f. Owner's effective federal and state dividend taxes on C corporation income available for distribution ☐ ☐ ☐
2. Was normalized PTE pretax income adjusted for the following? ☐ ☐ ☐
   a. Nonrecurring or extraordinary items ☐ ☐ ☐
   b. Errors in the calculation of reported income and expenses ☐ ☐ ☐
   c. Lack of consistency in the classification of similar transactions ☐ ☐ ☐
   d. Changes or inconsistencies in accounting and/or income tax methods ☐ ☐ ☐
3. Was the degree of control of the subject ownership interest considered when normalizing the PTE's pretax income? ☐ ☐ ☐
4. Does the state or locality in which the PTE operates impose an entity-level income tax on PTE earnings? For example, New York City imposes an entity-level income tax on unincorporated LLC and partnership income. In addition, New York City does not recognize S corporation status. ☐ ☐ ☐
5. Were the following factors impacting income retained in the business considered in connection with the inputs needed for the MDMM? ☐ ☐ ☐
   a. Working capital requirements ☐ ☐ ☐

(*continued*)

(*Continued*)

	Yes	No	N/A
b. Capital expenditures	☐	☐	☐
c. Business acquisitions	☐	☐	☐
d. Purchase of an ownership interest	☐	☐	☐
e. Hiring of additional staff	☐	☐	☐
f. Settlement of litigation	☐	☐	☐
g. Debt service	☐	☐	☐
h. Restrictive covenants in loan documents	☐	☐	☐
i. Uninsured claims	☐	☐	☐
j. Deferred maintenance and repairs	☐	☐	☐
k. Research and development	☐	☐	☐
l. Geographic and/or product line expansion	☐	☐	☐
m. Software development/purchase	☐	☐	☐
n. Development of e-commerce solutions	☐	☐	☐
o. Website upgrade	☐	☐	☐
6. Were the effective federal and state individual income tax inputs for the MDMM derived from the incremental income tax cost to the owner of the PTE ownership interest by applying the "with and without method"?	☐	☐	☐
7. Does the calculation of effective federal and state individual income tax rates take into consideration the following?	☐	☐	☐
a. Normalized reasonable compensation	☐	☐	☐
b. Normalized PTE pretax income	☐	☐	☐
c. Alternative minimum taxes	☐	☐	☐
d. Personal exemption phase-outs	☐	☐	☐
8. Does the calculation of effective federal and state individual income tax rates exclude the following?	☐	☐	☐
a. The attribution of itemized deductions and personal exemptions to PTE pretax income	☐	☐	☐
b. Reported owner's compensation	☐	☐	☐
c. Reported PTE pretax income	☐	☐	☐
d. The application of nominal statutory rates for each income bracket to PTE pretax income	☐	☐	☐
9. If the tax year was prior to 2003, was the input for the federal individual tax on dividend income the same as the input for federal income taxes?	☐	☐	☐
10. If the tax year was after 2002, was the input for the federal individual tax on dividend income less than the input for federal individual income taxes?	☐	☐	☐
11. For years after 2012, does the input for the federal individual tax on dividend income consider the applicability of the net investment income tax surcharge of 3.8%?	☐	☐	☐
	☐	☐	☐

12. Were the effective federal and state individual dividend tax rate inputs for the MDMM derived by applying the "with and without method"?

Income Approach and Investment Value

1. Have the individual investment requirements of the buyer been considered and explained in the valuation analysis? ☐ ☐ ☐

2. Was investment value measured by the risk-adjusted present value of future cash flows that the investor would expect a company to earn, in the way that the investor would operate it? ☐ ☐ ☐

3. Has the valuation analyst considered the degree of control and/or influence represented by the subject ownership interest? ☐ ☐ ☐

4. Does the subject ownership interest provide access to products, technologies, personnel, trademarks, research and development, and other intangible assets that enhance the cash flows of the acquirer's business? ☐ ☐ ☐

5. Was the synergistic benefit, if any, of the subject interest to the buyer considered as part of the valuation analysis? ☐ ☐ ☐

6. Will the acquirer of the subject interest enjoy the benefits of the subject interest's PTE status after the transaction? ☐ ☐ ☐

7. If so, was the MDMM methodology applied to determine the appropriate tax-affecting adjustment? ☐ ☐ ☐

8. Was the acquirer's cost of capital utilized to determine the investment value of the ownership interest? ☐ ☐ ☐

9. Will the acquirer have "inside basis" equal to "outside basis" post-transaction? ☐ ☐ ☐

10. Will the acquirer be able to amortize goodwill for tax reporting purposes post-transaction? ☐ ☐ ☐

11. If so, is the risk-adjusted present value of this tax benefit considered in the valuation analysis? ☐ ☐ ☐

12. If the acquirer is unable to enjoy the benefits of PTE status after the transaction, has this been explained in the valuation analysis? ☐ ☐ ☐

Income Approach and Fair Market Value

1. Has the definition of fair market value (FMV) as expressed in Revenue Ruling 59–60 been considered and referred to in the valuation analysis? ☐ ☐ ☐

2. Have each of the following characteristics of FMV, which distinguish it from value to the holder and investment value, been considered as part of the valuation analysis? ☐ ☐ ☐

   a. FMV assumes a willing buyer and a willing seller under no compulsion to effect a transaction; value to the holder and value to the buyer do not assume a lack of compulsion. ☐ ☐ ☐

(continued)

(Continued)

	Yes	No	N/A
b. FMV assumes hypothetical parties to a transaction; neither value to the holder nor value to the buyer assumes hypothetical parties.	☐	☐	☐
c. FMV assumes reasonable knowledge of relevant facts; the definition of value to the holder and value to the buyer does not include this assumption.	☐	☐	☐
d. FMV is defined as a price; neither value to the holder nor value to the buyer is defined as a price.	☐	☐	☐
e. Under FMV, the perspectives of two parties must be considered: the hypothetical seller and the hypothetical buyer. Under value to the holder and value to the buyer, only one perspective is considered.	☐	☐	☐
3. Was value to the hypothetical holder deemed to be the "floor" value under FMV?	☐	☐	☐
4. Was value to the hypothetical buyer deemed to be the "ceiling" value under FMV?	☐	☐	☐
5. Does the valuation analyst quantify the difference between floor and ceiling values?	☐	☐	☐
6. Does the valuation analyst consider the relative negotiating strength of the hypothetical buyer and hypothetical seller?	☐	☐	☐
7. Does the valuation analyst adequately justify FMV when the difference between floor and ceiling value is significant?	☐	☐	☐

Fair Market Value Court Decisions

	Yes	No	N/A
1. Has the valuation analyst considered each of the following six court decisions when applying the FMV standard of value (the six FMV cases)?	☐	☐	☐
a. *Gross v. Commissioner*	☐	☐	☐
b. *Estate of Heck v. Commissioner*	☐	☐	☐
c. *Wall v. Commissioner*	☐	☐	☐
d. *Estate of Adams v. Commissioner*	☐	☐	☐
e. *Robert Dallas v. Commissioner*	☐	☐	☐
f. *Gallagher v. Commissioner*	☐	☐	☐
2. The premise underpinning each of the six FMV cases is that PTEs and their owners incur lower income taxes. Was this considered and explained in the valuation analysis?	☐	☐	☐
3. Did the valuation analyst compare and contrast the principles underlying *Delaware Open MRI*, *Bernier*, and the six FMV cases and explain their similarities and differences?	☐	☐	☐
4. Did the valuation analyst consider the courts' reasoning in the six FMV cases for rejecting a 40% tax-affecting adjustment?	☐	☐	☐

5. Does the valuation analysis indicate that each of these six □ □ □
FMV cases does the following?
a. Involved the valuation of an ownership interest in a PTE □ □ □
b. Was prepared for estate or gift tax reporting purposes □ □ □
c. Had valuation dates prior to 2000 (except *Gallagher*, □ □ □
which had a 2004 valuation date)
d. Valued the subject interest pursuant to the income □ □ □
approach
e. Resulted in a tax-affecting adjustment of 0% □ □ □
6. Has the valuation analyst considered the MDMM impact of □ □ □
the individual and dividend tax rates in effect as of the
valuation dates noted in the six FMV cases?
7. Did the valuation analysis disclose that the six FMV cases □ □ □
never reported that an alternative to the all-or-nothing tax-
affecting methodology was considered?

The Market Approach

1. Has applicable authoritative guidance regarding the □ □ □
requirement to consider the market approach been
examined and referenced in the valuation analysis?
2. When applying the guideline public company method, has □ □ □
the valuation analyst performed the following?
a. Considered public companies comparable to the subject □ □ □
PTE
b. Explained the criteria used to determine comparability □ □ □
c. Compared the financial performance and relative □ □ □
strengths, weaknesses, threats, opportunities, and other
relevant factors of the subject PTE to the guideline public
companies
d. Considered guideline public companies whose shares are □ □ □
actively traded
e. Normalized the results of operations of the guideline □ □ □
public company for purposes of comparison to the subject
PTE
3. When applying the guideline public company method, has □ □ □
the valuation analyst considered applying different inputs
for value to the holder versus investment value if the subject
interest has the ability to influence management policies or
enjoy the prerogatives of control?
4. Has the valuation analyst also considered and explained the □ □ □
inconsistency of applying valuation metrics and multiples of
public C corporations to PTEs when applying the guideline
public company method?
5. When applying the guideline public company method under □ □ □
a value to the holder assumption, has the valuation analyst
developed valuation multiples for the subject PTE based on
investor net income after dividend taxes?

(*continued*)

(*Continued*)

	Yes	No	N/A
6. Has the valuation analyst considered and explained the potential consequences of relying on PTE valuation metrics other than investor net income when applying the guideline public company method under a value to the holder assumption?	☐	☐	☐
7. Has the valuation analyst considered whether, under investment value and FMV, the purchaser of the subject interest will be able to enjoy the benefits of PTE status under the guideline public company method?	☐	☐	☐
8. If so, does the valuation analysis disclose the reasons and justification for continuation (or loss) of the subject interest's PTE status?	☐	☐	☐
9. Has the valuation analyst considered the guideline transactions method?	☐	☐	☐
10. Have appropriate databases been examined to identify potential guideline transactions?	☐	☐	☐
11. When considering potential guideline transactions, has the valuation analyst examined the following?	☐	☐	☐
a. Sufficient information for each transaction to conclude that the subject PTE is comparable to the sold entity	☐	☐	☐
b. A sufficient number of comparable transactions to justify reliance on this method	☐	☐	☐
12. Has the valuation analyst considered the impact of the timing of potential guideline transactions on selling price, i.e., did the transaction occur before, during, or after the 2008–2009 recession?	☐	☐	☐
13. Has the valuation analyst considered the potential impact of relying on historical and not normalized financial information of potential guideline transaction companies?	☐	☐	☐
14. Has the valuation analyst considered the impact of the guideline transaction purchase price allocation to tangible assets, goodwill, covenants not to compete, employment agreements, and so on?	☐	☐	☐

Individual State Income Taxes

	Yes	No	N/A
1. Has the valuation analyst considered the valuation impact of state income taxes?	☐	☐	☐
2. Did the valuation analyst determine if the subject PTE files state and local income tax returns in all applicable jurisdictions?	☐	☐	☐
3. Has the valuation analyst considered the difference between state and local income taxes of the subject interest and the	☐	☐	☐

comparable state and local income taxes of guideline public companies and guideline transactions employed under the market approach?

4. Does the state or locality in which the PTE operates impose individual income taxes on PTE taxable income that pass through to owners? □ □ □

5. If so, has the progressivity of such state individual income tax rates been considered and explained by the valuation analyst? □ □ □

6. Certain localities, i.e., New York City, impose income taxes at the PTE entity level or add an additional layer of individual income taxes at the owner level. Has this been considered by the valuation analyst? □ □ □

7. The after-tax cash flows of an ownership interest in a business located in a high-tax location is less than it would be if the business were located in a low-tax location, all other things being equal. Has this been considered by the valuation analyst in connection with a determination of the FMV (or investment value) of a controlling PTE ownership interest? □ □ □

Discounts, Premiums, Bylaws, and State Laws

1. Has the valuation analyst read all PTE owners' agreements, bylaws, and other documents that define the rights and responsibilities of the subject interest? □ □ □

2. Has the valuation analyst identified the limitations or degree of control represented by the subject PTE ownership interest? □ □ □

3. If the subject interest is subject to limitations, has the valuation analyst considered their impact with respect to the following? □ □ □
   a. Discount for lack of control □ □ □
   b. Discount for lack of marketability □ □ □
   c. Other discounts □ □ □

4. Has the valuation analyst considered the impact of state law on the enforceability of provisions in owners' agreements that limit owners' rights and privileges? □ □ □

5. Have the provisions of IRC § 2704(b) been considered with respect to the valuation of PTE ownership interests for gift or estate tax reporting purposes? □ □ □

6. For estate or gift tax planning, has the valuation analyst considered the formation of a restricted limited liability company or restricted limited partnership pursuant to Nevada Senate Bill 350? □ □ □

7. Has the valuation analyst performed the following? □ □ □
   a. Identified any other states that adopted laws similar to that of Nevada Senate Bill 350 □ □ □

(continued)

(*Continued*)

	Yes	No	N/A
b. Become aware of any IRS challenges to (or acceptance of) Nevada Senate Bill 350	☐	☐	☐

Valuing Complex PTE Ownership Interests

	Yes	No	N/A
1. LLCs and partnerships permit special allocations. Have all special allocations of ownership rights, privileges, and interests in the subject PTE been considered and explained by the valuation analyst?	☐	☐	☐
2. Are there special allocations to owners of the following?	☐	☐	☐
a. Revenues	☐	☐	☐
b. Expenses	☐	☐	☐
c. Distributions	☐	☐	☐
d. Taxable income	☐	☐	☐
e. Voting rights	☐	☐	☐
f. Capital contribution requirements	☐	☐	☐
g. Proceeds on sale of the PTE	☐	☐	☐
h. Other rights and privileges	☐	☐	☐
3. Have the valuation implications of special allocations to different classes of ownership interests been considered by the valuation analyst?	☐	☐	☐
4. With respect to the valuation of an ownership interest in a PTE with a complex ownership structure, has the valuation analyst avoided multiplying the total value of the subject business by the percentage interest being valued to derive a conclusion of value?	☐	☐	☐
5. When there are special allocations of proceeds on the sale of a PTE, has the valuation analyst considered the applicability of the option pricing method to value the subject ownership interest?	☐	☐	☐
6. When applying the option pricing method, has the valuation analyst performed the following?	☐	☐	☐
a. Identified the amounts at which ownership allocations change (break points)	☐	☐	☐
b. Obtained all assumptions needed to apply an appropriate option pricing model	☐	☐	☐
c. Calculated the value of an ownership interest in the subject PTE at each break point	☐	☐	☐
d. Allocated each break point value to the respective ownership interests	☐	☐	☐
7. When valuing an ownership interest in an S corporation, has the valuation analyst identified any instances of the following?	☐	☐	☐

a. Unreasonable compensation paid to or on behalf of □ □ □
shareholders
b. Disproportionate distributions to shareholders □ □ □
c. Ineligible shareholders with an ownership interest in the □ □ □
subject company
8. If so, has the valuation consultant considered the valuation □ □ □
risk associated with the following?
a. An inadvertent termination of the S election □ □ □
b. The authority (legal and contractual) of the shareholders □ □ □
receiving disproportionate benefits to continue to receive
such benefits
9. Has the valuation analyst avoided opining on matters □ □ □
requiring legal expertise?

Case Study: Bob's Cruises

PART I: INTRODUCTION

"Welcome aboard! My name is Bob."

That is how I start most of my conversations these days, now that I am the proud owner of the most successful three-hour glass-bottomed, scuba diving excursion adventure in the Caribbean. I have more customers than I can handle, and they all want to learn how a former accountant from Long Island, yours truly, became the owner of a vacation dream-making machine. Well, here is how it happened.

My story began approximately five years ago. The date was July 16, 2013, and the time was 2:00 P.M. I was 35 years old, not married, and, as of one hour before, unemployed. The privately owned family business where I had spent the past 10 years had just fired me, and I was finding it difficult not to reflect on the events of the past few years.

I was a rising star in my company, a loyal and skilled accountant—but it didn't matter when the recession hit and the recovery never materialized. Although I survived several rounds of "rightsizing," my company was eventually swallowed by a much larger firm, a whale in comparison to our minnow. When the whale swallows you, unless your name is Jonah and you're from Galilee, don't expect to survive. Since I was only Bob from Long Island, I didn't.

When I thought about the past few years, I realized that it was time for me to move on. I had gotten tired of working at a desk and needed more interaction with nonfinancial people. I also learned that all fortunes don't rise and fall with the company's rising and falling tide. It seemed that when times were good, senior management—not those below—reaped the reward.

At this point, it was clear to me that a large part of my career and job risk was out of my control. I was dependent on the competency of the company's management and clients, the economy, tax laws, and many other factors. I know that risk is unavoidable, but I no longer wanted the risk/reward imbalance that I would surely continue to find in a formal big-business environment. What I needed was an opportunity that would allow me to identify and manage risk and to be rewarded for taking risk. I was open to purchasing a business. Now was the time, but where could I find the right situation?

Needing some time to sort my thoughts, I decided to not cancel the one-week vacation I had scheduled at my favorite hotel in Caribbea, a small (hypothetical) remote island in the Caribbean. Once there, I started considering my next steps.

Sam

Since I was a teenager, I have taken vacations in Caribbea every August. One of the things that I've most enjoyed while vacationing in Caribbea are the conversations that I've had with a local businessman named Sam. Sam and I first met at a hotel bar 15 years earlier. Although he was about 30 years older than me, we had a lot in common. Like me, he was from the United States, we shared a passionate interest in New York area sports teams, we had similar political points of view, and we both had an interest in business. When we first met, Sam had just started a local business, Sam's Cruises, that catered to vacationing hotel guests and cruise ship passengers looking for a scuba diving excursion; I was just starting my career in public accounting. For two guys in a bar, that was enough to start a friendship.

Over time, Sam and I stayed in touch via e-mail, and I would have dinner with him each year when visiting Caribbea. He was a friend, someone with whom I felt comfortable discussing work or personal issues. I found him to be very wise. So, I knew that we would be discussing my career crisis when I had dinner with him in August 2013.

Sam was blunt and direct. He told me that it was about time I left the corporate world and that I should be an entrepreneur—own my own business and do something financially and personally rewarding. That is what he did when he left his consulting job on the mainland to start Sam's Cruises, and he had not regretted it for a moment. Sam was right, and I agreed that it was time for a change. He had been lucky. It's not every day that you can find a Sam's Cruise opportunity.

And that is where my story gets interesting.

The Opportunity

Sam had anticipated our conversation. He knew that I was raised on Long Island where I spent my summers as a boy fishing, sailing, and racing motorboats. He also knew that I loved the beach and needed to escape from the formal business office environment. Coincidentally, Sam wanted to slow down and travel. Our timetables aligned, and so he offered me the chance to buy his business—fun-filled excursions on a glass-bottomed boat offering scuba diving to vacationers in Caribbea. We did not discuss price.

I needed a few days to digest Sam's offer. After returning back home to New York, I called Sam to tell him that I was interested.

Business Due Diligence

Sam and I agreed that I should work at Sam's Cruises for two months and learn how to operate the business, meet key business contacts, and understand the industry and the local economy. He would provide me with access to his tax returns, books, and records and answer any questions that I had regarding his company's historical economic performance. Equally important, I would experience what it was like to live in Caribbea. Sam agreed to show me the ropes so that I knew what to expect as the owner of Sam's Cruises.

Sam believed that the more I knew about the business, the more I would value it. We agreed that unless I had a clear understanding of the future lifestyle and benefits of owning Sam's Cruises, there would be no transaction.

During my two months working with Sam, I learned a great deal about Caribbea. Caribbea enjoyed a stable political environment, had regulations that created a relatively high barrier of entry into a new business (which limited competition), and had inflation and a bank-lending environment that closely matched that of the United States. Caribbea had also adopted the U.S. Internal Revenue Code for its federal income tax law. Unemployment was relatively low, and the island had little crime. The cost of living was very low, typical of a Caribbean island. Sam told me that he never had a problem finding competent, reasonably priced labor. He also introduced me to local regulators, politicians, cruise line operators, hoteliers, and business leaders. I was confident that I would be able to develop the same relationships with them that they had with Sam. The weather was mild, and the island appeared to be a relatively low-risk environment in which to own a business.

During my financial review of the company, I learned that the company's revenues were derived from two sources: U.S. vacationers visiting the island on cruise ships and U.S. vacationers staying at hotels on the island's main strips. I initially thought that revenues would vary based on the health of the U.S. and world economies, but I found that in good times and bad, through weak and strong U.S. currency fluctuations, revenues remained relatively stable.

Caribbea was comprised of two provinces: St. Christopher and St. Michael. Both provinces had popular, well-developed tourist areas. Sam's

Cruises was located in St. Christopher, which had a local tax structure that matched that of the State of New Jersey. Sam's Cruises had no competitors in St. Christopher, and it was unlikely that there ever would be a competitor due to local regulations. The other province, St. Michael, had a local tax structure that matched that of the City of New York. St. Michael had only one business like Sam's Cruises: Betty's Cruises. Betty's Cruises had been operating for approximately 20 years and did not compete with Sam's Cruises.

Sam's Cruises	Betty's Cruises
St. Christopher, Caribbea	St. Michael, Caribbea
New Jersey tax laws	New York City and State tax laws
15 years of operations	20 years of operations

Sam personally owned the building and dock from which the business operated. This site was where the boat was stored and maintained, where excursions originated, and where the company's back office operated. It was strategically located within a mile of where the cruise ships docked and where the hotels were located. Sam kept it in excellent condition, and there was no deferred building maintenance.

Sam's boat was critical to his success. Sam purchased a new boat every 10 years, without any debt financing. The boat that Sam purchased 5 years ago cost $1 million. Sam estimated that when he trades it in 5 years, it will have an estimated value of $200,000. Sam carefully performed all repairs and maintenance with his employees on an as-needed, timely basis. Sam made sure that the boat was never out of commission and presented well.

I found that I loved everything about operating Sam's Cruises. I enjoyed meeting and entertaining people and spending time outdoors in beautiful, sunny weather. Sam's employees were competent, friendly, pleasant, and extremely loyal.

PART II: SAM'S CRUISES

I read the cash-basis income tax returns and books and records of the company (there were no financial statements) to develop an understanding of the financial position, results of operations, and cash flow of Sam's Cruises.

My initial determination was that Sam was not making any money and that I should not bother with his business. But I knew that Sam was a wealthy man; had an expensive lifestyle; and lived in a magnificent, debt-free home. The reported numbers were inconsistent with Sam's spending habits. How could this be?

As an accountant, I had learned that reported results of operations are often different from the true economic financial performance of a company. Was Sam underreporting his taxable net income? I needed to dig into the numbers to find out.

Normalization

In order to predict the future results of operations of Sam's Cruises, I first needed to understand its true historical economic results of operations. The process of converting reported results to an economic basis is called *normalization*. Once normalized, Sam's Cruises' results of operations would be more indicative of the true economic activities of the business.

The following are four examples of normalization adjustments that I considered:

1. Correcting errors in the historical tax returns
2. Conforming accounting methodologies of Sam's Cruises to the accounting methodologies conventionally employed
3. Eliminating nonoperating and nonrecurring activities
4. Restating transactions that were not reported on an economic basis

My accounting background helped me perform this analysis.

Income and expense recognition and owner distributions are often classified in financial statements and tax returns in a manner that will generate lower income taxes. For example, distributions to owners can take the form of (regular and excess) compensation, perquisites, dividends, loans, compensation of no-show family members, and nonbusiness expenditures. I specifically focused on these types of adjustments in my analysis.

Sam was uneasy about sharing with me the information that I needed to prepare my normalization adjustments. This was out of character because he was willing to openly share information about all other aspects of his business. Eventually, he relented.

After digging more deeply into the numbers, I understood Sam's reticence. Let's just say that it looked like he operated by his own set of accounting rules.

The following are examples of the normalization adjustments that I identified:

- Large amounts of cash income (averaging $150,000 per year) were not recorded.
- Excessive building rent was charged to the company by Sam (averaging $75,000 per year).

TABLE B.1   Sam's Cruises—Schedule of Average Normalized Pretax Income (000s omitted)

	5-Year Average, as Reported		Normalization Adjustments	5-Year Average, Normalized	
Revenues	$ 750	100%	$ 150	$ 900	100%
Expenses					
Officer salaries	200	27%	(125)	75	8%
Other salaries	200	27%	10	210	23%
Rent	150	20%	(75)	75	8%
Depreciation	—	0%	80	80	9%
Personal expenses	50	7%	(50)	—	0%
Other operating and administrative	150	20%	10	160	18%
	750	100%	(150)	600	67%
Income before income taxes	$ —	0%	$ 300	$ 300	33%

- The company paid and deducted many of Sam's personal expenses (averaging $50,000 per year).
- The company recorded bonus depreciation and/or accelerated depreciation whenever it purchased a new boat or acquired other property and equipment.
- Sam reported an annual salary of $200,000 (he said that a replacement could be found that would cost the company $75,000).
- Sam did not record certain business expenses that were paid in cash (averaging $20,000 per year).

The net effect of all of these normalization adjustments during each of the five preceding years was that reported average pretax income was significantly increased to derive normalized average pretax income. Table B.1 summarizes my findings.

The *reported* average pretax income of $0 significantly understated the average, economic, normalized pretax income of $300,000. Moreover, during the past five years, pretax income and net cash flows from operations never varied by more than 5 percent (with an average annual increase in net cash flows during the five-year period of 3%).

I supposed that there were buyers who would continue Sam's practice of not reporting cash income and cash expenses and overstating business expenses. Not me; I planned on following the letter of the law.

Sam told me that his company was an S corporation and paid no income taxes at the business-entity level. Instead, the taxable income of Sam's Cruises passed through to the business owner (Sam). Since the source of funds that would be used to buy Sam's Cruises is after-tax cash flows, the next adjustment that I needed to consider was annual normalized income tax expense, a potentially significant adjustment.

In order to convert normalized pretax income into normalized after-tax cash flows, I needed to consider the following:

- Current and future income tax rates
- My expected individual income tax expense as an owner of Sam's Cruises
- Company retention of earnings

In addition, I needed to determine the appropriate valuation multiple to be applied to normalized after-tax cash flows in order to determine Sam's Cruises' value to me as buyer.

Income Taxes

The value of Sam's Cruises, or any business, is based on its risk-adjusted present value of anticipated future after-tax economic returns. If it is known (or knowable) that income tax rates will change, that should be taken into consideration. I knew that major revisions to the U.S. and Caribbea federal tax laws took effect on January 1, 2013. It would be foolish to ignore the possibility that there might be future changes. But what changes could be expected? It was anyone's guess. I would have to use rates presently in effect but be mindful that future changes in tax rates might increase/decrease my anticipated future after-tax returns.

I calculated the income tax cost associated with my ownership interest in Sam's Cruises.

1. I prepared an analysis showing what my income tax liability would be assuming that I resided in St. Christopher (New Jersey) earning $75,000 per year (normalized salary for working at Sam's Cruises and coincidentally what I had earned as an accountant), with itemized deductions consisting solely of state income taxes, a single filing status, and no dependents. This was Case 1, my tax cost without an ownership interest in Sam's Cruises.
2. I then calculated my income tax cost assuming a 100 percent ownership interest in Sam's Cruises. This was Case 2 and made the same assumptions as Case 1 except that there was also normalized pretax income of $300,000 that passed through to me as the sole shareholder of Sam's Cruises.

TABLE B.2　　Tax Cost of Owning Sam's Cruises ($000s omitted)

| | St. Christopher | |
	Without S Corp	With S Corp
Gross income		
Wages	$ 75	$ 75
S Corp pretax income	—	300
Adjusted gross income (AGI)	75	375
Deductions and exemptions		
State income taxes		22
Less: 3% AGI floor		(4)
Standard deduction	6	—
Personal exemptions	4	—
	10	18
Federal taxable income	$ 65	$ 357

| | St. Christopher | |
	Without S Corp	With S Corp
Income taxes		
Individual federal income taxes	$ 12	$ 102
Individual state income taxes	3	22
	$ 15	$ 124
Difference		$ 109
Difference as a percent of S corp pretax income		36.3%

3. The difference in total income tax costs (Case 2 less Case 1, or $109,000) was the tax cost associated with an ownership interest in Sam's Cruises. Expressed as a percentage of pretax profit, the individual combined federal and local tax cost of an ownership interest in Sam's Cruises for me was 36.3 percent. See Table B.2.

I could now calculate the normalized after-tax returns that I could expect as an owner of Sam's Cruises. Table B.3 calculates the net-of-tax cash flows from owning Sam's Cruises, after taking into consideration federal, state, and

TABLE B.3 Sam's Cruises After-Tax Cash Flows ($000s omitted)

Normalized pretax income	$ 300	100.0%
Less: Corporation income taxes	—	0.0%
Normalized taxable income	300	100.0%
Less: Income retained in business	—	0.0%
Normalized cash flows to equity	300	100.0%
Less: Individual income taxes	109	36.3%
Normalized returns, after all income taxes	$ 191	63.7%

local income taxes; itemized deductions; and other factors specific to me. Table B.3 assumes that 100 percent of all income is distributed to me as the owner and that no income is retained in the company.

PART III: VALUING SAM'S CRUISES

Having calculated the after-tax cash flows that I would receive as owner of Sam's Cruises assuming 2013 individual income tax rates ($191,000), I now had to develop the appropriate valuation multiple.

Valuation Multiple

I spoke with a number of friends, business brokers, and former business colleagues to learn about valuation multiples. The feedback that I received was that the valuation multiple that should be applied is, in large measure, a function of the risks associated with prospectively achieving the business's normalized historical after-tax cash flows. Stated differently, the greater the risk of achieving such cash flows in the future, the lower the multiple; the lower the risk, the higher the multiple. If I believed that there was high risk associated with achieving the projected after-tax cash flows, a reasonable multiple would be three times the after-tax cash flows. On the other hand, if I believed that there was a low risk of achieving the projected after-tax cash flows, a reasonable multiple would be five times the after-tax cash flows. I felt confident that as an owner of Sam's Cruises, I could achieve its projected after-tax cash flows. I based this on the due diligence that I performed and my understanding of the business.

Another factor was the number of years that I would be willing to work and not derive any financial benefits from owning Sam's Cruises. I believed that a three-times multiple of after-tax cash flows was unreasonably low and

TABLE B.4   Sam's Cruises—Goodwill Value ($000s omitted)

	After-Tax Cash Flows	Goodwill Valuation Multiple	Goodwill Value
Low	$ 191	3.5	$ 669
High	$ 191	4.5	$ 860

that a five-times multiple of after-tax cash was too high (i.e., I was unwilling to work for five years without a return on my investment). What appeared reasonable, at least to me, was a 3.5- to 4.5-times after-tax cash flows multiple. This calculation would provide me with a rough idea of the value of the goodwill of Sam's Cruises without regard to the purchase of any assets or assumption of liabilities.

Armed with my after-tax cash flows and valuation multiples, I was now ready to estimate the value to me of an investment in Sam's Cruises. Table B.4 reflects my calculation of the goodwill value of Sam's Cruises.

Based on Table B.4, the goodwill value of Sam's Cruises was $669,000 to $860,000.

The total value of Sam's Cruises was equal to the value of its goodwill and the value of the assets of Sam's Cruises that I would purchase as part of this transaction. I estimated the trade-in value of the boat to be $600,000 based on its age, condition, and discussions with a local boat dealer, and that all other assets and liabilities would have a net value of $50,000. Thus, I calculated the total value of Sam's Cruises to be $1.319 million to $1.51 million.

Sanity Check

The $1.319 million to $1.51 million range of value for Sam's Cruises was only a preliminary, though important, first step. It provided a rough estimate of a reasonable cost for Sam's Cruises, but it was far from the highly technical and sophisticated approach to valuation described in the various treatises that I had read. Being a novice at business valuation and not wanting to rely solely on my own interpretation of the treatises or my rough calculation of value, I thought it wise to reach out to a valuation consultant and spoke with Monica, whom I knew from college. Monica enjoyed an excellent reputation as a valuation consultant.

Monica derived an estimate of the cost of equity for Sam's Cruises using a traditional "build-up" methodology. She took into consideration publicly available data and the following company-specific factors. Each observation is followed by a + or − sign to indicate whether the observation would tend to increase (+) or decrease (−) the cost of equity capital.

- Sam's Cruises was much smaller than the average publicly traded company in decile 10 (+).
- The company depended critically on Sam's professional skill, personal contacts, and experience. Even the publicly traded companies of similar size tended to have more than one executive officer ("thin management") (+).
- The company had minimal revenue growth during the past 10 years, which was less than the average publicly traded company (+).
- Sam's Cruises did not prepare financial statements in accordance with generally accepted accounting principles (GAAP) (+).
- The company had no credit history or relationships with lenders (+).
- The company was dependent on the tourist industry for its revenues (+/−).
- There was a concentration of customer referral sources (+).
- The company was located on a small, remote island (+).

Based on these factors, Monica believed that Sam's Cruises should have an equity *capitalization* rate of 20 percent.

To derive an estimate of the value of Sam's Cruises, Monica then calculated the amount of normalized earnings available for distribution to me, assuming a C corporation structure and a C corporation income tax rate that would yield me the same after-tax cash flows that I would receive as an S corporation shareholder. For this, she utilized a method that she described as the Modified Delaware MRI Model.

Tables B.5 and B.6 present Monica's calculation of the fair market value of Sam's Cruises.

Monica concluded that Sam's Cruises had a fair market value of $1.329 million, which was within the lower end of the range of values that I had estimated.

Value to Sam

I spoke with Sam and told him that I thought the total value of the business, including its goodwill, boat, and other assets, was $1.4 million, and that was my offer. Moreover, I was not interested in buying Sam's company's equity (or capital stock); I only wanted to buy assets. This would limit my exposure to Sam's prior tax sins and generate a step-up in the tax basis of the boat and any other assets purchased.

TABLE B.5 Sam's Cruises—Calculation of Income Subject to Capitalization—
Income Approach ($000s omitted)

	S Corp		C Corp		
Normalized pretax income	$ 300	100.0%	$ 300	100.0%	
Less: Corporation income taxes	—	0.0%	(42)	−14.0%	[3]
Normalized taxable income	300	100.0%	258	86.0%	
Less: Income retained in business	—	0.0%	—	0.0%	
Normalized cash flows to equity	300	100.0%	258	86.0%	
Less: Individual income taxes					
Federal income taxes	(90)	−30.0% [1]	(51)	−17.0%	[2]
NJ income taxes	(19)	−6.3% [1]	(16)	−5.3%	[2]
	(109)	−36.3%	(67)	−22.3%	
Normalized returns, after all income taxes	$ 191	63.7% Table B.3.	$ 191	63.7%	

Notes:

[1]   Based on 2013 federal and NJ individual income tax rates.
Federal individual income taxes includes regular tax; alternative minimum tax; and high income HI, Medicare, and other taxes. See Table B.2.

	With K-1 Income	Without K-1 Income	Difference
Federal individual income tax	$ 102	$ 12	$ 90
NJ individual income tax	22	3	19
Totals	$ 124	$ 15	$ 109

[2]   Same assumptions as #1 above, except that instead of K-1 income we assume inclusion and exclusion of dividend income:

	With Dividend Income	Without Dividend Income	Difference
Federal individual income tax	$ 63	$ 12	$ 51
NJ individual income tax	19	3	16
Totals	$ 82	$ 15	$ 67

[3]   Calculated combined federal and NJ corporate income tax rate.

TABLE B.6 Sam's Cruises—Calculation of Fair Market Value—Income Approach ($000s omitted)

Distributable company earnings (Table B.5)	$ 258
Increased by long-term growth	3%
Divided by: Capitalization rate	266
	20%
Indicated FMV	$ 1,329

TABLE B.7 Sam's Cruises—Comparison of Values ($000s omitted)

	Value	Difference from Seller's Offer
Buyer's offer	$ 1,400	$ 250
Monica's calculated FMV (Table B.6)	$ 1,329	$ 321
Seller's offer	$ 1,650	

Sam had no problem selling assets and leasing me the business property based on its fair rental value (this was already incorporated into my normalized pretax income model), continuing to work with me in the business for some unspecified period of time, allocating a portion of the purchase price to wages, and providing a covenant not to compete.

Sam thought that the business had a goodwill value of $1 million plus the trade-in value of the boat ($600,000) and other assets of $50,000. His asking price of $1.65 million was $250,000 more than I offered for the business. Table B.7 reflects a summary of the values ascribed to Sam's Cruises so far.

I tried to understand Sam's thinking regarding why the business was worth so much more to him than it was to me. My estimate of normalized pretax income was equivalent to what he realized. What accounted for the difference? The answer was that Sam was not reporting as taxable income cash revenues ($150,000) and personal expenses ($50,000). The $200,000 of annual unreported income resulted in annual tax savings of approximately $72,000, assuming a combined effective federal, state, and local income tax rate of 36 percent. Adjusting the values ascribed to Sam's Cruises by the seller's avoided income taxes substantially narrowed the difference between each of the values (Table B.8).

TABLE B.8 Sam's Cruises—Effect of Unreported Taxable Income on Value ($000s omitted)

	Buyer's Methodology	FMV Methodology
Avoided income taxes	$ 72	$ 72
Increased by long-term growth	—	3%
	72	74
Buyer's multiple	4	—
FMV capitalization rate	—	20%
Impact on value	288	371
Difference from seller's original offer (Table B.7)	(250)	(321)
Revised difference	$ 38	$ 50

Then, from out of the blue, I had a surprise visit from Betty of Betty's Cruises. She had learned of my interest in Sam's Cruises from her contacts at several of the local hotels. She had performed a background check on me and knew that I was a serious, qualified potential buyer. Betty wanted to explore the possibility of selling her business to me. She had enjoyed working in the business with her husband and daughter. But now her husband was ill and could no longer work. Betty's daughter had graduated from college, joined the military, and expressed no interest in returning to the business. Working at Betty's Cruises had become a difficult chore for Betty, and she was open to selling her company to me whether or not I purchased Sam's Cruises.

PART IV: VALUING BETTY'S CRUISES

Betty started her vacation business in St. Michael approximately 20 years before as a partnership (the business converted to a limited liability company (LLC) five years ago). She operated her business in a manner very similar to Sam's Cruises. Her pricing was similar, the profile of her customers was similar, and Betty worked with the same cruise lines and hotel chains. The economy of St. Michael was similar to that of St. Christopher. The level of government regulation and the availability of workers was the same. Betty lived in a part of St. Michael that was just as nice as the area where Sam lived.

Betty purchased her boat from the same dealer as Sam did; and, coincidentally, her boat was the same year, make, and model as Sam's. Betty also paid cash for her boat when she acquired it.

I examined the tax returns of Betty's Cruises, which, unlike Sam's Cruises, accurately portrayed her company's financial position and results of operations. Betty's Cruises, like Sam's Cruises, never incurred debt when purchasing a boat and had an affiliated entity that owned and leased the dock, boat storage area, and office space used by the company.

The normalized results of operations of Betty's Cruises reflected the same level of normalized average revenues ($900,000) and normalized average pretax earnings ($300,000) as Sam's Cruises. The two companies' normalized pretax results of operations were almost indistinguishable. Although Sam's Cruises and Betty's Cruises were both pass-through entities, Sam's Cruises was an S corporation, and Betty's Cruises was an LLC. Accordingly, both companies were subject to the same federal income tax rules but not the same state and local income tax rules. The local income tax rules that Sam's Cruises operated under in St. Christopher were like those of New Jersey. The local income tax rules that Betty's Cruises operated under in St. Michael were like those of New York City and New York State.

I was getting more familiar with the process of valuation. I knew that in order to determine the value to me as a buyer of Betty's Cruises, I next needed to determine the normalized after-tax cash flows to me as the prospective owner. In order to determine that amount, I needed to first understand the tax consequences of owning a St. Michael LLC that had normalized pretax profits of $300,000. Then I could apply the same 3.5- and 4.5-times valuation multiples that I used to value Sam's Cruises.

Normalized After-Tax Cash Flows

From my analysis of Sam's Cruises, I knew that I needed to consider the impact of 2013 federal, state, and local unincorporated and individual income tax rates. St. Michael imposed an unincorporated business tax on LLC and partnership taxable income (St. Michael also did not recognize S corporation status at the local level). I then prepared Tables B.9 and B.10 to calculate the tax cost associated with an ownership interest in Betty's Cruises and the after-tax income that I would realize from an investment in Betty's Cruises. Table B.10 also calculates the income subject to capitalization under the income approach.

Like Sam's Cruises, the total value of Betty's Cruises to me as a buyer was equal to the value of its goodwill plus the value of the assets, net of liabilities, that I would purchase as part of the transaction. As noted in Table B.11, I estimated the goodwill of Betty's Cruises to be $599,000–$770,000.

The $600,000 trade-in value of the boat plus $50,000 of other assets and liabilities assumed yielded a total value for Betty's Cruises of $1.249 million ($599,000 plus $650,000) to $1.42 million ($770,000 plus $650,000).

TABLE B.9   Tax Cost of Owning Betty's Cruises ($000s omitted)

	St. Michael	
	Without LLC	With LLC
Gross income		
Wages	$ 75	$ 75
S Corp pretax income	—	300
Less: LLC local income taxes	—	(12)
Adjusted gross income (AGI)	75	363
Deductions and exemptions		
State income taxes	6	37
Less: 3% AGI floor	—	(3)
Standard deduction	—	—
Personal exemptions	4	—
	10	34
Federal taxable income	$ 65	$ 329

	St. Michael	
	Without LLC	With LLC
Income taxes		
Individual federal income taxes	$ 12	$ 93
Federal alternative minimum tax	—	5
Individual state income taxes	6	37
	$ 18	$ 135
Individual income tax difference		$ 117
NYC unincorporated business tax		12
		$ 129
Difference as a percent of S corp pretax income		43.0%

Sanity Check

I again wanted a sanity check and asked Monica to calculate the value of Betty's Cruises, just as she had done with Sam's Cruises. Table B.12 summarizes her calculations.

Monica's estimate of the fair market value of Betty's Cruises was again within the lower end of the range of my approximated estimate. I decided to make an offer of $1.3 million.

TABLE B.10 Betty's Cruises—Calculation of Income Subject to Capitalization—
Income Approach ($000s omitted)

	LLC		C Corp		
Normalized pretax income	$ 300	100.0%	$ 300	100.0%	
Less: Corporation income taxes	(12)	−4.0%	(53)	−17.7%	[3]
Normalized taxable income	288	96.0%	247	82.3%	
Less: Income retained in business	—	0.0%	—	0.0%	
Normalized cash flows to equity	288	96.0%	247	82.3%	
Less: Individual income taxes					
Federal income taxes	(86)	−28.7% [1]	(49)	−16.3%	[2]
NJ income taxes	(31)	−10.3% [1]	(27)	−9.0%	[2]
	(117)	−39.0%	(76)	−25.3%	
Normalized returns, after all income taxes	$ 171	57.0%	$ 171	57.0%	

Notes:
[1] Based on 2013 federal, NYS, and NYC individual income tax rates.
   Federal individual income taxes includes regular tax; alternative minimum tax;
   and high income HI, Medicare, and other taxes. See Table B.9.

	With K-1 Income	Without K-1 Income	Difference
Federal individual income tax	$ 98	$ 12	$ 86
NYS and NYC individual income taxes	37	6	31
Totals	$ 135	$ 18	$ 117

[2] Same assumptions as #1 above, except that instead of K-1 income we assume
   inclusion and exclusion of dividend income:

	With Dividend Income	Without Dividend Income	Difference
Federal individual income tax	$ 61	$ 12	$ 49
NYS and NYC individual income taxes	33	6	27
Totals	$ 94	$ 18	$ 76

[3] Calculated combined federal, NYS, and
   NYC corporate income tax rate.

TABLE B.11   Betty's Cruises—Goodwill Value ($000s omitted)

	After-Tax Cash Flows	Goodwill Valuation Multiple	Goodwill Value
Low	$ 171	3.5	$ 599
High	$ 171	4.5	$ 770

TABLE B.12   Betty's Cruises—Calculation of Fair Market Value—Income Approach ($000s omitted)

Distributable company earnings (Table B.10)	$ 247
Increased by long-term growth	3%
	254
Divided by: Capitalization rate	20%
Indicated FMV	$ 1,272

TABLE B.13   Betty's Cruises—Comparison of Values ($000s omitted)

	Value	Difference from Seller's Offer
Buyer's offer	$ 1,300	$ 250
Monica's calculated FMV (Table B.12)	$ 1,272	$ 278
Seller's offer	$ 1,550	

Betty thought that her business had a goodwill value of $900,000 plus other assets of $650,000. Her asking price of $1.55 million was less than Sam's asking price but far greater than what Monica and I thought the business was worth. Betty also had no problem selling me the company's assets, leasing me the business property based on its fair rental value (this was already incorporated into my normalized pretax income model), continuing to work with me in the business for some unspecified period of time, allocating a portion of the purchase price to wages, and providing a covenant not to compete.

Table B.13 summarizes the values ascribed to Betty's Cruises so far.

PART V: CLOSING THE DEAL

I was new to the process of negotiating a purchase price for a business. It was obviously much more complicated than agreeing on a sales price based on

TABLE B.14   Comparison of Sellers' and Buyer's Offers ($000s omitted)

	Buyer's Offer	Seller's Offer	Difference
Purchase Price			
Sam's Cruises	$ 1,400	$ 1,650	$ 250
Betty's Cruises	$ 1,300	$ 1,550	$ 250
Purchase Price Includes Goodwill of			
Sam's Cruises	$ 750	$ 1,000	$ 250
Betty's Cruises	$ 650	$ 900	$ 250

what the parties think the business is "worth." Judging by the preliminary differences between the offer and counteroffers for the assets of both Sam's Cruises and Betty's Cruises, it appeared unlikely that any deal could be made. Table B.14 summarizes the initial positions of buyer and sellers.

After-Tax Purchase Cost

I realized, though, that what was important to me was not the pretax purchase price cost; rather, it was the after-tax purchase cost. If by structuring the transaction in a particular way I could reduce the after-tax cost of a purchase of either Sam's Cruises or Betty's Cruises, this could help narrow the differences. Three opportunities for reducing the after-tax purchase cost of each transaction were (1) amortizing goodwill over a 15-year period for income tax reporting purposes, (2) depreciating the $600,000 cost of the boat, and (3) allocating a portion of the purchase price to currently deductible salary expense.

Goodwill was a significant cost of each transaction and yielded a tax benefit over an extended period of time. In addition, I decided to request that $200,000 of the purchase price be converted to salary ($50,000 per year for four years).

I was beginning to feel optimistic about my chances of closing a deal with both Sam and Betty when I received some bad news: the license to operate each business was not separately salable and could only be sold with the business. Accordingly, I would be unable to structure either transaction as a purchase of assets and could only purchase the equity of both Sam's Cruises and Betty's Cruises. This had a substantial effect on the after-tax cost of Sam's Cruises, an S corporation, but no impact on the after-tax cost of Betty's Cruises, an LLC. This was because as a single-member LLC, Betty's Cruises was a disregarded entity for income tax reporting purposes. Thus, the transaction would be treated as if I personally purchased the assets of Betty's

TABLE B.15 Net of Tax Cost of Each Counter-Offer Assuming Purchase of Equity With $200K of Wages in Lieu of Goodwill ($000s omitted)

	Sam's Cruises (S Corp)		Betty's Cruises (LLC)	
	Pretax	After-Tax	Pretax	After-Tax
Purchase Price Allocation				
Boat [1]	$ 600	$ 600	$ 600	$ 342
Net Assets	50	50	50	50
Goodwill [2]	800	800	700	608
Salary [3]	200	151	200	142
Total Cost	$ 1,650	$ 1,601	$ 1,550	$ 1,141
Buyer's Offer		$ 1,400		$ 1,300

Notes:
[1] Assumes expensing in year of acquisition at overall effective tax rate of 43.0% (see Table B.9).
[2] Assumes 15-year straight-line amortization, discount rate of 23% (Monica's capitalization rate of 20% plus long-term growth of 3%), and overall effective tax rate of 43%.
[3] Assumes 4 years of salary at $50K per year, discount rate of 23%, and effective tax rates for each company (36.3% for Sam's Cruises and 43.0% for Betty's Cruises, see Tables B.2 and B.9).

Cruises even though I was purchasing the equity. This effectively placed me in the same position as if I purchased the assets of Betty's Cruises outright.[1] See Table B.15.

Comparison of Transactions

It was finally time to weigh the positives and negatives of each transaction.

First, I considered the advantages of buying Betty's Cruises. Betty's Cruises was a better opportunity than Sam's Cruises for the following reasons:

- The after-tax cost of Betty's Cruises ($1.141 million) was $460,000 less than the after-tax cost of Sam's Cruises ($1.601 million).
- The after-tax cost of Betty's Cruises was $159,000 less than my pretax offer of $1.3 million. The after-tax cost of Sam's Cruises was $201,000 more than my pretax offer of $1.4 million.

---

[1]The result to the buyer is no different if a single-member LLC purchases the equity of an LLC from another LLC with two or more members.

- I was concerned that I could inherit potential income and/or payroll tax audit adjustments for Sam's past reporting practices.
- Although I could still inherit payroll, sales, excise, and/or unincorporated business tax problems as well as potential legal liabilities by buying the equity of Betty's Cruises, this was not a concern to me because Betty appeared to report all revenues and expenses and file all required tax forms on a timely basis. There was no indication that she ever had any legal issues.
- The books, records, and income tax reporting of Betty's Cruises reflected its true economic results of operations, making it easier to finance.

On the other hand, Sam's Cruises was a more desirable acquisition because of the following factors:

- I knew the operations of Sam's Cruises better than the operations of Betty's Cruises, having worked there for several months.
- I knew Sam for many years and believed him when he said that he would be available to assist me in the future. I was not as sure that Betty would be available.
- St. Christopher had a lower income tax environment than St. Michael.

On balance, although both options were desirable, I thought Betty's Cruises was a better deal.

Another option for me was to purchase *both* companies. I considered the positives and negatives of this alternative. On the positive side, I considered the following:

- I could achieve economies of scale owning both companies. I could reduce total boat fuel costs through enhanced buying power from the sheer volume of my purchases. I could achieve lower payroll and advertising costs. I might even be able to achieve some cost savings by purchasing two boats.
- Owning both companies would further limit the possibility of future competition.
- If either Sam or Betty were unavailable to help me, at least having one of them would be beneficial.

On the negative side, I considered the following:

- I was uncomfortable incurring such a significant amount of debt.
- I knew that I still had a steep learning curve to climb managing one business; two businesses from day one might be too risky.
- There was an old joke that circulated on Long Island when I was a young boy. What are the two happiest days of a sailor's life? The answer: the day

TABLE B.16 Financing the Purchase of Betty's Cruises ($000s omitted)

Equipment financing	$ 500
Salary	200
Cash	400
Seller financing	450
Total	$ 1,550

that he buys his first boat and the day that he sells his last boat. It just didn't seem right to jump into this business by buying two companies.

I concluded that I would only buy one of these companies, Betty's Cruises, at this time.

My final step was to figure out how to pay for Betty's Cruises. I prepared Table B.16, indicating how each component of the gross selling price would be paid.

I decided to pursue this option. Betty agreed to the salary adjustment, and I arranged the necessary equipment and seller financing with Betty's cooperation.

After concluding my deal with Betty, I spoke with Sam. Although he understood why I chose Betty's company and not his, he was very upset and angry with me.

I told Sam that I might be interested in purchasing his company in another two years after I had fully adjusted to owning Betty's Cruises. I told Sam that I might be interested in purchasing an option to buy or having first refusal rights with respect to his company. We started negotiating the price, terms, and conditions but never finalized any option deal. Sam wanted to continue to operate his business his way, did not want to move from his $1 million goodwill asking price, and was unwilling to provide any seller financing. Perhaps with the passage of time, he will be more open to change.

PART VI: LOOKING BACK

It was approximately five years ago that I purchased Betty's Cruises, now known as Bob's Cruises. It has been a wild ride.

Nothing had prepared me for the emotional rollercoaster ride that I experienced as an entrepreneur. The normalized earnings projection that I developed five years ago approximated my actual five-year average. But that is like saying that if you have one foot on ice cubes and the other foot on hot coals, on average you should be feeling all right. Remember Hurricane

Hillary in 2015? My business was closed for two months. Then, when the worldwide economic recovery finally arrived in 2016, I scrambled to find new people to hire just to keep up with the unexpected demand. Today, there still remains a lack of clarity on future tax laws, and that uncertainty will likely continue for many years to come.

I still root for my favorite New York sports teams, and I continue to stay in touch with my stateside friends through social media. It seems like every month another friend comes to visit me. During the winter months, my beautiful new home is always packed with guests.

Betty worked part-time with me until her husband passed away last year. She now travels and is enjoying her retirement. I've repaid all monies owed to her and to the bank; except for the boat debt, I now own the business free and clear.

I never purchased Sam's Cruises. Sam continues to express a desire to sell it to me, but with its lack of growth and the poor condition of its financial reporting, Sam's Cruises is still not worth $1 million plus the boat and other assets. Sam has slowed down, and he has hired more people to relieve him of some of his duties. We remain close friends, and one day, when he really wants to sell his company, we'll try once again to work things out.

During my five years in Caribbea, I've investigated several new expansion opportunities. As a result of my strong relationship with the major cruise lines and hotel chains, I was introduced to several new locations on nearby islands. Currently, I am negotiating the development of two new Bob's Cruises locations. I plan on managing the back office of these new sites through one central office in St. Michael. The financing will be available because of the credibility I've developed with local banks.

After acclimating to St. Michael, I found that there were only two parts of my life in Caribbea that were incomplete. The first was to find someone who could work with me as I expanded Bob's Cruises; the second was finding a life partner. Well, when I attended Betty's husband's funeral last year, I finally met Betty's daughter. Let's just say that my life is no longer incomplete.

About the Website

This book includes a companion website that can be accessed at www .wiley.com/go/valuingptes (password: barr123). Here you will find the Appendix A Checklist included in the book, along with seven key cases referenced in the text that have significantly influenced pass-through entity valuation theory.

The text of these seven cases can be accessed on the companion website:

1. *Gross v. Commissioner*
   T.C.M. 1999–254, 78 T.C.M. (CCH) 201, T.C.M. (RIA) para. 99,254, 1999 Tax Ct. LEXIS 290 (July 29, 1999). The U.S. Court of Appeals affirmed the decision of the Tax Court, 272 F.3d 333 (6th Cir. 2001).

   This case involved the fair market valuation of 1992 gifts of less than 1 percent of the common stock (a noncontrolling interest) of an S corporation that was highly profitable and distributed nearly all of the company's income to its shareholders. The company's shareholders' agreement contained restrictions on transfers and prohibitions on terminating the S election. There was no mention of any expectation to sell the business or terminate the S election of the subject company. In its 1999 decision, the tax court applied a 0 percent tax-affecting adjustment when applying the income approach; this decision was affirmed by the U.S. Court of Appeals in 2001.

2. *Estate of Heck v. Commissioner*
   T.C.M. 2002–34, 83 T.C.M. (CCH) 1181, T.C.M. (RIA) para. 54,639, 2002 Tax Ct. LEXIS 38 (Feb. 5, 2002).

   This case involved the 1995 estate tax fair market valuation of a 39.6 percent noncontrolling interest in an S corporation that was highly profitable. The company's shareholders' agreement contained restrictions on the sale or transfer of the subject ownership interest. The business appraisal experts for the decedent and for the IRS disagreed over many issues in connection with the valuation of the subject ownership interest—but both experts agreed that the cash flows to equity derived from their respective discounted cash flow analyses should not be tax affected for federal income tax reporting purposes.

3. *Wall v. Commissioner*

T.C.M. 2001–75, 81 T.C.M. (CCH) 1425, 2001 Tax Ct. LEXIS 97 (Mar. 27, 2001).

This case involved the 1992 fair market valuation of 20 gifts of nonvoting, minority interests in an S corporation to irrevocable trusts for the benefit of the donors' children. The court found flaws with the income approach methodologies and conclusions of both the donors' expert and the IRS expert; as a result, tax-affecting S corporation income was ultimately not an issue decided in the case because the court placed little weight on the income approach.

4. *Estate of Adams v. Commissioner*

T.C.M. 2002–80, 83 T.C.M. (CCH) 1421, T.C.M. (RIA) para. 54,696, 2002 Tax Ct. LEXIS 84 (Mar. 28, 2002).

The subject interest in this case was a 61.59 percent controlling interest in an S corporation, valued as of 1995 for estate tax reporting purposes. The valuation issue presented to the court in this case was whether the taxpayer could tax-affect the discount rate and capitalization rate, rather than the cash flows of the taxpayer; the taxpayer's expert tax affected such rates, but the IRS expert did not. The court concluded that taxpayer's expert should not have converted the capitalization rate from after-corporate tax to before-corporate tax.

5. *Robert Dallas v. Commissioner*

T.C.M. 2006–212, 2006 WL 2792684 (T.C. Sept. 28, 2006).

This case involved the fair market valuation of below-market 1999 and 2000 sales (in effect, gifts) of nonvoting, minority interests in an S corporation to trusts for the benefit of the owner's children. In its 2006 decision, the court decided that it was not appropriate to tax-affect the S corporation's earnings for valuation purposes.

6. *Gallagher v. Commissioner*

T.C.M. 2011–146 (June 28, 2011).

This case involved the 2004 fair market valuation of a 15 percent noncontrolling member interest in a limited liability company for estate tax reporting purposes. Citing the *Gross* decision and finding no explanation for ignoring the benefits associated with S corporation status, the court applied a 0 percent tax-affecting adjustment.

7. *Delaware Open MRI Radiology Associates, P.A. v. Howard B. Kessler*

898 A.2d 290 (Del. Ch. 2006).

This case involved the 2004 valuation of a minority ownership interest in a very profitable S corporation that distributed substantially all of its earnings. The plaintiff in the lawsuit was the minority ownership interest that was subjected to a squeeze-out merger and the fair value standard was applied by the court. Experts for the plaintiff opined that a 0 percent tax-affecting adjustment was appropriate; experts for the defendant opined that a 40 percent tax-affecting adjustment was appropriate. Citing *Gross, Adams, Heck,* and other cases, the court disagreed with both experts and applied a 29.4 percent tax-affecting adjustment based on a methodology that effectively "reverse-engineered" an appropriate tax rate.

Index

Page numbers with *c* and *t* indicate chart and table, respectively.